Published by ABC Enterprises for the
AUSTRALIAN BROADCASTING CORPORATION
20 Atchison Street (Box 8888) Crows Nest NSW 2065

First published 1990

National Library of Australia
Cataloguing-in-Publication entry
Frith, David, 1937-
By his own hand: a study of cricket suicides

Bibliography.
Includes index.
ISBN 0 7333 0089 8.

1. Cricket players—Suicidal behaviour. I. Title.

796.3580922

Edited by Glenda Downing
Designed by Trevor Hood
Set in 11½/13 pt Goudy Old Style by Midland Typesetters, Victoria
Printed in Australia by The Book Printer, Victoria
5.5-2999

The following friends and acquaintances—and even a couple of relatives—have provided help of varying magnitude in this project, and the author's sincere gratitude is extended to them: Jonathan Agnew, Maurice Alexander, Chris Aspin, Jack Bailey, Brian Bassano, John Bishop, Robert Brooke, Jack Burrell, Don Cameron, Donald Carr, Richard Cashman, Geoffrey Copinger, Brian Croudy, Brian Crowley, John Day, Hubert Doggart, Anandji Dossa, Alan Dowding, Duggie Ettlinger, Robin Feather, Ric Finlay, David Foot, Debbie Frith, John Frith, David Green, Imogen Grosberg, Walter Hadlee, Bob Harragan, Chris Harte, Reg Hayter, Jonathan Heher, Andrew Hignell, Eric Hill, David Jowett, Jack McLaughlin, John McMahon, Ken Mills, Barbara Moor, Pat Mullins, Don Neely, Brian O'Gorman, Ossie Osborne, Peter Parfitt, Mudar Patherya, Gordon Phillips, Terry Power, Qamar Ahmed, Wanda Reynolds, Michael Ronayne, David Roylance, Subroto Sirkar, Alan Smith, Mike Spurrier, John Thicknesse, Philip Thorn, Ern Toovey, Richard Williams, Wendy Wimbush, Geoff Wright. Thanks also to Melbourne Cricket Club. A number of others offered to assist but never got around to doing so. My thanks to them all the same for the kind initial thought.

Contents

Foreword

by Peter Roebuck

This is a remarkable book: a study of 80-odd cricketers who have taken their own lives, and yet not, thankfully, a study of cricketing suicides. Or not, at any rate, for the most part.

In truth, every man mentioned here needs a book to himself. Here we read of Fred Bull, a 'chucker' who tied a 7–lb stone around his neck and sat waiting for the sea to drown him, having first returned his key to his landlady. We hear of Richard Humphrey, who, poor man, 'did not accomplish half of what was expected of him', of Woodcock, a fast bowler who liked to 'bump the ball up a bit', and of Wardill, an embezzler. David Frith tells us about a bookie who took bets after the race (he went broke), of a cricketer who was suspected of being Jack the Ripper, of another who thought he had Aids, and of many others who endured the gentle slide-down which, as Terence Rattigan wrote, is 'not so gentle sometimes; it makes one feel so ruddy useless and old'.

We meet a range of extraordinary characters—at least we hope they are extraordinary—and follow them, sometimes from a distance, sometimes closely, as they move inexorably towards their tragic conclusion. Time and again we remember that far and away the most interesting part of a sportsman's life arises when his playing days are over, a period seldom documented. For how does a man manage who, from 20 to 35, enjoys the applause, the spotlight and the rapture, and for whom, midway through his life, all is suddenly silent?

John Sullivan, a member of Lancashire's vibrant team of the early 1970s, contemplated his own happily-arrested downhill slide after his cricket career ended and said that 'I couldn't accept that part of my life was over'. It is a common trait which tens of thousands of cricketers have had to endure. County cricket, in particular, is a private world and to leave it is to leave a community of monastic self-absorption. Nor is there any second, third or fourth division to enter, no subsidiary world in daily contact with the county scene. An English county cricketer lives an all-or-nothing life, which is why so many turn to umpiring, coaching or writing when their skills begin to fade. Everything else is darkness.

So far as cricket goes, suicide has been a burden of white Protestants, nearly all of them from middle-class backgrounds and many of them from respected professions outside cricket. We find here lawyers, parliamentarians and members of the Stock Exchange.

We also find a surprising number of Australians, South Africans and New Zealanders, for each a tale to be told. Out of the years of his Australian youth, Frith recounts the sad demise of Jack Iverson, freak bowler, 'rum sort of character', and apparently contented businessman. Sid Barnes, *enfant terrible*, a calculating, difficult man, yet immensely generous to his friends, killed himself, as did Jim Burke, a frail, stubborn cricketer whose bowling action is best described as idiosyncratic. In these stories, as in most others, poor health, business worries, and sexual disappointment and problems played their part as a man lost his confidence, his desire to live. In cricket, self-respect can fall dangerously low when failures, often due to more bad luck, heap upon each other, for a batsman's very purpose is to score runs. Inevitably, failure in this self-absorbed world leads men to feel humbled in the eyes of their peers. And for a cricketer who has known glory, to fail in later life is hardly less of a humiliation.

South Africa, too, has tales of overwhelming sorrow to relate. Aubrey Faulkner, a war hero but a 'very temperamental' man felt a want of support and purpose. Vincent Tancred took his own life at 29, while Zulch, Glen Hall ('the reclusive chemist') and Joe Partridge ended days of misery with self-destruction. Partridge, a Test cricketer in the 1960s, had become a heavy drinker and was in debt to his remaining friends. Stuart Leary was a fine, resilient cricketer for Kent, though colleagues thought him vain about his appearance; but darker days followed his retirement, and in 1988, 17 years after leaving county cricket, he died on Table Mountain. Friends said he was worried about a forthcoming investigation into juvenile vice. Perhaps he could not bear to see his public fame destroyed by his private preferences; perhaps he could not meet his friends again. Cricketers are supposed to be simple, even gung-ho, in sexual matters as in everything else. And yet cricket—and most cricketers—has its dark secrets, its skeletons; and while players sound aggressive, they are seldom macho, for let him who is without sin cast the first stone.

Somerset, too, has its painful list of premature deaths: Percy Hardy, who could not face returning to the trenches, and so slit his throat; Arthur Sanders, 19 years of age, educated at Harrow, took his life in 1920; and Tom Hall, who played for Somerset in 1953, a popular man, educated at Uppingham, and a worried businessman who died in a fall from a train in 1984. More famously, that loveliest of writers and unsung bowlers, Raymond Robertson-Glasgow, took an overdose of pills during a bout of nervous depression, deepened, friends remember, by a snowstorm which drove this splendid fellow to despair, for he suffered from claustrophobia too. And gifted, tormented Harold Gimblett, who so wanted to be loved and yet found himself rejected by those who, arriving late in his career, saw only a tetchiness brought on by years of worry, years of carrying his team's batting. Finally he could bear it no longer, packed his bags and left. This country boy, this uneasy, sensitive man who had burst upon county cricket with terrible simplicity, was never really happy again, for Somerset cricket had meant so much to him, had taken him to the heights, and to the depths. Twenty-five years after his career had ended in bitter dispute with Somerset officials, Gimblett swallowed his pills.

And so the list continues, across the world, down the generations. Gimblett is one of those studied in detail, as are those Victorians Stoddart ('that son of grief'), Shrewsbury, who could not face his own obscurity, Scotton, the intense blocker, and 'turnip-head' Trott, that mixture of joy and cruelty, fun and disappointment. Trott, they say, was interviewed by police, though not as a suspect, after a Taunton lady with a somewhat doubtful reputation was found murdered. His powers in decline, his pockets emptied by gambling and drink, his belly big, Trott killed himself at the age of 41. All of these Victorians died within a decade of losing fame and finding an anonymity for which they were not prepared financially or psychologically. They, more than most in this book, were *cricketing* suicides.

Not, of course, that every depressed cricketer kills himself. Sir Richard Hadlee has talked helpfully about his own nervous breakdown. Many others have sought solace in chaplains, psychologists, special diets, mentors, anything which will bring comfort and hope. Cricket can be a *lonely* game, for a player is surrounded by comrades and so must be adaptable; and yet in performances he is utterly isolated.

David Frith has been kind enough to mention *It Never Rains . . .* , my own tale of a difficult cricket season. Many fellow-cricketers, including some surprising ones, had told me how close to their own bone they felt it to be. To me it was a way of saying Goodbye To All That. Once written, it was no longer true about my life, though it remains true about others. Cricket no longer touches me quite so deeply— and in a way I am sorry about this because I believe a man must care, must tackle those very parts of his life which worry him most, otherwise he is cheating his talent.

Since *It Never Rains . . .* some people have predicted a

gloomy end for this writer. One former colleague said so to my face in September 1986. It will not be so. The art is to find other things which matter just as much, which stretch you just as far. Certainly a man needs beliefs. Principles are not enough. But belief can spring from satisfaction in his own work, for to believe in yourself is an act of faith. Since 1983 I have led a stable, remarkably untroubled life, and such vicissitudes as have occurred have been connected with cricket form rather than temperament. Apart from anything else, I keep seeing the funny side of things. It is wise, and surely a sign of maturity, to keep these two things—form and temperament—apart.

Mr Frith has written a carefully researched and passionate book about a few dozen first-class cricketers who took their own lives. He leaves it to the statisticians to say if these suicides are above or below the average rate, and concludes only that cricket itself was very seldom the cause. He seems to reject my idea that cricketers are especially vulnerable because the game, by its nature, attracts sensitive men of aesthetic temperament, the very men who are, in the end, least well served by it. Instead, he shows us flawed characters who happened to play cricket and whose ends could not be avoided even by the tenderest of ministrations. It is a book I can warmly recommend as a study of a group of characters interesting for the extremities of their emotions.

Taunton 1990

1

By His Own Hand

Self-destruction is fairly commonplace on the cricket field. 'Unplayable' balls, in the strictly scientific sense, are extremely rare. More often than not a batsman gets himself out, as much through a lapse in concentration as absence of co-ordination. He pokes a bat at the wider ball and gives the wicketkeeper a catch, or loses all self-control and launches a wild drive at a delivery deserving of more respect. The price is paid: the mental aberration, the rush of blood, has proved fatal. The life of that innings is at an end.

Each time a cricketer arrives at the crease and takes his guard, whatever the odds may be, whether he be a Bradman or a hopeless No. 11, that first ball could get him. Not for him the assurance known to golfers: that however much of a disaster the first or second or third hole may be, there will be 18 altogether. The footballer, barring a broken leg or the humiliation of being sent off by the referee, knows he should have 90 minutes' play ahead of him, with the chance of a good second half to offset a poor first half. In tennis, in a five-setter, you can still come back to win after losing the first two sets.

Cricket is not unique in its perpetual uncertainty. No boxer, even be he a Mike Tyson, can guarantee he will stay on his legs for 12 or 15 rounds. The sturdiest steeplechaser may not make it to the finishing line.

But cricket is Uncertainty on the grand scale. A match—even a humble club match—takes a lot of time to unfold. While standing for hours on end in the field, and perhaps having taken a long time travelling to the ground, a batsman can only imagine what fate awaits him when he eventually takes his turn to bat. He may be all confidence, buoyed up by much recent success; he may be dreading his moment on centrestage, the threat of a further sickening link in a chain of failures weighing heavily upon him.

Nor is it just the batsmen who wait and wait before being summoned into the spotlight to show their skills. Bowlers have been known to seize up completely, or to the point where taut mind and muscle play grotesque havoc with length and direction. It is perhaps the very combination of the passive with the active during the drawn-out process of playing serious cricket which imposes a strain on the nerves such as is known in few other sports. Uncertainty may lend excitement, but prolonged periods of boredom interspersed with acute tension can also be insidiously corrosive.

It is not claimed here that cricket has a higher rate of real, human self-destruction than other sports. Boxing has its Randolph Turpin, football its Hughie Gallacher, horse-racing its Fred Archer, and a full-scale survey on any of these or other sports may reveal an unexpectedly high rate of suicide among its leading players. Meanwhile, this work will represent over 20 years of research and observation on the subject as it applies to cricketers, with over 80 cases cited, half of them concerning players of some eminence. There must be others undiscovered or covered up in misguided shame.

There are three so-called classic causes of self-destruction: matrimonial/romantic disturbance, financial anxiety, and breakdown or fear of breakdown of health. Many of the cricketers who killed themselves were prey to one or more of these haunting factors. But there is a fourth factor, and this is the inability to cope when the athletic peak is passed and the adulation vanishes. Sam Palmer, the Test veteran, played by Jack Warner in the 1953 film *The Final Test* (written by Terence Rattigan), sums it up perfectly when he muses: 'The trouble with making a game a profession is that you're at the top too young. The rest of the way's a gentle slide down. Not so gentle sometimes. It makes one feel so ruddy useless and old.'

Palmer (Warner), with his aldermanic waistline and awkward forward defensive shot, did indeed look somewhat 'useless and old', but any cricketer would have seen beyond the miscasting and recognised the sadness bordering on grief which assails all who love the game, when the signals indicate that reflexes are slowing and breath gets shorter. Lucky are they who slip gradually and gratefully down through the ranks, still playing in slow-motion when in their fifties and sixties.

First-class cricketers, alas, seldom continue to play into their later years. Relief at escaping that nerve-racking uncertainty at least lessens their sadness. They spent years enough with churning stomachs before going on stage. Vanity also features in their rationale: Ian Chappell refused to play beyond his early forties: 'I reckon I wasn't a bad hooker, mate, but I'm damned if I'm going out there now to have some smart-arse young tearaway going for my skull!'

'Chappelli' is lucky. He remains fully engaged in the game at top level as television commentator and writer. He is still often asked for his autograph as well as his opinion. His deeds are well recorded: even in moving colour, on video. He is not forgotten. And that makes acceptance of retirement from athletic pursuit many degrees easier.

Footballer Jackie Milburn said, after Hughie Gallacher, 54, had thrown himself under an express train near Gateshead in 1957: 'How a man so loved and so idolised could feel so alone I'll never know.' And yet the answer to that was fairly straightforward: Gallacher, an alcoholic whose second wife had recently died, was facing a court charge over an assault on his son. The 'balance of his mind' would have seemed to have been 'disturbed', yet it might appear more a case not so much of all reason lost as found. Often the test of courage, as a certain Conte Vittorio Alfieri suggested, is not to die but to live. Or, as S.N. Behrman stated at the age of 75, 'I have had just about all I can take of myself.'

Leaving aside the oddness of spending a large portion of one's life standing motionless in a field—sometimes before only a handful of spectators, sometimes before vast, cheering crowds—the basic question begs: might there not have been a better way of spending those God-given days and years? While the answer may be predictable from a Derbyshire fast bowler who might otherwise have been underground inhaling coaldust throughout his twenties and thirties, how seriously we should take Colin Cowdrey's anguished self-questioning at the end of his glorious career. Captain of England, scorer of 107 centuries, 22 of them in Tests, he asked, in a confessional in a Surrey newspaper in 1976, how he could conceivably justify 'having spent a quarter-of-a-century standing at first slip'. As Ian Wooldridge said, having brought this remark to a wider audience through the *Daily Mail*, 'As understatements go that probably ranks with Menuhin dismissing his life as one long fiddle.'

Cowdrey had developed heavy reservations years earlier, and had referred his self-doubt to no less a person than the Archbishop of Canterbury. His Grace would presumably have pointed to the pleasure given to countless thousands in their relaxation, and to the shining example of sportsmanship displayed daily and naturally by Cowdrey. He might have pointed to Cowdrey's ambassadorial merits and to his frequent projection, in pulpit and at gatherings of cricket-lovers, of Christian virtues and beliefs.

In the dozen years which followed, Colin Cowdrey was to be headline news in a particularly painful divorce which rocked the cricket world. Working in the public affairs department of Barclays Bank, he became chairman of the International Cricket Council, and stood to guide the troubled world game into the 1990s: all surely enough to keep a man from brooding on the 'wasted' hours which he once felt, selfflagellatingly, would have been far better spent saving lives as a surgeon or perhaps growing crops for the hungry.

Desperate doubts and inescapable depression must have caused many a cricketer to contemplate suicide, alcohol often deepening the plight and exacerbating the condition. Jemmy Shaw, the prominent Nottinghamshire left-arm bowler of the early 1870s, tried to bury his disappointment after taking a battering from the Gloucestershire batsmen. He sank a lot of ale and eventually got into a noisy argument with his team-mates over a game of cards. Shaw smashed glasses and stormed from the room, shouting that he was going to 'do for meself'. His fellow players instantly thought of the nearby Clifton Suspension Bridge, from where so many defeated souls had leapt. (In 1988, Peter Lowe, aged 53, who played once as a wicketkeeper for Warwickshire in 1964, was found dead at the bottom of Avon Gorge.)

Peter Lowe — death at Avon Gorge.

In the early hours of the following day, one of the opposing players, out for a stroll, came across Jemmy Shaw's prone body under a tree. He was fast asleep. A few hours later still he excelled himself by batting for over an hour-and-a-half, probably his longest innings ever, and helping Notts save the follow-on.

However muddled or sincere Shaw may have been in his alcoholic haze, Billy Bates was unquestionably at the end of his tether after a fierce hit from a neighbouring practice net at Melbourne cannoned into his cheekbone, severely damaging an eye. Repatriated by ship soon after Christmas 1887, devoid of hope now that his livelihood seemed to have been snatched away, this normally cheerful and charming Yorkshireman, the first Englishman to take a Test hat-trick, tried to end his life. The attempt was unsuccessful, but much misery lay ahead. His wife died in 1891, and he struggled to live off the interest on a sum collected for him and his son, still playing league cricket as a professional, his vision greatly restricted. When he died in 1900, at the age of 44, it was written of him that 'he had his failings—who has not?—but he had also trials that fall to the lot of few men. He was a great cricketer, and a most kindly soul.'

Bates's son grew up to play for Yorkshire and Glamorgan, and *his* son was football manager Ted Bates.

Only a few years before Bates's career came to such a shuddering halt, Joseph Wells, father of H.G. Wells and the first player to take four wickets with consecutive balls in first-class cricket, fell some distance while pruning his grapevine, and suffered a compound fracture of the thighbone. He had endured a marriage which had become little short of an ongoing war, his business had failed, and, just as significantly, his beloved cricket could bring him no further success and satisfaction. Members of his family were convinced that the fall was a suicide attempt. He found later solace in books and the company of his son, and lived on until 1910, but the 1877 'accident' left him with a limp, an affliction that always seems an unnecessarily cruel mockery among infirm old sportsmen.

The mental equilibrium of top-flight slow left-arm bowlers Johnny Briggs (Lancashire and England) and Colin Blythe (Kent and England) was subject to severe upset through epilepsy. Briggs, who had a fit on the Test match field in 1899, was to die in Cheadle Asylum in 1902, aged 39, and Blythe was killed in 1917, when 38, in the fighting near Passchendaele. Australians Harry Trott and Harry Graham, both heroes of the 1890s, and Anglo-Australian Billy Midwinter were to die in mental institutions, while earlier champions such as Ted Pooley, the Surrey wicketkeeper, and John 'Foghorn' Jackson, the terrifying Notts fast bowler, died in Lambeth and Liverpool workhouses respectively. It is unlikely that either of them, representative as they were of the ill-educated 'breadline' class, did not entertain thoughts at some time or other of exercising man's ultimate prerogative.

Since the Second World War, with poverty less widespread but nonetheless a threat, depression rising from this and other combined factors has caused cricketers anguish of such depth that suicide has been contemplated. Lancashire's Geoff Edrich, brother of the more famous Bill, managed to get by on a war disability pension after three-and-a-half years of imprisonment and deprivation at the hands of the Japanese: to which was added the unspectacular wage of a professional cricketer. Recovering his strength gallantly (his weight during captivity had dropped from 11½ stone to 6½), he carved out for himself a creditable career in county cricket for over 10 years, but when he was sacked by Lancashire in 1959, he took it hard. It has been the acid test for many a professional player. In Edrich's case he was plunged into deep depression which lifted only as he learned to put what he regarded as pettiness by the Lancashire committee behind him and started anew with league cricket at Workington and then as coach and head groundsman at Cheltenham College, where he worked until retirement.

A more clearcut case of a cricketer finding his career ended and the future consequently bleak concerned another Lancashire player, John Sullivan, an all-rounder who played an important part in the county's thrilling successes in the

1970s in one-day cricket. He had played cricket professionally for almost half his life when, at only 31, his contract was not renewed. 'Somehow I couldn't accept that part of my life was over.' Like many a cricketer before him, he took charge of a pub. The venture failed. His wife left him, unable to stand the strain of the regular rough-and-tumbles in the saloon bar and of her husband's increasing personal intake. For 10 days Sullivan shut himself away with bottles of brandy and port. 'I suppose I was trying to kill myself.'

He was found to have tuberculosis, and spent three months in hospital. He renounced the booze, met and married Freda, and was last heard of in the late 1980s hoping to complete his rehabilitation: one of cricket's near-misses.

Barry Knight, the Essex, Leicestershire and England all-rounder of the mid-1960s, was another to find his world crumbling around him. In 1968, in a newspaper article, he told of his bankruptcy, his marriage break-up, and how he had contemplated suicide. His salvation came in emigration: to Australia, where he had toured with two England sides in the 1960s, and to a successful indoor cricket school venture. Rebirth in a land faraway.

Knight shrewdly stayed with cricket. Some are disenchanted with the game after ceaseless involvement at professional level. Others continue to need it, though they can only get from it substitute joys, as from coaching, umpiring, committee work, or journalism. Yet others depend upon it as a spectacle and as a sublimation of their lives, and when things go wrong, their mental stability collapses. Gordon Piper, a 23-year-old science graduate from Adelaide University, was found with his throat cut at his lodgings in Harpenden, Herts in 1930. He managed to dictate his will to a fellow lodger while a doctor was summoned, and he gave as one of his reasons for his action Australia's recent loss against England in the Trent Bridge Test match (Bradman's first in England: the game was turned by substitute fielder Copley's diving catch to dismiss McCabe). Piper, the grieving Australian patriot, died in St Albans Infirmary.

Almost 50 years later, a Nottingham man took an overdose

during the 1989 Ashes Test at Trent Bridge, where Mark Taylor (219) and Geoff Marsh (138) put on a record 329 for Australia's first wicket, the eventual total of 602 for 6 before Allan Border declared being sufficient for victory by an innings and 180 runs, Australia's heaviest ever in England. The distraught man explained, after he had been revived, that he had committed his act because of 'the situation at the Test match'.

There could hardly be a sadder case then that of Arthur Wills, a former sailor and prison warder, who threw himself onto a railway line near Portsmouth in April 1956. Only 35, he explained his plight in a letter for the coroner which survived the impact of the train:

> I know, sir, that you will have in your mind that I took my life while the balance of my mind was disturbed. Maybe that is what you will think, but now I will tell you that two years ago, in July 1954, I was overtaken by haemorrhage of the brain. I have tried to get fit, so as to play cricket again, but now I know I will never be fit enough to play that most enjoyable game again. If there is no cricket to live for, then I would rather be out of the world. It was all to me. I am convinced that I shall never play that finest and most glorious game again. I thank you for bearing with me so long.

His brother-in-law later said that cricket was Arthur's 'one passion in life' and that he was an outstanding bowler who 'was always improving his batting'. He said he had played for clubs in South Africa and for the Royal Navy and several clubs around Portsmouth.

This poignant story prompted Imogen Grosberg to include in her privately published collection of verse, *Run Chase*, a poem entitled 'The Cricketer's Farewell'. It begins:

> I think I have played my last
> At England's greatest game
> And life, now all that has passed,
> Will never be the same.

Its tenth and final verse runs:

Not that, for I cannot live
Without our summer play;
A coward, I ask 'Forgive'.
My life runs out today.

Opinions will conflict as to whether suicide or attempted suicide over sport is proof of insanity. Yet if the victim is overwhelmed by the situation, he is . . . overwhelmed. The nature of motivation alone varies. Cricket can mean as much to a man as his wife, his employment, his physical well-being. So, judging from an incident in Los Angeles in 1989, can baseball. Donnie Moore, 35, simply could not shake off the 'taint' of large-scale sporting failure after his pitch, for the California Angels against the Boston Red Sox, was hit out of the ground for a home run that turned impending victory into ultimate defeat and elimination from the 1986 World Series. The media and the fans never let him forget his misfortune, and when the Angels dropped him, and a contract with minor league club Omaha Royals failed to last, he shot and wounded his estranged wife and then turned the gun on himself, ending his life.

'Everything revolves around one pitch,' said a former teammate. 'It destroyed a man's life. The guy was just not the same after that. He was never treated fairly. He wasn't given credit for all the good things he did. It's a tough drop from the top of the world to the bottom.'

That's what former Treasurer of Pennsylvania, Budd Dwyer, 47, must have felt before blowing his brains out in front of television cameras in 1988, having protested his innocence of a bribery charge.

The heartbreak that sport can inflict was dramatically demonstrated by a London club cricketer before the First World War. Charlie Skipwith played mainly for Honor Oak between 1892 and 1906, and also for Alleyn's during that time. He had some rich seasons with the bat, an innings

Charlie Skipwith —
amok with the cricket bat.

of 182 not out accruing in 1902, when he was 34. But the intensity of the man towards his cricket is revealed in notes left by the Surrey cricketer and music-hall entertainer Joe O'Gorman, who recalled that Skipwith suffered a drastic loss of form with the bat, and had to endure a lot of 'mickey-taking'. At last his luck turned. He made a century in his usual forceful, stylish manner. Then, wrote O'Gorman, 'the triumphant hero returned home and proceeded to destroy the contents of the house with his bat, smashing pictures and ornaments as he had scattered the bowling that afternoon. His mind completely deranged, he was confined to Cane Hill Sanatorium.' He was never to emerge from being in care, and died in 1921.

It so happens that an Honor Oak contemporary of Skipwith's committed suicide later in life. George Harrison was a good enough batsman to play two or three times for Hampshire in their pre-first-class days. In club cricket he was a regular century-maker, and had some stunning successes as a bowler too: 9 for 4 and 8 for 7 were cited in a local newspaper profile in 1896. By 1933, when he was 67 and listed as a shopfitter, Harrison's life had changed beyond

George Harrison —
fine club cricketer: gassed.

recognition. His death certificate records: Asphyxiation—Coal Gas Poisoning—Suicide—Unsound mind.

Just as a certain level of stress is necessary in producing a maximum of concentration and sporting performance, so an excess poses dangers. The response of the body takes the form of stimulation of that part of the brain—the hypothalamus—which controls emotions, appetite, thirst, temperature, the autonomic nervous system, and the pituitary gland. Brainwave activity is altered. There is no conscious will about this. Physiological and chemical alterations of the brain-functioning occur. It goes almost without saying that levels of tolerance to stress vary enormously from person to person. Modern medical thought would have us believe that stress can be reduced by exercise, which releases endorphins or opiates into the system, heightening a feeling of well-being and warding off depression.

A medical advisor familiar with one or two of the strands of this book has suggested that not only do retired cricketers miss (and sometimes yearn for) the acclaim and camaraderie of old, but they could also be lacking the beneficial endorphins released during physical endeavour. The gentler game of golf often helps to fill an old cricketer's aching vacuum.

Studies go on. In 1988 *The Observer* published a map of England and Wales which showed the varying intensity of male suicides. Surprisingly, Cornwall, Devon and western Wales bore the heaviest patches, while the lowest rates were reflected in central and eastern districts. London, of course, had a 'heavy' patch of its own. Concern at the rising rate of suicide among teenage schoolchildren continues to cause great anxiety, as does the rate in gaols and among rural communities where the tranquillity of old has been overtaken by latter-day business pressures.

Alvarez, in his classic *The Savage God: A Study of Suicide,* which takes a broad historical view of the subject, quotes Professor Joad's aphorism that 'in England you must not commit suicide, on pain of being regarded as a criminal if you fail and a lunatic if you succeed'. Suicide ceased to be a criminal act in the United Kingdom in 1961, and today's more compassionate attitudes have led to greater understanding; which is not to say that the traditional stigma and sense of shame and taboo have disappeared.

Certain scientists have even professed to have found a link between suicidal tendencies and particular astrological signs. Others are convinced that behaviour follows weather patterns, with violence, sexual offences, alcoholism *and suicide* reaching peaks during spring and early summer, though for anyone who has truly loved cricket, whether internationally successful at it or not, the onset of a fresh season stirs the emotions in such a way that legions of poets have tried to capture the magic.

Perhaps it is time for a forced, if not hollow, laugh, courtesy of the wonderful Dorothy Parker, whose 'black' verse on the subject ran: 'Razors pain you; rivers are damp; acids stain you and drugs cause cramp. Guns aren't lawful; nooses give; gas smells awful; you might as well live.'

2

Eminent Victorians

There could be no more sharply defined example of a famous sportsman lonely and depressed in middle age than A. E. Stoddart. The finest wing three-quarter of his or probably any other age, he captained England at Rugby and on two cricket tours of Australia in the 1890s. He once held the world record for the highest score in any class of cricket, 485 for Hampstead one summer day in 1886. The Stoics fielders ran around while 813 runs were scored. No declarations were permitted then, and the visitors eventually went home without picking up a bat. 'Stoddy' had prepared himself for the match in fairly typical fashion the night before. With friends, he went dancing; then played some poker; then, at dawn, his winnings considerable, he had a warm bath and took his friends off to the swimming-baths to freshen up. A hearty breakfast followed, then off he went to the Hampstead ground to perform his awesome batting feat. That evening, far from exhausted, the young man from South Shields took part in a doubles tennis match, had another bath, then attended the theatre before going on to a supper party. 'After that,' he said, 'I got to bed all right, and it wasn't nearly three!'

He had already played for Middlesex, and by 1887 he was ready for his first tour of Australia, where he played in the first of his 16 Test matches—and met the girl (already married) whom he eventually wed in 1906. He toured again in 1891–92 with W. G. Grace's side, and scored a brisk and attractive 134 in the Adelaide Test. He was the natural choice as captain of England at Lord's sixteen months later when W. G. was indisposed.

In an uncanny juxtaposition of people and events, Drewy Stoddart and Arthur Shrewsbury, both subsequent suicides, walked out to open the batting for England on July 17, 1893, passing another suicide-to-be in Billy Bruce of Australia on the way to the wicket, the funeral of former England batsman William Scotton, who killed himself, having taken place a week previously.

Grace returned for the second and third Tests, taking Stoddart to the crease with him each time. As on so many occasions, the younger man lost nothing in comparison with the mighty Gloucestershire champion when it came to style and speed of run-making.

In 1894 Stoddart was approached to take an English team to Australia to play a series of five Test matches that winter, and by the end of a rubber which, by its grip on the public's imagination, established international cricket on the grand scale recognised today, Stoddart had become the toast of both countries. The first Test, at Sydney, was won sensationally by England (by 10 runs) after they had followed on. They went two-up at Melbourne, thanks principally to Stoddart's 173, the highest score by an England captain in a Test in Australia until 1975. Albert Trott (another future suicide) destroyed them at Adelaide and Harry Graham's century set up an innings victory for Australia at Sydney to make it 2–2 with one to play, and in another classic encounter, England pulled the match round at Melbourne, J. T. Brown smashing 140 and Albert Ward making a resolute 93 when England, needing 293 to win, had lost two for 28. Stoddart was a handsome, smiling hero across the Empire, and faced rounds of celebratory dinners, presentations and back-slapping upon his return to England, bronzed, elated, but modest of bearing, and with a banjo conspicuous in his baggage.

So sensitive was he to newspaper allegations that he took payments for playing, although he was an amateur, that he withdrew from the final Test of the 1896 series, having opened with W. G. Grace in the previous two. Worse was to follow. Having toured West Indies with great success and made runs steadily in 1897 before a knee injury slowed him down, he took his second team off to Australia aboard *Ormuz*.

There was much sickness on board, and Stoddart was confined to bed during the first match. In Brisbane his watch and chain were stolen. Then he lost his keys and offered a reward for their return. And on December 8 he received a cable telling him of his beloved mother's death. Distraught to the point of collapse, he withdrew from the forthcoming Test match, Archie MacLaren taking over the captaincy. The tour had lost all meaning for Drewy Stoddart.

Though scoring 111 at Ballarat when he finally felt well enough to play again, he was to make a negligible impact on a series which a young and confident Australian side made their own. While the gossip columnists went on suggesting that 'Stoddy' was searching for a wife, he solemnly placed into his cuttings books an apparently irrelevant but mesmeric cartoon of a 'tired pessimist' committing 'fish suicide'. Rifle muzzle in mouth and fishing-line tied to the trigger, he waits for a hungry fish to do the rest. It is the only item non-romantic or non-sporting in the entire album.

Stoddart's popularity slipped at the end of the tour when he gave an interviewer several paragraphs of criticism of Australian barrackers, whom he considered 'insulting'. His deep, multi-sided anguish was unlikely to be understood, and many branded him a bad loser. Such a description of this much-loved sportsman would have been inconceivable prior to the tour.

His one piece of luck on the 1897–98 tour was a sweepstake win which returned him a massive £1350, a prize he split up among his players and some of his hosts. But his homecoming this time was muted. English cricket was deflated

Drewy Stoddart — record innings of 485; England captain against Australia; fatal disenchantment in middle-age.

by the 1–4 drubbing, and Francis Thompson, in reviewing Housman's *A Shropshire Lad*, referred to Stoddart as 'that Son of Grief'.

He averaged 52 for Middlesex in 1898, his last full season, but at 35 he was beginning to feel that first-class cricket was losing its appeal for him. He was 'still a batsman whom it is worthwhile going 100 miles to see', but stocks and shares and club cricket claimed him. He helped Middlesex in one match in 1899, and made a duck, and did little in the Hastings festival. After a tour of the United States with Ranjitsinhji's team, he prepared, the following spring, for a season of club cricket. Middlesex, stuck for a player, persuaded him to turn out against Sussex late in May, a few days after the relief of Mafeking, and Cyril Bland (another future suicide) bowled him for 1.

Then, on Whit Monday, as a gesture of admiration for the great medium-pacer J. T. Hearne, Stoddart played in his benefit match, Middlesex v. Somerset, at Lord's. He was out for 12 in the first innings. Next day, an inspired A. E. Stoddart made a glorious 221 at almost a run a minute before 10,000 spectators whose applause often was tinged with near-delirium. He finally fell as he tried for his thirty-seventh boundary, and that evening, responding to repeated congratulations, he said the innings would be 'a consolation for my old age'. Old age never came.

Becoming secretary to Neasden Golf Club and then to Queen's Club, he, with his young bride, lived in St John's Wood Road, and then in Clifton Hill, Maida Vale. He passed the time at the club in quiet and gentle conversation, and attended Lord's occasionally for matches and dinner gatherings. His weight increased. Whisky-and-soda became a familiar companion. Number 115 Clifton Hill was said to be haunted, and the adjoining property, once owned by the artist W. P. Frith, housed a poltergeist.

A neighbour often saw Stoddart sitting at his front window, gazing distantly down the quiet street, perhaps hearing the crowd's roar at Blackheath or at Lord's or Melbourne. The year 1914 brought much sadness. In June his brother, Harry, who had lived for years in America, died there. To the passing of R. E. Foster and A. G. Steel was added the loss, by self-inflicted gunshot, of Albert Trott, a Middlesex colleague, hours before the outbreak of the Great War. Stoddart's finances seemed in jeopardy, and his marriage had become joyless. A severe bout of influenza followed his resignation from Queen's, and a convalescent voyage to Australia was arranged; but he could not be bothered going through with it. His nerves were in ruinous condition.

By April 1915, just past his fifty-second birthday, he had reached the end of his tether, and told Ethel so. It was the momentous month of the Gallipoli landings, of fear that the Zeppelins would bomb London; giant Jess Willard knocked out Jack Johnson; George Joseph Smith was arrested for the 'brides in the bath' murders; and gas was being used at Ypres.

Stoddart was out all day on Easter Saturday, April 3. In the evening he told his wife that he was tired of everything, and took a pistol from his pocket. Ethel tried to reason with him. Things could be sorted out; they would talk with friends in the morning. She reached for the pistol, but he wrested it from her grasp. Reckoning the chamber to be empty, and holding the box of cartridges, she felt that at least he could do no harm. Perhaps he would calm down. Indeed, tucking the pistol into his pocket, he seemed in control as he bade Ethel and her female companion goodnight.

It was just before midnight when Ethel Stoddart went to his bedroom and switched on the light. Drewy was in bed. No shot had been heard. There was no trace of explosive smoke. Yet there was blood trickling down his cheek. She cried out, and Isabel Dalton ran upstairs. The police were summoned, and the constable found the revolver tightly gripped in Stoddart's right hand. A second box of ammunition lay nearby, missing one cartridge.

The inquest jury at Marylebone returned a verdict of 'suicide while of unsound mind'. They had been told how moody, forgetful and restless he had grown, and how money worries had preyed on his mind. So irritable had the once good-humoured husband become that the rustling of paper threatened to drive him mad. A doctor testified that the lungs had shown signs of impending pneumonia, which always induces despondency. The *Pall Mall Gazette* mourned:

> In how many country houses is his portrait at this moment hanging with those of the other great sportsmen of our time! Had his admirers but known of his difficulties would they not gladly have ended them? Something forbade it, perhaps pride. It is all too sad for words.

After the cremation at Golders Green, his ashes were conveyed to Radford, near Coventry, there to be buried in his mother's grave in the parish churchyard of St Nicholas. A Luftwaffe bomb demolished the church 25 years later, killing children and blasting away part of the Stoddart memorial cross. Then, in the late 1970s, even the base was removed as the run-down burial ground was cleared.

If Stoddart was at one time the finest amateur batsman in the world, Arthur Shrewsbury, seven years his senior, must have been the best of the professionals. From 1875 until 1902 he played for Nottinghamshire, the Players, and England, displaying a patience and a shrewd selection of shots which combined to make him seemingly undislodgable. He drove bowlers to despair with his innovative use of his pads. Anything pitched off-line which he felt he couldn't trust he would pad away—a safe ploy at a time when lbws could be achieved only from balls pitching wicket-to-wicket. Shrewsbury was a master of leaving the ball alone when attempting contact could only present danger.

The batting style betrayed characteristics of the man. He was intense. He was an accumulator, notwithstanding the risks he might have had to take in his successful sportsgoods business (with Alfred Shaw) and the tour ventures he undertook with Shaw and James Lillywhite junior.

Arthur Shrewsbury — best professional batsman in the world, but dead at 47.

He took part in four Test tours of Australia, leading England in seven Tests, of which five were won and two lost. Two of his three Test centuries against Australia were made at Lord's, the 164 in 1886 being the highest for either side on that ground until 1926. His river of runs for Notts contained many a huge partnership with the gangling William Gunn (398 against Sussex at Trent Bridge in 1890—still a second-wicket record—being the highest), and his first-wicket stand of 391 with A. O. Jones against Gloucestershire at Bristol in 1899 remains a record for the county. So too does the 266 he and Gunn put on for the fifth wicket at Hove in 1884. He compiled as many as 10 double-centuries in an era when such scores were comparatively rare.

Born in New Lenton on April 11, 1856, it soon became apparent that not only was he an exceptional batsman, but he had a strong will. Initially in the lace trade—who in Nottingham then was not?—he soon became a leader among his fellow professionals at the county cricket club, instigating 'industrial action' in protest against inequitable match payments. Nor was he always in completely good health, and the escape from the English climate must have been just as potent a factor in his tours of Australia as the financial reward.

He had his peculiarities. Whenever possible, he would return to sleep at home (which was the Queen's Hotel in Arkwright Street from 1869 to 1902) in Nottingham, even if it meant a long journey from where he was playing and late arrival. Prematurely bald, he tried never to be seen without a cap on—rather in the later manner of Australia's spin wizard Clarrie Grimmett. To go a step further, George Lyttelton, in a letter to James Agate in 1944, wrote: 'Do you know a queer fact about Shrewsbury?—that no-one ever saw him naked.'

Whatever the case, bowlers saw his back all too seldom. When he set up camp at the wicket it was usually for a lengthy campaign. He had this and at least one other thing in common with Geoffrey Boycott of Yorkshire and England: extended bachelorhood.

Surviving letters by Shrewsbury suggest a blunt,

uncompromising man in terms of business and of his judgments upon fellow cricketers. There seems to be no evidence, either photographic or written, that he was greatly endowed with a sense of humour either. What gradually emerged, as middle age approached, was a suspicion of hypochondria. There was an ominous ring to his remark in a letter written early in 1900: 'Am pleased to say my health, *as far as I know*, is all right.' A few weeks later he declined to play in a match in mid-April because of the risk of contracting a cold or something worse.

After 32 years at the Queen's Hotel, Shrewsbury was forced to move out early in 1902, the new landlord of the pub having given him notice. He moved into the home of his widowed youngest sister, in Trent Boulevard, and had a highly successful 1902 season, at the age of 46, averaging 50, with four centuries, two of them in the same match against Gloucestershire, and all at Trent Bridge, where his spirit must float to this day. The Notts committee launched a testimonial in appreciation of his splendid year, and he received £177.

But soon he was aware of pain around his kidneys. Several doctors were consulted, and then he went to London to see a specialist and stayed briefly in a nursing home. Nothing untoward could be identified. He transferred his lodgings to the home of Amelia, another of his sisters, at The Limes, Station Road, Gedling. His health seemed to improve, but he stayed away from the indoor winter nets, and by March 1903 he was indicating that there was little likelihood of his playing county cricket in the approaching summer. He was patently a despondent man.

Shrewsbury went into Nottingham on May 12 and bought a revolver at Jackson's in Church Gate. A week later he returned, having bought the wrong calibre bullets. That evening, May 19, he went up to his bedroom, having asked his girlfriend of several years, Gertrude Scott, to make him some cocoa. Soon she heard a strange and loud noise from upstairs, and called out; was everything all right—what was it? 'Nothing,' Arthur retorted. In fact, he had shot himself in the left side of the chest. Soon, fearing the job had been botched, he placed the pistol to his right temple and squeezed the trigger. Death was assured and almost instantaneous.

At the inquest, Gertrude recalled Shrewsbury saying, on the afternoon before his death, 'I shall be in the churchyard before many more days are up.' He had been convinced he had an incurable disease, but still there was no evidence to support this fear. The *Wisden* obituary offered the belief that it was not this alone which 'quite unhinged his mind'. That he knew his long career in the cricket field was over was surely most relevant?

Four years later his business partner, Alfred Shaw, who bowled the first ball in Test cricket, died from natural causes, and was buried in Gedling cemetery—not, as legend has it, 22 yards away from Shrewsbury, but several yards further. Some say it was to allow for Shaw's bowling approach. Perhaps it was symbolic of the extra distance that had grown between them as their friendship cooled in later years.

Nottinghamshire's match at Hove had been abandoned when news of Shrewsbury's sudden death arrived by telegram, and no major cricketer in the land could have felt anything less than an awesome sorrow such as is evoked by the loss of any great technician. Stoddart's mind might have projected pictures of his opening stand of 266 with Shrewsbury in the MCC Centenary match at Lord's in 1887. And only months earlier, in Melbourne, Shrewsbury (236) had posted 196 for the Non-Smokers' first wicket against the Smokers. His partner then was local man William Bruce. Suicides all.

William Scotton was at school with Shrewsbury at the People's College in Nottingham, and they both made their debuts for Notts in 1875. A notoriously dour left-hander, Scotton played in 15 Test matches for England, and toured Australia three times with the Lillywhite, Shaw and Shrewsbury combinations during the 1880s.

He fell foul of Shrewsbury's rigid rules of friendship in 1888 when, having missed the 1887–88 tour of Australia himself, he asked Shrewsbury to chase up a debt of £40 which he claimed was still unsettled from the 1886–87 tour. Shrewsbury

William Scotton — pathological worrier.

went out of his way to recover the money for his old schoolfriend, only to establish that not only had the sum been remitted, but Scotton must have known it had been remitted. Chastised, Scotton petulantly let rival sportsgoods firm Gunn & Moore display his cricket trophies in their shopwindow.

One view of Scotton at the time of his death was that he was 'a wonderfully quiet, harmless fellow, and what many people used to regard as "side" was mere mannerism'. It was a pointer to the likelihood that he belonged to the hordes of humanity who remain misunderstood all their lives.

As a youngster he was employed by MCC on the Lord's ground staff, and was also a good enough footballer to be engaged by Notts County. For years he was a pub landlord, and after retirement he took to umpiring. His career as a professional batsman took a strange turn after 1883. To that point he had been adept at both defence and attack, using his long reach to deal with speed and spin with equal facility.

After a hand injury (while catching W. G. Grace) and a spell of ill-health, he emerged in 1884 as one of the 'Stonewall brigade', blocking and nudging, ignoring the bad ball.

It seems certain that beneath the dreamy eyes and elegant moustache lurked a pathological worrier. As with Hobbs and Sandham in a later generation, there was never any doubting who was the senior partner in the on-going partnerships for Nottinghamshire between Shrewsbury and Scotton. Differentiation never bothered Sandham of Surrey, but Scotton of Notts tried to offset it by speaking invariably of 'I and Arthur'.

Twice in Tests against Australia, both times at The Oval, he drove the bowlers to distraction by his continuing occupation of the crease and refusal to play shots. In 1884, after Australia had piled up 551, Scotton opened England's innings with W. G. and was still there when Walter Read came in at No. 10 (an absurd position for such a major batsman). Together they put on 151 for the ninth wicket, the oldest surviving partnership record in Ashes Tests over a century later. Scotton's highest Test score of 90 was spread over five hours and 40 minutes. Two years later he opened the batting again with Grace (who went on to 170) and lingered for three-and-three-quarter hours for 34, seizing up on 24 for such a period, 67 minutes, that it must have seemed to the Australians that time was frozen. It was not the only time Scotton stayed scoreless for an hour or more.

His 1886 performance, when England's first wicket realised 170 before Tom Garrett ejected him by breaching his barndoor defence, led to *Punch*'s parody 'tribute':

> Block, block, block, at the foot of thy wicket, O Scotton!
> And I would that my tongue could utter my boredom.
> You *won't* put the pot on . . . But one hour of Grace
> or Walter Read were worth a week of you!

Some could have shrugged this off, but from what we know of the man, he would have seen his self-denial for the sake of his country merely mocked. He had a fearful dread of making mistakes, and, for his pains, here he was, suffering humiliation. It was nothing, of course, when compared to the scathing headlines and cowardly drivel churned out by the tabloids of the late twentieth century. But it was enough to increase Scotton's anguished introversion. Nor was he able to rehabilitate his reputation at the highest level, for his final two Tests, in Australia that winter, produced scores of 1, 6, 0 and 2.

His pride was damaged seriously in 1891 when Notts dropped him from the team, and it was never to be restored, since no recall was to be issued. Depressed and unsociable, he played in minor matches and did some umpiring. Soon it became known that he and his wife had divorced, which surprised many who had not known in the first place that he was married. On May 2, 1893 he took lodgings at 91 St John's Wood Terrace, a short walk from Lord's, a terrace house owned by Joseph and Ethel Lansdown. James Chandler, maker of bat-handles, was a fellow lodger.

On Sunday morning, July 9, Mrs Lansdown knocked on Scotton's door and went in. Clad in only a nightshirt, the 37-year-old cricketer's body lay on the floor swamped in blood. He had slit his throat. The razor was still in his left hand. Chandler was called, and felt the calf of Scotton's leg, which was still warm. It could not have been a quick death. Blood and the evidence of desperate upheaval were everywhere, and near the body was a basin, the wretched victim having tried to confine the messy consequences of his deed.

(One might reflect here, not entirely unconnectedly, that the horrendous scene awaiting Mrs Lansdown that morning bore similarities to that which awaited the police less than five years previously when they beheld the result of Jack the Ripper's carnage over in Whitechapel. One of the prime Ripper suspects has long been Montague John Druitt, 31, a fast bowler and all-round athlete. A barrister who preferred to teach at a school in Blackheath, he played cricket for Winchester College, Incogniti and Dorset, and was a playing member of MCC. He drowned himself in the Thames in December 1888, his body being washed ashore at Chiswick. He explained in

Montague Druitt —
Jack the Ripper suspect.

a suicide note to his brother that he feared he was going mad, a fate suffered by their mother six months earlier.)

At the inquest on William Scotton at Marylebone Coroner's Court, Mrs Lansdown said that he had been cheerful until the Thursday before his death, but when he returned from umpiring a match at Clifton he seemed depressed, and spoke of having wrongly given a batsman out. He remained in bed all day Saturday, and when she tried to talk with him he was rambling and incoherent as he tried to express his resentment at his treatment by MCC. He was also convinced he was being followed, and it was revealed that this once-abstemious man was given lately to 'sly tippling', though the landlady said she was certain that he never drank at home.

James Chandler testified that, on the Friday evening, Scotton had remarked to him while staring out of the window: 'By God! There's my brother John's voice!' John, a licenced victualler in Nottingham, was nowhere in the vicinity. Scotton then broke down, and begged Chandler to let him sleep on his couch. He was persuaded to return to his own room, and went to bed around 11 pm.

George Francis Hearne, pavilion clerk at Lord's and a friend of the lonely Scotton, asserted that he would weep at the slightest provocation. He had written to Scotton in the hope of helping him out of his spiritual trough, but the letter backfired in rendering him suspicious that MCC were about to terminate his employment.

A week or two earlier, Scotton had let another incident upset him seriously. Playing in a match at Mitcham, he had damaged—inadvertently, of course—one of young Tom Richardson's fingers, forcing him out of cricket for two weeks. Imagined guilt added to his burden. There was a striking echo of this kind of sportsman's over-consideration in Barbados in 1981, when England's deeply loved and admired coach and father figure Ken Barrington hit a high practice catch to Graham Gooch which split a finger. Already weighed down by the trauma of Robin Jackman's expulsion from Guyana and sundry related anxieties, Barrington refused to dismiss the Gooch injury as purely bad luck. He condemned himself for the incident . . . and died a few days later after a massive heart attack.

Scotton's landlady had gone into his room, in the rear parlour, on the evening before his death and found him seemingly refreshed and brighter. Late that night she and her daughter went in again and served him a fish supper, which he enjoyed. Smiling, she believed, for the first time in the three days, he said he would have the leftovers for breakfast, and expected now to have a good night's sleep. That sleep was to be eternal.

A few days before his death, Scotton had sat for a photograph at the studio of R. W. Thomas in Cheapside, and ordered four dozen copies for relatives and friends. Instead, they were to behold the face of the deceased when the Midland Railway train reached Nottingham and the coffin was unlidded on the platform. In torrential rain, Scotton was laid to rest at Nottingham General Cemetery while his son, Harold, his brother and three sisters, and John Selby of Notts stood by. We shall never know what was passing through Selby's mind as he saw his tormented team-mate into the next world. On the 1881–82 Australian tour the two of them had had a fist-fight while the team was in Cootamundra, the clouded cause either a proposed bribe or 'marital jealousy'.

We go further back, to a carpenter's shop just outside Guildford, Surrey, in May 1879. Another left-hander, George Griffith, one of the best batsmen in England not so very long before, had left his days in the sun well behind him.

'Oh, you're hard at work,' Griffith said to the carpenter, who later described his visitor as 'dirty and rough' and looking very ill, as if he'd had nothing to eat. 'I want to come and look at you to amuse myself. I don't know what to do with myself. I feel very ill from diarrhoea.'

Griffith and the carpenter had a pot of beer together, and time passed, until the 45-year-old cricketer noticed a piece of cord hanging in the shop. 'I should like to beg a bit of cord,' he said, and the carpenter told him he could cut off as much as he wished.

As he left the shop, Griffith looked back and said, 'Do you know what I'm going to do with myself?' The carpenter could only shake his head. 'Well,' said Griffith, 'I'm going to hang myself.'

George Griffith, known through much of his adult life as 'Ben' or 'old Ben', was born in Ripley on December 20, 1833,

George Griffith —
'I'm going to hang myself.'

and in the 1851 census was listed as 'helper in the stables'. By 1861 he was a baker by trade but a big-hitting batsman by reputation, preparing to board ship with the first English cricket team to visit Australia, one of seven Surrey players chosen. In the opening match, against XVIII of Victoria at the Melbourne Cricket Ground, he scored 61 and took nine wickets before daily crowds of 15,000, and went on to make more runs on the tour than anyone else. No more than 5 ft 7 ins tall, he was very powerfully built, with, according to fellow tourist Billy Caffyn, a short neck, his head partially buried between immense shoulders. A slight stoop added somewhat to the effect of a rather menacing stature.

Nonetheless, Griffith was seen at his peak as a 'most cheery as well as keenest of cricketers' by Surrey secretary Charles Alcock. He bowled fast roundarm with a lot of break (later adding underhand slows to his repertoire), and was a safe catcher, who could throw a ball over 100 yards. While bowling, he once killed a dog which was running across the pitch. Among his prodigious hits was a sequence of four clean out of the ground at Hastings off a four-ball over from 'Farmer' Bennett in 1864. Griffith was playing for the United All-England XI, and one observer said that all four hits landed the ball on the same house, some 115 yards away. For the fourth ball, Griffith skipped down the pitch and swung extra lustily to send the battered leather thing onto the roof of the house. When the hat was passed round for a sizable collection, grateful spectators must have taken into account not only the thrilling power of the man but his talent for grouping those sixes so well.

In Australia the crowds took to him, dubbing him 'The Lion Hitter'. But when it came to making a speech, as was required of him during that inaugural Melbourne match, he was seized by nervousness, and his words were mumbled inaudibly. Back in the cricket field, where he belonged, 'Ben' bowled out for one run (and that a no-ball) an entire eleven at Beechworth, 140 miles inland, in a special challenge match between the 'very inferior' locals and just himself (with three to field for him). He made a comfortable six in reply.

His personal best with the bat came at Hove in 1863, when he followed 89 in little more than an hour for Surrey against Sussex with 142 in the second innings, the higher of his two first-class centuries. In 1867 he returned his best bowling figures, 9 for 130, against Lancashire at The Oval. A year later he toured North America with Willsher's team, making the tour's highest score, 69 against XXII of Canada at Montreal, and returning proudly as one of only three players to have resisted seasickness either way.

Record survives of an astonishing catch he made at Lord's in 1869, when playing for the South of England against MCC. He parried Tom Hearne's sizzling hit with one hand and caught the ball with the other.

His troubles began as the 1870s unfolded. In Dublin he threw his left arm out, rendering it next to useless for bowling, and at The Oval he badly sprained that broad back in attempting a catch. By 1872, Surrey, with some sympathy, awarded him a benefit match, which raised around £400. He would have been gratified to read in his one-shilling copy of *Wisden* that spring that 'Surrey's committee never granted The Oval to a worthier fellow, a more popular professional, or harder-working cricketer'.

For a short time landlord of the Queen's Head in Brodie Road, Guildford, and an umpire for a season or two, Griffith also coached at Oxford for a few years, as well as at Rugby, Winchester, Harrow and Cheltenham College. For another cricketer, the hoarse roars of applause had died away.

The carpenter saw George Griffith that night in the Row Barge pub down by the river, drinking beer and speaking to nobody.

At half-past-noon, PC Prior was called to Griffith's house in Stoughton Lane and found him dead, hanging by a piece of rope tied to the two sidepieces of a bedstead. His little daughter had discovered the body.

The coroner heard that Griffith's wife, Eliza, had last seen him alive in the washhouse the previous morning, before he left the house. Her husband had been unwell and 'very strange' for the past two months, and had suffered an attack of yellow jaundice. She had heard him but not seen him the night before, and again the next morning, when he was moving about upstairs. She went on with her work. She had stayed downstairs at night for the past nine weeks, as George had shut himself in his room every night and had not eaten in the house for nine weeks. PC Prior stated that he had been sent for often by Mrs Griffith to remove her husband from the house after drinking bouts.

The jury, after a short deliberation, predictably returned a verdict of 'suicide whilst in a state of unsound mind', and Griffith, professional cricketer, was buried in the local churchyard at Stoke on May 10, 1879, a week after his death. Fourteen years earlier, Sir James Stirling, first governor of Western Australia, had been laid to rest in the same churchyard.

3

Australian Falling Stars

It seems to be generally held that the nineteenth century, from all its poverty and alcoholism, saw the darkest age for suicide among cricketers. Yet the names of three Australians whose careers blended for a season or two in the early 1950s might dispel this conviction, so large was their impact on the game. For Stoddart, Shrewsbury and Scotton read Barnes, Burke and Iverson.

Jack Iverson etched his name into one series of Ashes Test matches (1950–51) with an extraordinary return of 21 wickets at 15.24, crowning it all with 6 for 27 as Australia took the third Test at Sydney by an innings to retain the Ashes. 'Big Jake' was in his thirty-sixth year, and had had a mere 12 months' experience of the first-class game.

He had been a Second XI fast bowler as a youth at Geelong College, and during war service in new Guinea he began playing around with a ping-pong ball, flicking it with his huge middle finger and making it hop alarmingly and unpredictably. Moving on to the cricket ball, he found he could make it spin either way off the middle finger, imparting a propulsion as if disposing of a dead cigarette.

Jack Iverson — mystery bowler; mystery end.

The next step came when, strolling through the park with his wife one day, he saw some blind cricketers at play. Admiration for their courage swept over him, and he announced that he was game to try his unusual bowling action in subdistrict cricket for Brighton in Melbourne.

Soon he was touring New Zealand with an Australian 'B' team in 1949–50 and bamboozling the local batsmen to such an extent that he finished with 75 wickets at a ridiculous seven runs apiece. His 46 wickets for Victoria in the Sheffield Shield that summer (seven more than anyone else) cost only 16.61 each, starting with 6 for 47 against Western Australia on a plumb Perth pitch, with 7 for 77 in his second match, at Adelaide, followed by 6 for 46 at home against Queensland. He finished with a 6 for 30 in New South Wales's second innings at Sydney and a 5 for 48 at Brisbane. The big guns may well have been away with the Australian side in South Africa, but it was obvious that something special had arrived on the scene.

Iverson was a tall, lumbering sort of chap, a hopeless No.

11 batsman, and clumsy in the field, often kicking the ball to somebody else to collect for him. But this, in days before the embarrassingly earnest slide-all-over-the-place fielding which came with the advent of limited-overs cricket, merely added to this cricketer's box-office attraction.

Cinesound newsreel did a 'special' on this freak bowler, and lips were licked in anticipation when thoughts turned to his impact on international cricket. Came Hutton, Washbrook, Compton and Simpson, and the answer was soon revealed. They were puzzled, often to destruction.

Towards the end of the 1950–51 series several of the Englishmen, notably Len Hutton and Reg Simpson, began to fathom him, treating him as fundamentally an off-spinner. But something else had happened, just after the third Test, to hasten the bursting of a dream. At Sydney, in a Shield match, the New South Wales batsmen went after him, and it was soon apparent that he was confused by cold-blooded punishment. His 20 eight-ball overs cost 108 runs, and although he picked up three wickets—and 5 for 32 against a weak Western Australia a few weeks later—cricket seemed a crueller game.

He had been an innocent victim of interstate bitterness. At net practice before the Tests, his Victorian (and Australian) captain, Lindsay Hassett, had stopped him from bowling to Arthur Morris and Keith Miller, lest they work him out and then maltreat him when he played against New South Wales. The two batsmen were incensed, and devised a plan to disrupt Iverson when the Shield match took place. Standing wide of leg stump, they destroyed his direction, his confidence, and his late-flowering career.

He did take his faded magic to India on a Commonwealth tour, Paul Gibb later writing that this man of unparticular habits had a handshake so strong that 'you wondered what had got hold of you', but soon he put his old twine-bound brown bat away for good and entered the family real estate business, one of his last odd gestures in the game being an underarm delivery on the Indian tour which actually took a wicket.

The man whom Colin McCool once described as 'a rum sort of character' had written to an enquirer in February 1952 that he had recently taken over his father's real estate business and that meant the end of any ideas about making the 1953 Australian tour of England: 'So you will not be seeing the Freak in action.'

Years later, when asked what sort of man Iverson was, Keith Miller replied jovially that he 'didn't have a brain in his head'. He was a 'bit of a loner', but the great all-rounder contended that Iverson 'would have murdered England in 1953'. Ian Johnson, a Victorian team-mate and future Australian captain, while agreeing that Iverson was a 'loner', went on to say:

> However, I think Keith may have been a little hard in saying he didn't have a brain in his head. Had he qualified this generalisation by specifying a cricket brain, I would agree. This, however, is understandable as he really had no background in the game.

Johnson likened him to a bowling machine, every ball pitching in the same spot, doing the same thing, with a constant trajectory. His action gave the impression of leg spin, though the ball always came from the off or went straight on: 'not because of anything Jack did—simply because the odd one did not grip'.

Iverson returned to the Victorian side in the 1952–53 season, but batsmen were handling him with comparative ease. When he shared a cabin of the train with Ian Johnson after an interstate trip, they opened a couple of beers, and 'the Freak's' first words were: 'I'm going out to graze, back to Melbourne fourths.' Johnson asked why. 'I've lost it,' said Iverson. 'They're playing me easily.'

Johnson knew that here was a man who lacked the power to take the challenge further. When batsmen worked him out, he should have probed further for other weaknesses, setting them fresh problems. 'It was a classic case,' he says, 'of a bowler who was different in technique—unique, in fact—

but not knowing the first thing about the game.' He rejects, too, the suggestion that Iverson would have carried all before him in England:

> He may have done well against mediocre county batsmen, but not against good players. He was too automatic and relied upon the bounce of Australian wickets. He would have come off too easily (as I did), and he did not have the ability to dig the ball in.

On October 23, 1973 Jack Iverson shot himself in the head in his Brighton home, leaving a wife and two daughters in their twenties. The nature of his death was not made public, and no-one outside the family seems able to point to a reason for the 58-year-old former Test cricketer's action in the face of an apparently successful business and contented family life.

Two months later, on December 16, 1973, after several earlier attempts, Sid Barnes, Test average 63, aged 57, succeeded in ending his own life with an overdose of tablets at his home in Collaroy, a northern-beach suburb of Sydney. Or, as Keith Miller claims a 'cop' put it to him (he lived close by): 'Hey, Nugget, your mate's just knocked himself off!'

S. G. Barnes created smaller or larger storms wherever he went. Described in the Australians' 1938 tour brochure as a 'taxi-owner', by the time he returned with Bradman's all-conquering 1948 side he was regarded by many of those within range as, in post-war parlance, a 'wide boy' or a 'spiv'—in the nicest possible way. He was alert to a deal, forever looking for the main chance, blunt, sometimes reclusive, determined that no-one would stand in his way once his mind was made up. And it showed in his batting.

He backed himself (£8 at 15 to 1) to score a century in the 1948 Lord's Test, a landmark he was all the keener to reach because MCC had snubbed him a year before when, in England as a wine-and-spirits rep, he asked to have a net at Lord's and was refused. In the Test, Hutton caught him off Coxon for a duck; but in the second innings he made

Sid Barnes — top batsman; rebellious film-maker.

141. The newsreel shows him reaching his century, eyes blazing, oblivious to Don Bradman's extended hand.

In the previous Test, at Trent Bridge, he had grabbed a souvenir stump and run from the field, thinking the winning run had been made. He had to return sheepishly to the middle, having hurled the stump back onto the field, and was disgusted when Hassett eventually made the winning hit and he, 'Bagga' Barnes, was left amidships with no souvenir after all. He could have made a few bob out of that historic little piece of ashwood.

His fearless fielding—in pre-helmet days—only a few feet from the batsman at forward short leg irritated the English crowds as well as the batsmen themselves. When he was suspected of having a foot illegally planted on the cut pitch, he teased the onlookers by ostentatiously plonking a boot well into the sacred area, and failing hopelessly to conceal his own amusement at their agitation.

Not everyone, therefore, was humanely sympathetic when Barnes was hit around the kidneys by a massive heave by

England tailender Dick Pollard. He was carted off and taken to Manchester Infirmary, where a bruise the size of a dinner plate was revealed, and when he courageously tried to bat later, he collapsed at the crease after running a single. He was back for the fifth Test, and after England had been bowled out by Lindwall for 52, the magnificent opening partnership of Morris and Barnes was seen for the last time in a Test match. They put on 117, Morris 196, Barnes 61. Two balls after Barnes had unknowingly taken his leave of Test cricket, caught behind by Evans off Hollies, Bradman, in *his* final Test innings, was bowled.

The two, Bradman and Barnes, had created an enormous stand against England at Sydney in December 1946. Replying to England's 255, Australia were 159 for 4 when Barnes was joined by his captain. They each scored 234 and the fifth-wicket stand swelled to 405 before Bradman was out. Barnes impishly—or impishly claimed as much—terminated his innings at the same score as Bradman's so as to be linked

Barnes (right) during his stand of 405 with Don Bradman against England at Sydney.

with him numerically for all time. He had laboured for ten-and-three-quarter hours.

Sid Barnes's Test career had started at The Oval in 1938, when Hutton ground out 364 runs in thirteen-and-a-quarter hours and England declared at 903 for 7, leaving Australia to take strike minus Bradman and Fingleton, who were both injured. Barnes made a gutsy 41 and 33 in his side's feeble 201 and 123. A broken wrist on the voyage to England had delayed his international baptism.

It took a very good batsman indeed to keep the cool and elegant Bill Brown from a regular place in the Australian XI in the late 1940s, but Bradman, as shrewd a judge as ever lived, backed Barnes all the way—though he would have winced at some of his antics. It was all very well to let a 30-lb block of ice from the ice-box slide down the pavilion canopy and onto the verge in front of the England dressing-room during a Brisbane thunderstorm in 1946, causing gasps of astonishment, but to film at Lord's—the King being among the selected subjects—in defiance of ground regulations caused discomfort; though not to 'Bagga'.

He learned to wrestle; was expert at the waltz and tango; once hit 40 runs off a nine-ball over in a first-grade match; sped a racing car around Brooklands at over 100 mph; took strike with a miniature bat in the Bradman testimonial match at Melbourne; bowled straight leg-spin with fair success; kept wicket; wrote an outrageous newspaper column headed 'Like It or Lump It'; told the Australian Board of Control for International Cricket that their fee for the 1949–50 tour of South Africa was inadequate and declared himself unavailable; teased and terrified English umpire Alex Skelding by thrusting a mongrel dog under his nose, saying it would go with his white stick. He was an enfant terrible who renders Ian Botham and Fred Trueman almost ordinary by comparison.

It was the rare action of the Australian Board in overturning his selection to play for Australia against West Indies at Adelaide during the 1951–52 series that halted Barnes in his tracks. He was omitted for reasons other than his cricketing ability. Was it that the elders objected to the filming at Lord's three years earlier, or his leaping over the Melbourne Cricket Ground turnstiles when a gateman refused him entry without a pass?

Almost certainly the core of the Board's objection sprang from the events of 1948, filming at Lord's (though Barnes had obtained permission from Lord Gowrie), travelling separately from the team (though he had his captain's permission), 'abducting' Ernie Toshack, twelfth man in the match, away from a game of tennis not far from the dressing-room. On top of that was the turnstile incident. A Board official branded all this as 'childish' and 'undignified'. It didn't help matters, either, that he had lampooned officials in his newspaper column. The overall conclusion remained, nonetheless, that he was rejected simply for daring to be his own man.

All his lifelong insecurities must have risen like serpents at that time, and the humiliation would surely have swirled with an anger that blotted out all his attained aims in life.

A Mr J.L. Raith was responsible for giving Barnes an opportunity, out of the blue, to challenge the Board without taking them to court—an inconceivable step even for Barnes to have taken. Raith wrote to Sydney's *Daily Mirror* in support of the Board. His published letter stated, in part, that 'in declining to meet his request to publish reasons, the Board may well be acting kindly towards him'.

Sid Barnes sued a later-repentant Raith and won his case, with damages, setting almost every newspaper in Australia at the throats of those Cricket Board members who were revealed as narrow-minded, petty and unfair. VINDICATED thundered the *Mirror*'s front page of August 22, 1952.

But he still never played for Australia again.

Neither did he 'go straight'. Within weeks he was acting as twelfth man for New South Wales against South Australia at Adelaide Oval. At drinks time, he went out with the steward, and 9000 spectators saw Barnes, in a grey suit, carrying a wireless set, a box of cigars, a mirror, clothes brush and deodorant spray. He stopped in the outfield and raised his hand to the crowd on one side of the ground and then the other, then proceeded to the middle, where he turned on the radio and began to 'look after' the New South Wales fieldsmen. He combed the long, dark hair of his old pal Keith Miller, then skippering New South Wales, and held the mirror up to his face. His offer of cigars all-round was declined. Then the deodorant was squirted over certain players.

By now the steward had left the field and the players were returning to their places. The crowd, having enjoyed the joke, now wanted to see some cricket, over five minutes having elapsed already. There was silence, broken by the odd cry of 'Take him off!' There was rather too much for Barnes to carry off all at once, what with his special equipment and a few jugs the steward hadn't managed to carry off. Barnes walked off to an embarrassing silence, and eventually the field was clear for play to resume. Young Dean Trowse was out almost immediately, his concentration probably disturbed. The locals didn't like that.

Nor did the South Australian Cricket Association, whose president sent a letter of protest to the New South Wales Cricket Association. Sid was in the doghouse again.

His was a tale of wastage on a gigantic scale. He finished with an average of 70.50 against England and 54 in all first-class cricket. Had his behaviour been more orthodox he would have played more often, broken more bowlers' hearts with his firm method of self-denial until his eye was thoroughly in. But he wouldn't then have been Sid Barnes.

His father had died before Sid was born, but adversity was there to be overcome. By early manhood the urchin had transformed himself into a smart, chirpy (when he chose to be) Sydneyite who thrived on clever deals and brooked no argument. So prosperous an image did he radiate when playing Lancashire League cricket that the collections for his fifties (and there were many) were poor. A friendly team-mate pointed to the reason: Sid's Sunbeam Talbot and Savile Row suits. Next Saturday he parked some way from the ground and arrived for the match wearing a grimy raincoat and cloth cap. The £10 collection of previously swelled to £28.

The great S. F. Barnes, England's master bowler of the Edwardian age, was as strong-willed as they come, but not even he could have been said to have had a more calculating mind, a thicker streak of stubbornness, or a more dedicated tendency towards self-interest than his later Australian namesake. Sydney Barnes, proud as he was of his copperplate handwriting, would never have resorted to S. G. Barnes's ploy of having a rubber stamp made of his signature. He carried it in his pocket, along with an inked pad, and lined up the kids, satisfying them with an autograph much faster than could Lindsay Hassett, Ray Lindwall and Bill Johnston with their own particular flowing signatures. One thing the two Barneses did share, however, was an acute sense of self-valuation. Aussie Sid's portrait was missing from a cigarette company's souvenir calendar in 1948. He had been offered £5, refused it, and suggested—being 'a reasonable fellow'—something nearer £50. No deal.

So much for the mean image. To his few trusted friends, the real Sid was a golden character. Without fanfare, he had sent food parcels after the war to pals in austerity-squeezed London. When Bill Alley, the promising New South Wales all-rounder, was badly injured in an accident at net practice, and then lost his wife, Sid financed him to England, where he found partial escape from trauma by playing in the leagues and laying the foundations for a remarkable late flowering in county cricket with Somerset. And better known—because Sid made it clear in his autobiography—was his charity work as he showed his tour films all over Australia, often with Bill O'Reilly helping with the commentary. Over £10,000 was raised.

R. C. Robertson-Glasgow summed him up perfectly with a few lines:

> And there is so much that is American about him; the native jocularity that lies close under the surface of purpose; the natural kindness; the tendency to puncture authority; the mischievous inclination to being a minority of one.

His cunning was deeply ingrained, another manifestation of it coming when he and Bradman batted together, each keen to manipulate a favourable proportion of the strike. To many a batsman keen to run a single off the last ball of an over, Sid's broad back was as a red traffic-light.

In writing of the dangers of fielding at short leg (the position was often referred to around 1948 as the 'suicide' position), Barnes declared himself a 'fatalist': 'I knew that a hit on the temple, for instance, would bring the Barnes bones to their rest at last in some English cemetery.'

He gave up cricket—or it gave him up—while he was still in one piece. Various business ventures followed, one in building with Keith Miller. But the clouds gathered, and his mind took punishment. Towards the end he suspected he had heart trouble, and an appointment with a specialist was made. Events overran it. His family found him, on the lounge-room couch. Life had gone. Sid Barnes had employed the strictly modern method of a tablet overdose, the gentlest form of self-murder though the coroner chose to return an open verdict. Barnes left a widow and three children.

The warning to be absorbed from the case of Jim Burke was that a beaming smile and a jaunty step are no guarantee of a serene interior. Just three weeks after Burke had responded to a query on slow scoring with a loud laugh and a throwaway line of response, and very soon after his last cricket broadcast on ABC Radio, he was dead from a self-inflicted rifle wound. He was 48, and had played 24 times for Australia.

It was hardly an instance of a man who could not live without the activity of cricket and the applause which surrounded it, but it certainly was a tragic compound of those three familiar causes of self-destructive thought: reverses in health, marriage and finance. To which, in Burke's case, has to be added the grief of recently having lost his father.

James Wallace Burke was born in Mosman, Sydney on June 12, 1930, and was spotted at school as a cricketer of obvious talent. He made the New South Wales side at 18, and was chosen for Australia at 20, for the Adelaide Test of the

1950–51 series, scoring 101 not out in the second innings, becoming only the eighth Australian batsman to record a century on debut against England.

There followed a period in the international wilderness as others were preferred in the two succeeding series and for the 1953 tour of England, and it was not until the 1954–55 rubber against Hutton's Englishmen that he was chosen again, and then only intermittently. His 'comeback' innings was a determined 44 in the Sydney Test which Frank Tyson made his own with 10 wickets, but the selectors' lack of confidence in Burke was answered by a tightening in defence and a

Jim Burke — dour and brave opening batsman.

notorious reluctance to play the artistic shots which friends such as Peter Philpott, with whom he had grown up, knew and admired.

One of the most upsetting sights in cricket was to see the frail Burke hit in the chest by a lifting, fast delivery. His cap at a jaunty angle, his alert 'Irish' eyes darting, he would rub his insubstantial ribs ruefully and chirp a morsel of trench humour to the close fielders before resuming. He even smiled when an onlooker whose impatience was matched by his stentorian lung power bellowed from the Sydney Hill: 'Hey, Burke! I wish you woz a statue and I woz a pigeon!'

His dour batsmanship and durability finally paid off. He went to England in 1956 as an opener and forged what was to become a solid and successful partnership with Colin McDonald of Victoria. The Australians may have been mowed down time and time again by off-spinner Jim Laker that summer, but Burke finished top of the Australian Test averages (271 at 30.11) and made most runs on the tour (1339 at 47.82), his experience in Lancashire League cricket standing him in good stead. He scored most centuries on the tour as well: four, 194 against Warwickshire, two in the match against Somerset, and 123 against Leicestershire, joining with Ken Mackay in a century stand which, as a vision of eternity, caused a frustrated slow handclap. Batting for the Australians, in an era when Test victories were very few and far between, was a serious business.

It is often forgotten that Australia were one-up after two Tests of 'Laker's series' in 1956. The victory at Lord's was launched by McDonald (78) and Burke (65), their stand amounting to 137. The stolid Burke, to the amusement of his critics, was actually out stumped—by Evans off Laker. He joint-top-scored with 41 in the first innings at Headingley, and derived more perverse amusement in Laker's match by becoming the only one among 20 victims in the encounter not to hang from Laker's belt: Cowdrey caught him at slip off Lock, who then caught him off Laker in the second innings.

On the way home Australia played one Test in Pakistan and three in India, and it was there that Jim Burke reached his second Test hundred at Brabourne Stadium, Bombay. It took him 368 minutes, and he went on to 161 in 504 minutes, adding 204 with Neil Harvey for the second wicket.

It was this long, drawn-out hundred which was the object of the enquiry to Burke at the top of the M. A. Noble Stand at Sydney in January 1979. Graeme Wood and Derek Randall had both recently scored very slow Test centuries, and in recalling other tedious efforts Burke's name was among the first to be thrown up in the Press-box. It just so happened that he passed along the narrow concourse at that very moment. His reply was cheerful enough, but inside he must have groaned. The boring-stonewaller image was his for life. And surely inside every Boycott there is a free-flowing Trumper trying to get out.

Burke headed the tour averages in South Africa in 1957–58, the only Australian to reach 1000 runs (average 65.06), and in the Test series (won 3–0 by Australia), apart from Benaud's two centuries, only Burke reached three figures—though his partner, McDonald, was caught at the wicket for 99 in that same innings. The pair put on 190 to start Australia on the road to eventual innings victory at Cape Town, and Burke's 189 stretched over nine hours 38 minutes, the highest and last of his three Test centuries.

There remained just one more Test series, the 1958–59 drubbing of England, four matches to nil, under inspiring new captain Richie Benaud. Burke played in all five Tests, doing what he saw as his duty, making a 66 at Adelaide, where he and McDonald (170) posted 171 for the first wicket, but managing only 28 not out as his next-highest score in 10 innings in the series. And that 28 placed his name not only among the legendary sloths, but in infamy. It spanned four hours and 10 minutes, and, matched with Trevor Bailey's 458-minute encampment for 68, threatened to kill the series and, for that matter, the game of cricket itself. The number of television viewers in Australia was growing daily (this was the first Test to be shown on TV in the country), but this was no advertisement for the game. Norm O'Neill saved this Brisbane match towards the end with a dashing 71 not out to steer Australia to victory. As for Burke, he remained part of Australia's strategy, seeing the series through to the end, bowling a startled Peter May for 92 in the drawn Sydney Test, and having the pleasure of being at the wicket at Adelaide when Les Favell's hit saw the Ashes back in Australia's possession again. There had not been one 'duck' in Burke's 44 innings in Test cricket.

The legacy of rib injury during the South African tour together with the necessity of making a living persuaded Burke to retire from first-class cricket at 29. He had abundant good memories to index with the taunts of exasperated opponents and spectators. When only 19 he had carried his bat for New South Wales at Melbourne in making 162 not out against a Victorian side which included the mysterious, probing Iverson. At Adelaide in 1956–57, against South Australia, his personal score reached the heady heights of 220, a career-highest. And at the end of the 1956 Trent Bridge Test, when his unbeaten, highly disciplined 58 in four hours staved off England's attack on the final day to save the match, the applause of his team-mates will have rung in his prominent ears long and loud, to be resurrected in years to come, perhaps, as the temples turned grey.

This son of a Kentish man so loved the game that he carried on playing first-grade for Northern Districts, in Sydney. He was a fine golfer too, as was his mother. For some years yet Jim Burke was able to enjoy his sport, even if the largest crowd would now be no more than a few relatives and friends at a suburban oval.

The author played several times against him in grade cricket during this period. Placed at leg slip for Ted Cotton's brisk inducker, he waited in vain for the fabled Burke leg glance as the shot was eschewed for four hours while a century was composed. Then, to the swift new-ball bowling of Bill Jocelyn, Burke stood deep at first slip, and nonchalantly held a fast nick with his right hand, the gleeful grin helping the batsman on his way with a slightly less heavy heart than would otherwise have been the case.

A year later there came the chance to sample Burke's dart-throwing off-spinner's action. He took over 100 wickets in first-class cricket, and bags of them in grade cricket, and one of the game's miracles is that he was never called for throwing. The explanation has to be that he was so chirpily charming to umpires. Jollying them along after every ball with some quip or other, he usually had them in the palm of his hand by the time the shrill appeal rent the air. He had me fired out by an obliging umpire when the leaping ball came through high on the hipbone.

But he was good value after the match. He would organise a nine-gallon keg of beer, and do a bit of mimicking, and talk genially about big battles gone by. If a piano was available he would tinkle it as felicitously as Hoagy Carmichael; and his Al Jolson impression was all right too.

By early 1979 life was looking anything but all right for Jimmy Burke. His second marriage had hit a rocky patch. His hip had degenerated and an operation was imminent, threatening, as he thought, his precious golf, which had filled the vacuum left after cricket. His investments, to add to his anxieties, seemed doomed.

In 1978 he had resigned from Vinton, Smith & Dougall, a stockbroking firm in which he was a partner, and then relinquished his seat on the Melbourne Stock Exchange. He was now working as a client advisor for J.M. Bowyer & Company in Sydney. On Thursday, February 1, 1979, he had been most untypically perturbed, even distressed, in the presence of a work-mate. Next morning, first thing, he chatted with the chief scrip clerk and was his customary perky self again, looking for a verbal jest. Then he left the office and took the ferry to Manly.

There, at Manly Beach police station, he paid two dollars for a gun licence, having answered the standard questions, and walked to a nearby sports shop and bought a Savage .22 rifle. He then drove to St Patrick's College around lunchtime, pinned a note to his lapel, and shot himself near the heart. His body was found on the grass by his car.

Former Test star found dead in car

Former Test cricketer and ABC cricket commentator, Jim Burke, was found dead in his car in the grounds of St Patrick's College, Manly, on Friday.

News of his death was revealed only yesterday.

A rifle, which Mr Burke bought, apparently on Friday, was found nearby.

Police said there were no suspicious circumstances.

His death has shocked cricket followers.

Mr Burke, who was 47, played in 24 Test matches for Australia between 1950 and 1958.

He was an opening bat and scored 8000 runs in first-class cricket in a career lasting from 1948 to 1959.

A former team mate and president of the NSW Cricket Association, Mr Alan Davidson, described Mr Burke as one of the greats of Australian cricket — and one of the most talented opening batsmen who played for Australia.

"It's a tragedy," he said yesterday. "He was held in the highest regard by all who knew him."

Mr Burke worked in Sydney for a Melbourne sharebroking firm.

JIM BURKE . . . PLAYED IN 24 TESTS

He took part in the ABC's television coverage of the 4th Test in Sydney and was due to do the commentary on the 6th Test beginning in Sydney next Saturday.

He was twice married and had four children, two daughters and two sons.

Burke's death came as a dreadful shock.

The cricket fraternity could hardly have been more sickened and stunned, for Burke's nature had seemed so inviolably sunny. The *National Times* used his death as a means of introduction to a study of Australia's suicide problem, disclosing it as being higher than that in either Britain or Japan at 11.13 per 100,000 in 1977, and until recently higher than in the United States. The key reason? It could only be supposed that the ethos of 'mateship' and 'manliness' in

Australia bound a man to keep his emotions to himself for fear of a response which would almost certainly be scornful and mickey-taking and embarrassing.

The torment of Jim Burke had gone undetected. Father of four, Test battler, honorary MCC member, a *Wisden* Cricketer of the Year, he had, according to Richie Benaud, been patently afraid of firearms, and, according to Ian Meckiff, he had been too afraid to leave the wagon when on safari in a South African game reserve. Fear, after all, may have dragged down to lethal depths a man who faced the missile attacks of Tyson, Trueman, Statham, Heine and Adcock without a visible tremor. The most pathetic of ironies was that, after his death, Jim Burke's investments in gold futures, which were showing a loss of over $150,000 at the time of his death, later turned round and would have made him a fortune.

4

Simply Through Sadness

It may be coincidence, but Sussex cricketers number comparatively highly in the ranks of those who have terminated their own lives: Sussex, the county where the sweeping green downs slope to the sparkling sea, and cricket is played with a carefree gladness before rows of euphoric men, women and youngsters in deckchairs. The very departure from these surroundings as age reduces athletic ability and consigns mature players to the category of back numbers must be a telling influence. Retirement from the darkness and claustrophobia of a coalmine is one thing; expulsion from the agreeable 'workplace' of a cricket field is another, especially if it be the handsome expanse of Hove.

Albert Relf probably coped well enough when retirement came. His demise seems unrelated to any inability to cope with the loss of youth and the excitements and privileges that went with touring with the England Test team during the Edwardian years. He simply loved his wife deeply, and could not take the prospect of losing her through illness.

He was by now, 1937, coach at Wellington College, Berkshire, a popular long-serving mentor who was content enough with his lot to have stayed at the college for around 20 years. He had become an institution there, a kindly coach who could still surprise the boys at the practice nets with his ability to whip the ball through off a testing length which had become almost automatic in his days as a professional all-round cricketer with Norfolk, Berkshire and principally Sussex. That professionalism inclined him to preach solid defence rather than flamboyant aggression, which comes more readily to schoolboys. His predecessor at Wellington, Willie Hearne, had urged the boys to go after the ball. Relf, hoping to develop a Test cricketer or two, concentrated on the foundations. G. J. Bryan, of the Kentish brotherhood, was probably his best product: he scored 124 on his first-class debut for Kent in 1920, when he was only 17.

Bert Relf himself was one of a distinguished brotherhood. R.R. (Bob) was a regular for Sussex from 1905 to 1924, numbering three double-centuries among his 24 three-figure scores. E.H. (Ernest) played for the county a dozen times. And Albert Edward Relf, the eldest, in his quiet, determined way, served Sussex for just over 20 years from the turn of the century. As he put over 22,000 runs into the book (26 centuries) and took almost 1900 wickets, he saw not only a lot of his native land but of the old Empire too.

He missed most of the English winters of his peak years, being in Australia with Plum Warner's Ashes-winning side in 1903–04, in South Africa with two MCC Test tours, in West Indies in 1912–13, and in New Zealand, where he played domestic cricket for Auckland for three seasons from 1907–08. He instantly won honours with Auckland by scoring 157 and taking eight wickets against Canterbury in the inaugural Plunket Shield match. To complete a cricketing atlas, he also coached in India.

Relf had a springy walk, and bowled medium-pace with a fine flowing action that enabled him to keep going through long spells (he once bowled for seven hours without a break against Essex), bending and spinning the ball and mixing in clever variations of pace. His best first-class return was 9 for 95 against Warwickshire at Hove in the midsummer of

Albert Relf — overwhelmed by conjugal anxiety.

1910, his best all-round performance a century and 15 wickets against Leicestershire in 1912, and the best figures of his 13 Test matches were 5 for 85 in the 1909 Lord's Test against Australia, every one of those wickets a world-class batsman: Bardsley, Armstrong, Trumper, Noble and Gregory. Thereafter, Relf was overlooked in favour of the great S. F. Barnes.

His very first Test match had been a momentous affair. A fortnight before Christmas 1903, he went in at No. 10 at Sydney to join R. E. Foster, who was on his way to a final score of 287 in his maiden Test innings. England were 332 for 8 in reply to Australia's 285, and when Relf was out for 31, a further 115 had been added. Young Wilfred Rhodes then went in as last man and made a proud 40 not out while a further 130 runs accrued, 'Tip' Foster finally being caught 13 short of a triple-century. England went on to win by five wickets, and recovered the Ashes in the fourth Test of the series. Relf played only in the first two Tests.

His highest Test score came in his final series, in South Africa in 1913–14, when he made 63 at Johannesburg, opening the innings with Rhodes (who had moved up from No. 11) and putting on 141 before Jack Hobbs came in at No. 3. Relf also had the pleasure of taking a wicket with his final ball in Test cricket, the South African No. 11 in the fifth Test, at Port Elizabeth. How desperately he would have striven for a wicket eight years earlier, at Johannesburg, when Dave Nourse and Percy Sherwell snatched a one-wicket victory by making 48 runs for the tenth wicket, the winning hit coming off a Relf full-toss.

In international cricket as in county cricket the adjective for his play was 'steady'. He was dependable, skilled in a reliable sort of way, not given to extravagance of gesture or ambition; kindly, and good to have around—which made his ending all the more surprising and shocking.

His diary notes during the 1903–04 Australian tour, written by fountain pen and erratic of spelling and punctuation, reveal a lively relish for travel and sightseeing, even though separation from his family was for many more weeks, in pre-airline days, than is the norm for today's complaining tourists. The ancient sights of Naples thrilled Relf—except for the disgusting sanitation arrangements—and he was forever on the lookout for gifts for 'darling Aggo', Agnes, the wife he left behind.

Far out at sea, the phosphorous glow on the water reminded him of 'a lovely seafront at night at Brighton', but the longing for home was only intermittent, for 'my opinion of Colombo is great. I would like to live there for a few months in one of the bungalows.' Having read a number of books and written countless postcards during the voyage and enjoyed the deck sports and the social life, Relf was impressed with his first glimpses of Australia. Soon they were practising, and enduring the rounds of civic receptions, the one in Adelaide being followed by, of all things, a visit to the fire station, where the firemen 'gave us a show of their abilities'. Throughout his diary entries he is fond of using the word 'nice', though not in reference to Warner's underuse of him as a bowler, or the bad luck which followed Relf innings after innings (he was caught in Brisbane, for instance, when his bat split up the middle and the ball was caught at point at the second attempt, while in Newcastle he was given out lbw after edging the ball).

Between-times he spent many hours out shooting—anything that moved: seagull, plover, kingfisher. His familiarity with a gun was established this early. Thoughts of idling the time away were soon put to one side as the first Test match approached. 'Mr Warner asked me to play in the Test so I feel rather pleased.' This famous Sydney match, blessed not only by Foster's record 287 but by 185 not out from Victor Trumper, was Relf's maiden appearance for England, as it was for Foster, Bosanquet and Ted Arnold (who dismissed Trumper with his first ball in Test cricket).

Relf's debut Test innings, a crucial 31 in a stand of 115 in 84 minutes with Foster before a crowd of 40,000, is recorded economically in the diary as 'very useful assistance'. His captain, in his book on the tour, goes a little further by writing that 'I cannot praise him enough for his cool head at a trying time'. Next day Relf received a cable informing him that his wife had given birth to another daughter, and that 'all is going well'.

The hardened professional in him emerges again and again as he bemoans further controversial dismissals ('did not think I was out when caught in the slips' in the Victoria match) and records with satisfaction another haul of wickets and more slips catches (he was an expert there, and held 537 catches in his first-class career).

Relf and his team-mates went often to concerts and the theatre, and although *A Desperate Game* at Melbourne's Theatre Royal was 'much too dramatic for me', he derived much enjoyment from this and other social occasions. The pleasure of touring beams unmistakeably from the diary, which terminates on January 2, 1904 and is now in the custody of Sussex County Cricket Club.

Bert Relf played on until he was 47, having appeared nine times for the Players against the Gentlemen and achieved the double of 1000 runs and 100 wickets in eight seasons.

Statistically his best year was 1913, when he made 1846 runs and took 141 wickets. He was in his fortieth year, and his effort earned him a place among *Wisden*'s Five Cricketers of the Year. *Wisden*'s essay includes a telling summary of his batsmanship:

> He has a way of letting the ball hit the bat that is certainly not impressive to the eye. Still, the fact remains that season after season he makes as many runs as men who look twice as good as he is.

Coaching the sons of soldiers at Wellington became the natural course to take as his playing career closed, and the 'adornment to the game' became a respected figure at the college, the schoolboys who had hero-worshipped the all-rounder with the jet-black hair and luxuriant moustache having grown to adulthood by now. Relf's travels had come full circle, for, although he was Sussex-born, he had played his boyhood cricket at Finchampstead, his father then being chief coach at Wellington.

By March 1937, Albert Relf's mind was in turmoil. Though secure financially, he was so devoted to Agnes, whom he had married at Godalming, Surrey, almost 40 years before, that the thought of losing her or of her suffering played heavily on his mind. She had been in Reading Hospital, making a slow recovery from a gallstone operation; but he was convinced he was about to lose her. From his Crowthorne home, where a daughter shared accommodation with her parents, Relf had consulted a doctor about his own abdominal pains. Dr Lambert found nothing organically wrong and put it down to nervous strain brought on by the prolonged worry over his wife, whose operation had been postponed twice. Relf's depression seemed, according to the doctor, to have every chance of lessening as his wife slowly recovered.

On Good Friday, March 26, the doctor was called to the cricket pavilion at Wellington College by Ross Willmott, a fitter, who knocked on the door at 12.55 pm after Relf's daughter had told him that her father had not come home for lunch as expected. Willmott found Relf lying on the floor of his office, a 12-bore sports gun across his feet. PC Mortimer was called and searched the room and Relf's clothing, but found no letter or note. A stick, 23 inches long, was by the shotgun and had evidently been used to activate the trigger. When Dr Lambert arrived and examined the body he found a wound between the fourth and fifth ribs, near the breastbone, 'which would be through the middle of the heart'. Relf had been dead about two hours.

The last person to see him alive was Fred Streat, the assistant groundsman, who had called through the office window mid-morning, seeking permission to go home. Streat testified at the inquest, which was held in the pavilion, that Relf had been 'rather strange' for the past week, and seemed to have lost interest in his work and everything else. He had remained in his office most of the time—which Streat thought was unusual—and had kept three or four guns there. Relf's brother-in-law told the coroner that he had 'seemed to go to pieces, more or less'.

Returning a verdict of 'suicide while of unsound mind', the coroner expressed sympathy to the family, and hoped Mrs Relf would soon recover her health. The beloved wife whose feared death brought such inconsolable sadness to her husband did indeed recover, and inherited a handsome estate.

Almost half-a-century later, Australia's popular scorer and baggage-master, Dave Sherwood, committed suicide for reasons not dissimilar to those in Relf's case. Both men might be regarded as 'uxorious'—defined in the *Oxford English Dictionary* as 'excessively fond of one's wife', and surely no crime. It is thought, too, that—as in Relf's case—Sherwood suspected or even knew that he had a serious illness. Worry at the recent ill-health of his wife seems to have been the decisive factor.

He had been Australia's official scorer for over 20 years, touring England seven times, and generating much affection wherever he went by his friendliness and willingness to help with statistical matters. He had scored for the Randwick club, in Sydney, since 1926, and scored his first match for New

Dave Sherwood — kindly Australian scorer.

South Wales in 1932–33, in the match in which Tim Wall took all 10 wickets for 36 for South Australia at Sydney. (Wall, in passing, is thought by at least one close acquaintance to have taken his own life in Adelaide in 1981, after years of suffering with Parkinson's disease—though the death certificate does not support this belief.)

Dave Sherwood, a caterer and then office manager, studied the immaculate scorebooks and stroke charts left by a noted predecessor as Australia's scorer-baggageman, Bill Ferguson, and his own elegant hand kept the tradition going for decades more. He served with the RAAF in New Guinea during the 1939–45 war.

On his last tour of England, in 1981, Sherwood was carrying out yet another of his countless acts of kindness, gaining admission to the Australian dressing-room at Lord's for the author after an attendant had been particularly difficult. Then he gave me the team autograph sheet. While there, I decided to get Dennis Lillee's signature in his latest book, a paperback on family fitness, with a photo of the great fast bowler and two youngsters running up the beach. Dave Sherwood saw it and called across to Lillee, 'Hey, Fot, are these your two nippers?' Lillee asked him to repeat the question, which he did. Mis-hearing, Lillee shouted back, 'Yeah, of course they're my nipples. Who else's?'

On March 12, 1985 a woman jogger saw Sherwood, resident at Double Bay, sitting on the edge of the Gap at Watson's Bay, a notorious suicide spot on Sydney's South Head. Later she saw only what turned out to be a pile of his clothing and some identification. His body lay on the rocks far below, but had been washed out by rough seas when police went to the spot, and it was a week before it was recovered. Kind, gentle, brave Dave Sherwood was 73.

A Sussex fast bowler who often took the field with Albert Relf in the first few seasons of the new century was Cyril Bland. He was very fast for a summer or two, and brought much-needed bite to the Sussex attack, while Ranjitsinhji made enough runs for two for the county. Bland, born in Lincolnshire, at Leake, outside Boston, qualified for the southern county (playing for Horsham), and was one of the sensations of 1897, when he took 129 wickets in his maiden season, 95 of them for Sussex. Over the next three summers he took another 302.

He was seen by some as the new Tom Richardson. Wirily-built, with ears that stuck out like satellite-television dishes, Cyril Harold George Bland went all out for pace at a time when the expansion of the county program was persuading many of the fast bowlers that less physical effort and a greater concentration on accuracy would prevent breakdown and lengthen their careers. Bland, for a few seasons, went on being explosive.

In June 1899, in Kent's second innings at Tonbridge, he blasted out all 10 wickets for 48 off 25.2 overs after his side had been forced to follow on. Kent eventually needed 227 to win, but Bland got rid of them for 114 in one of the most remarkable bowling performances in county cricket history, delivering at top speed and getting the ball to kick on a third-day pitch. Two years earlier, against the same opposition at the same venue, he had taken 8 for 65.

As he approached 30 he began to lose pace and consistency,

Cyril Bland — meteoric career; suicide in old age.

and by 1905 he was a 33-year-old ex-county cricketer, whose successes had started to be overshadowed by whispered accusations that he threw the ball. He was among those named at an enquiry at Lord's in 1901. The fast bowler who had started with Hertfordshire and the Yorkshire leagues (where the great J.T. Brown had helped his development) returned to obscurity, to live with his memories of Sussex successes and of the terror he spread in club cricket as he returned such grotesque figures as 9 for 3 (twice) and 8 for 1 for Skegness.

His first-class cricket behind him, he served in the Army Veterinary Corps in the First World War, and was wounded. And in Lincolnshire's flat, broad acres he lived for many more years, until, one Saturday in 1950, the first day of July, his body was recovered from the Greenlands Drain in the Maud Foster Canal.

He had gone to a great deal of trouble to end it all. His feet were tied together with twine, knotted at the front up to the knees, which were also tied at the front; likewise his waist, in front of which his hands were tied together. He was fully clothed, and his cap was tucked neatly into his pocket. Outside involvement was ruled out. Bland was 78, and it was made known that for some time he had been a heavy drinker.

If his spent days of fame and glory were a source of mental strain, he had lived with it for the latter half of his life and then some.

In the same year, 1950, another Sussex cricketer, though of a later vintage, took his own life after bouts of ill-health and an inability to escape from traumatic memories had shattered all remaining hope. Tommy Cook, born in Cuckfield, Sussex, on February 5, 1901, was at first an outstanding footballer, playing at centre-forward for Brighton & Hove Albion (and later Bristol Rovers), and representing England in an international against Wales in 1925, when Albion were a Third Division club. His total of 113 League goals for the club remains a record.

At the end of the season before his England cap was won, he and his Sussex team-mates had been shocked by the death of their little wicketkeeper George Street. His motorbike had crashed into a brick wall by the Southwick crossroads as he tried to avoid a lorry and applied the throttle instead of the brake. He was returning home from watching Brighton's football team in action—his favourite player, naturally enough, having been Tommy Cook.

Cook's professional cricket career began by accident. Playing for Cuckfield, he did enough when invited to the Sussex nets to be included, more as a camp supporter than prospective player, in the happy party which took off for the County Championship match against Lancashire at Liverpool in July 1922. Suddenly his name appeared on the team sheet, and he was making his debut in first-class cricket, going out to bat at No. 9 after his illustrious team-mates higher in the

Tommy Cook — traumatic memories.

order had collapsed before his opposition namesake 'Lol' Cook's bowling on a rain-affected pitch. Thomas Edwin Reed Cook, product of Brighton Municipal School, aged 21, made an instant impression with 50 not out, helping the total to 231, before taking in the proud delights of treading the same field as household names from his own county, such as the Gilligans, Ted Bowley, Maurice Tate, and George Cox senior, and from Lancashire in Makepeace and Hallows, Ernest and Dick Tyldesley, and Cec Parkin.

By the end of that summer Tommy Cook had had 29 Championship innings for Sussex, averaging 22 to finish third in the county's batting. For the next 15 years he was to be a favourite in the side, holding the opposition at bay or pressing for runs, bowling occasional medium-pace, and moving in the outfield like the top-class soccer player that he was.

He was far from being the most colourful player on the circuit, but was a pleasing enough study for those who watched keenly from the stands and terraces. Life was good for a young man who excelled at cricket in the warm season and football when the overcoats came out. His batting matured to the point where he amassed some tall scores in the early 1930s: 278 (in a long-sleeved sweater on a warm day) against

Hampshire at Hove in 1930, 214 against Worcestershire at Eastbourne in 1933, and 220 against the same county at Worcester a year later. In that year, 1934, he made 2132 runs at 54.67, with four three-figure scores: steadiness personified.

Arthur Gilligan, his captain, was thrilled at Cook's progress, and put much of it down to his willingness to listen to advice and to absorb from observation. Cook studied Patsy Hendren's alert and educated footwork against slow bowling and built it into his own game. (Hendren, it might be remembered, gave the world the ultimate cricketer's suicide story: the one about the fellow sitting miserable and all rugged up in a railway compartment, whispering to the fellow across the aisle that he had just played in a match where his bowling was hit for over 100 runs without reward, his visit to the crease had been scoreless, and he had missed two catches, both batsmen going on to make centuries. 'Goodness me,' said his sympathiser, 'if that ever happened to me I think I'd cut my throat.' 'I just did,' croaked the poor chap.)

The closest Tommy Cook came to being a double international was a Test trial at Old Trafford in 1932 when, not getting in until six South wickets had fallen, he scored 22. The seven batsmen above him give some indication of the class of England batsmanship at the time: Woolley, Gubby Allen, Duleepsinhji, Hammond, Jardine, Ames and O'Connor. When given the chance to stretch himself against international opposition, he generally looked good. His playing of Australian spin masters Mailey and Grimmett in the tourists' Sussex match in 1926 was considered excellent.

Cook made just over 20,000 runs at just over 30, with 32 centuries, and held 169 catches. His 80 wickets cost 36 apiece, with a best return of 5 for 24. And if there should be any doubting the fulfilment known to the Sussex players of that era, Cook's own words, penned for a magazine in 1929, seem to pin it:

> We of Sussex, all Sussex-born and -bred, seem to have a county spirit that can never be so strong in teams of

mixed counties and nationalities. This county spirit seems to give us a will to win stronger than the incentive of the £2 bonus.

Among those 169 catches was one at Hastings in 1926 which might have overwhelmed even one of today's television cameramen. Arthur Carr of Notts, England's captain against Australia that year, and a mighty hitter, straight-drove Bowley and had the crowd applauding a six: until Cook, fielding in front of the sightscreen, leapt up and parried the ball goalkeeper-fashion before catching it in an outstretched right hand. Dudley Carew wrote that he would never forget 'the almost comical look of anxiety upon Cook's face as he judged the flight of the ball before jumping for it'.

Another of his special catches was made at Hove in 1932. Jack Mercer of Glamorgan hit a high one into the sun, and Cook ran for it, waited for it, and held it, rolling over and losing his cap. Above the full-throated applause—for this meant that the visitors would have to follow on—came the shrill cry of his mother, seated on a seat on the roof: 'He's my son! He's my son!'

That son had put his age up in order to join the Royal Navy in the First World War, winning a gallantry medal after diving over the side in Archangel Harbour to rescue a shipmate. When the Second World War broke out he was coaching in Cape Town, having played his last for Sussex in 1937. He joined the South African Air Force, and it was while on a training flight that his life was changed tragically and irreversibly. Returning to the airfield because of engine trouble, the aeroplane crashed on the runway, all aboard perishing in the flames, except Cook, who was thrown clear, and was to spend months in hospital.

He had left his wife before the war, but now he returned to England and moved back in with his family. He became manager, briefly, of his old club, Brighton & Hove Albion, but, like many thousands of other ex-servicemen, he was a different man. The burning aircraft and screaming young airmen trapped within came back to him in nightmares.

Worsening his condition was the onset of chronic bronchitis. On January 15, 1950 he went to the local hospital in the hope of lessening his pain and misery, only to be told that he should see his doctor instead. He went back home and took a fatal overdose of tablets. He was 48.

Fifteen years on, in 1965, another Sussex player died by his own hand, a relatively young man who had shown considerable talent on the cricket field while at school at Winchester and in his handful of games for the county. Son of the distinguished footballer (and later chairman of the Football Association) and cricketer (Cambridge Blue 1921–22) A.G. Doggart, and brother of Cambridge, Sussex and England batsman (and later MCC president) Hubert Doggart, A.P. (Peter) Doggart was also gifted in sport, representing England at squash 'despite the nervous strain', as an obituary observed.

He was in the Winchester College cricket XI in 1944–45, and after making a lot of runs for Sussex 2nd XI he played for the county's senior side for the first time in 1947, when he was 19. There were to be nine appearances altogether

Peter Doggart — clinical depression from boyhood.

in 1951, with a top score of 43 and an average of 17.54, and there seems little doubt that he was a prime example of a batsman whose talents tended at times to be smothered by nervousness.

He had a fortnight, in 1947, such as few cricketers have known. Rejoicing in the best possible way in the time available to him to play cricket, he scored 107 for Middleton against Guildford in a club match, 131 for Sussex II against Essex, 70 not out for Sussex Club & Ground against United Hospitals, 87 for Incogniti against Sutton, 151 for the Incogs against United Services (adding an analysis of 7 for 57 with his medium-pacers), and 94 for Butterflies against the Bank of England.

In June of that year he was involved in a remarkable piece of sportsmanship, typical of the great and gracious New Zealand left-hander Martin Donnelly, then captain of Oxford University. Doggart, batting for Sussex at Chichester, was given out lbw, but was recalled to the crease by Donnelly when it became clear that the batsman had first played the ball with his bat.

Peter Doggart collated the public school reports for *The Cricketer* magazine for several years from 1950, until a breakdown in health forced him to resign. He committed suicide on March 17, 1965, at the age of 37, dying in Epsom Hospital from an overdose of tablets. He left a widow and three children.

His brother Hubert remembers Peter as a 'lovable person'. 'We grew up playing cricket all summer and soccer in winter, and my father built a squash court at Selsey,' he recalled. But his younger brother wrote sad letters home from school. Clinical depression was diagnosed early; he was unable to stand pressure of any sort.

When Peter made over 2000 runs in a season, Hubert gave him a pair of gold cufflinks with the statistics engraved on them. It may be safely supposed that cricket, murderous on the nerves though it can be, for once brought exquisite pleasure and relief for one young man from the hard world and its hazards.

5

Springbok Shocks

'What a pity we can't stay young!' said Aubrey Faulkner in the course of a radio interview in 1930 with Jack Hobbs to mark the master batsman's retirement from Test cricket. Faulkner himself had last played Test cricket, for South Africa, six years earlier, when he had made a sort of comeback at 42. 'These young fellows today don't know how marvellous it is to be young enough to get on with things,' he went on. If he sounded disgruntled, it had something to do with having been an all-rounder himself of the highest quality, though now 48 and worn out by interminable work at his indoor cricket school in London, where he bowled to his pupils with his left arm if his right arm seized up through fatigue.

Towards the end of the Hobbs interview, when the Surrey and England maestro spoke of having had 'a good innings', with fine times to look back on, Faulkner reacted curiously: 'You're lucky. The majority of us are not so fortunate.' Only a minute earlier he had said, 'You make me feel I want to start cricket all over again.'

A few days later, Major George Aubrey Faulkner, DSO, Order of the Nile, batsman, bowler, fielder, theoretician, coach, journalist, was dead. He left a note for the secretary of the Faulkner School of Cricket: 'Dear Mackenzie, I am off to another sphere via the small bat-drying room. Better call in a policeman to do the investigating.'

The military precision of his last order came as no surprise, for he was a soldier too. As a young man who had once been forced to beat up his alcoholic father for assaulting his mother, he was both gregarious and something of a loner. Relationships did not come easily. He threw himself into the Boer War and saw action in the relief operations at Mafeking and Ladysmith as a gunner whose unit was attached to the Imperial Light Horse.

Strongly-built, intelligent and sensitive despite the brusque exterior, he absorbed early coaching and developed into a correct batsman, straight of blade, powerful of shot, and, equally memorably, an expert at the new form of spin-bowling deception, the 'googly', as popularised by Bosanquet of Middlesex and England. Faulkner and three other South Africans, Schwarz, Vogler and White, stunned England with this phenomenon which revolutionised the game.

Aubrey Faulkner — South African allrounder supreme.

He took 6 for 17 in the Headingley Test, turning the ball mystifyingly both from leg and off with apparently the same action. His performances with bat and ball in the home series of 1909–10 against England, and in Australia a year later, were stupendous. He must have been the most effective all-rounder in the world at that stage. Crowning his 732 runs in the Australian series was a double-century at Melbourne, and when he played against Australia on neutral soil, at Manchester during the 1912 Triangular Tournament, he scored 122 not out. Soon he was taking 7 for 84 against England at The Oval. During that season he made 1206 first-class runs and took 163 wickets. How South Africa could have used him just over a year later, when S. F. Barnes massacred them on their own matting pitches, taking 49 wickets in four Tests.

But by now Aubrey Faulkner was settled in England, playing with huge success around Nottingham, where the millionaire cricket-lover, Sir Julien Cahn, Packer-style, soon signed him on.

Then came the Great War, and Faulkner was soon charging the enemy, starting in France and Egypt before engaging in some tough mountain fighting in Macedonia. Finally, in Palestine, he saw action in the capture and defence of Jerusalem, and was awarded the Distinguished Service Order. The Order of the Nile, fourth class, followed. His competitive qualities at last had been formally acknowledged.

While his one-Test comeback in 1924 is best forgotten, his reputation had been revived and strengthened in 1921 when Archie MacLaren, then 49, included him in his specially chosen team to take on Armstrong's all-conquering Australians at Eastbourne, determined to show the dithering Test selectors that the steamrollering invaders were not unbeatable. As well as taking six wickets in the match, the 39-year-old Faulkner, who had had little recent practice, scored 153 in 210 minutes in high heat, setting up a victory which excited Englishmen more than any other event that season. Armstrong was far from amused. MacLaren was exultant. Faulkner returned to his coaching, leaving the

Australians wondering what kind of man could talk to himself all the way through his innings. In truth, he got by 'by coaching myself as I went along'. Yet the wicketkeeper thought he was out of his mind.

In 1925 he abandoned schoolteaching and established his cricket school—the first of its kind—in Richmond, south-west London, later moving to a larger garage in Farm Lane, Walham Green. Some great cricketers in the making passed through his academy, young men such as Duleepsinhji, Jardine, Freddie Brown, Doug Wright, Fred Bakewell, Tom Killick, Walter Robins, and Maurice Turnbull. He had as assistants at various times Ian Peebles, R.E. S. Wyatt and Tom Reddick, Peebles remembering him with great affection and a certain sadness, adding wryly that, among an interesting assembly of qualities, he was convinced that Faulkner was highly sexed. A teetotaller, the veteran soldier and cricketer denied himself any bar profits at his school by simply refusing to have a bar. He feared it would attract layabouts to whom cricket was barely material.

He enjoyed expressing himself on paper, writing with feeling about the courage and skill of Don Bradman and Archie Jackson as they joined together in a stand of 243 on an Oval pitch not altogether trustworthy in August 1930. His praise for the two young Australians was near to being the last thing he wrote.

In 1926 he had written *Cricket: Can it Be Taught?*, a model instructional book, perhaps even a masterpiece of its kind, with scores of thought-provoking paragraphs, penetrative statements on technique and conduct, and numerous pictures of the author, broad of waistline, showing how it should all be done—and indeed, how he once did it.

His body was found on that chilling morning in September 1930. PC Horace Scott told the inquest jury at Fulham that Faulkner had died with his mouth over one of the gas-radiator jets. He was fully clothed, and in his pockets there was a chequebook, £2.6.6 in cash, and other articles. The police surgeon, Dr Orchard, examined the body at 9.45 am and calculated that 'the Major' had been dead between one and

Faulkner in later life:
still battling on.

four hours. Death was attributed to suffocation through inhaling carbon monoxide.

Faulkner's widow, Alice, his former secretary, who was a good deal younger than her husband, and was his second wife, said that he had been a healthy man until the previous year, when he 'had an illness due to overwork'. He had had two operations at the end of 1929, and they left him very depressed. He was 'very temperamental'.

The coroner, H. R. Oswald, asked if it was not unusual for a cricketer to be like that; to which Mrs Faulkner replied, 'Yes, very.' Asked if she had ever heard him threaten to take his own life, she replied that she had, 'only once definitely'. 'Did he ever indicate in what way he would do it?' asked the coroner. 'Yes,' she replied, 'in exactly the same way as he did do it—by gas.'

Ronald Mackenzie, the secretary of the Faulkner School of Cricket, said he had known his managing director for about a year and described him as 'healthy' and a man of 'sober habits', but felt that he had a 'peculiar temperament, and used to have fits of depression.'

Tom Reddick, one of Faulkner's pupils who later played for Middlesex, Western Province and Notts, wrote of the much-admired Faulkner, just on half-a-century later:

> It was never discovered why he killed himself. He was a courageous man, so something must have severely disturbed his mind. I do recall an early incident after Faulkner had been particularly disappointed with the broken promise of some financial assistance for the school from one of cricket's hierarchy. 'You know,' he said, 'this sort of thing sickens me. I wonder sometimes if all this is worthwhile: perhaps it would be better for everyone if I moved on.' It never occurred to me that he might have been serious.

In the year before he died, Faulkner, having played no outdoor cricket for four years, agreed to appear at the opening of the Chelmsford ground. On the train, Reddick, fearful at the prospect of the old maestro humiliating himself or doing himself an injury, asked him where his cricket bag was: where was his kit?

'I haven't brought any,' he said. 'I'm much too old and fat, so I shall not play.' He told his young companion that he would explain when he reached Chelmsford, and knew that Walter Warsop, the bat-maker and organiser, would understand. But when they reached the ground, Faulkner's name appeared in large lettering in the match posters, and Warsop would not hear of the great veteran's withdrawal. So, in borrowed clothing and equipment, Faulkner took the field, stood at slip for a time, and eventually had a bowl. His leg-breaks, wrong'uns and topspinners were dropped on a length and claimed seven victims, one of them young Essex opening batsman Dudley Pope, who was to be killed in a car accident in 1934. Pope was shaking his head as he passed Faulkner on his way back to the pavilion, and said, 'I don't know who you are, sir, but my word, you bowl a bloody good wrong'un.' Reddick wrote: 'Faulkner just smiled. Perhaps Victor Trumper had said much the same thing to him in Sydney many, many years before.'

Aubrey Faulkner's estate, left to Alice, amounted to £273.16.6 though she later reclaimed his Springbok blazer from Reddick, to whom Faulkner had presented it only weeks before he died. The widow would have valued it not for sentimental reasons alone. Its buttons were solid gold.

Five other South African Test players are known or believed to have committed suicide. Three of them played for their country only once: either a blessing and an honour or a frustratingly short brush with the highest glory, depending upon one's disposition.

Vincent Maximillian Tancred was one of five brothers, three of whom played for South Africa in some of that country's earliest Test matches. Louis was the best cricketer among them, playing 14 times, with a top score of 97, while Augustus Bernard Tancred was his side's major scorer in the first of all South African Tests, against England in Port Elizabeth (birthplace of the Tancreds) in March 1889. He made 29 in each innings, and within a fortnight had become the first batsman to carry his bat through a Test innings, holding on against Johnny Briggs (7 for 17) for 26 not out in South Africa's first innings of 47 at Cape Town. They didn't do as well in the second innings, Briggs's 8 for 11 wiping them out for 43. They probably all had a good laugh about it. If not, then they should have done. Bernard Tancred's reputation grew over the next two seasons as he averaged 74 in the Currie Cup tournament, but cricket thereafter took second place to his business as a solicitor.

Louis, the youngest of the three Test-playing Tancreds, was on the second of his four tours of England in 1904 when news of Vincent's death came through. The Springboks were at Worcester, where Louis scored 61 in the second innings. It was nine days before he played again, and then scored 97 in two hours against Gloucestershire, as if in honour of young Vincent. Then came a century against Warwickshire, and on July 18 he hammered 250 against Scotland at Edinburgh. Grief may even have intensified his concentration.

Why Vincent Tancred should have ended it all on June 3,

1904, back in Johannesburg is not altogether evident. While Louis went on to hit 148 against Dublin University and further centuries against Leicestershire and Notts, *Cricket*, the weekly which published scores and all kinds of news snippets, was silent on Vincent's demise. The stigma then attaching to suicide was more intensive—if only just—than in modern times, though *Wisden* for once made no bones about it. In its 1905 edition 'Mr Vincent Tancred . . . shot himself' left no room for misunderstanding. The confusing euphemism 'died tragically' caused the world to believe (almost certainly wrongly) that Tom Richardson, the great Surrey and England fast bowler, had cast himself down a French hillside in 1912. His young son had understood that Richardson had had a heart attack, but a suicide theory was put about in the late 1920s. It seems to have been dispelled with Ralph Barker's examination of police and medical records in 1966. No such confusion ever existed over V. M. Tancred.

Vincent Tancred was 29 when he took his exit in Florida, near Johannesburg. He had played for Transvaal against Lord Hawke's 1898–99 English touring team and in the opening Test match, at the old Wanderers ground, Johannesburg, when he was one of 14 debutants in the match, Plum Warner and

Vincent Tancred — dead at 29, having just missed the 1904 tour of England.

Johnny Tyldesley among them. Tancred, regarded as South Africa's best outfielder, opened with Jimmy Sinclair and made 18 of an opening stand of 46 before Schofield Haigh bowled him. South Africa went on to secure their first-ever first-innings lead in a Test match, but in the second innings, when they needed 132 for a totally unexpected victory, Haigh had Tancred caught behind for 7, and nobody did much better in an all-out total of 99.

Was it a disappointing denial of a further chance to do well at international level? Could he have been oppressed by the thought of being third-best to brothers Louis and Bernard? He had been known to keep pace with Bernard—then regarded as South Africa's best batsman—in Eclectics' match against Union (who had Brockwell, the England bowler) at Pretoria in 1896, making a century; but Bernard made *two* of them in the match.

Vincent had failed twice for Transvaal against the 1902–03 Australians, and was merely a reserve for the 1904 tour of England, which was a few weeks old when he shot himself. It possibly, probably had nothing to do with cricket at all. Only a suggestion of financial anxiety has drifted down through the years.

Norman Reid played once for South Africa, against the visiting Australians, at Cape Town, his home town, in November 1921. His brilliant cover fielding as much as his batting and bowling earned him his place, and he came away from that Test match not quite empty-handed with scores of 11 and 6 and two wickets (Mayne and Pellew) for 63 off his 21 overs.

Reid, whose father was Western Province's chairman for a quarter of a century and had much to do with the acquisition of the Newlands ground, had two cricketing brothers, Alan, who toured England with the 1901 (non-Test) Springboks, and Frank, who also played for Western Province and became a QC.

'Normie' Reid played in the Western Province side which won the Currie Cup in 1920–21 and he had a score of 81 not out against Orange Free State a year later. He was, if anything, a better Rugby player than cricketer, winning Blues in the strong Oxford University sides of 1912 and 1913, and playing for the Barbarians. He served in the Imperial Light Horse in South-West Africa in the First World War, transferring to the Royal Field Artillery in France, being wounded twice and winning the DSO and the Military Cross.

Many years on, at the age of 56, having retired as a solicitor in 1944, he died in June 1947, in Cape Town, while in faraway London the South Africans were about to embark on the Lord's Test match of the Compton-Edrich summer. His countrymen were saddened to hear that Reid died in 'tragic circumstances'.

Facts were and still are hard to come by, so effectively were the details of Reid's death covered over. Historians have assumed it was suicide, the cause probably 'standard'. However, South African cricket researcher Brian Bassano remembers Herby Taylor, long ago, saying that Reid's wife, 'a rather intense Scandinavian woman', killed him and then herself in their large house near Newlands.

Norman Reid — marital murder/suicide.

In the preparation of this book, further attempts were made to clarify the Reid case, and eventually an inquest report was found, together with a death certificate. The facts are not so far removed from those handed down to Bassano by H. W. Taylor: Norman Reid's body, clad in pyjamas, was found in his bed 'in an attitude of sleep' on June 18, 1947. He had been shot in the head. In the loungeroom, his wife lay dead from a gunshot wound in the stomach. She had left a note apologising for the inconvenience caused, and had been suffering from severe depression arising from her wartime experiences in Belgium all those years ago during the First World War. Reid's death certificate states that death was 'due to a gunshot wound of the head' and concludes that 'from the evidence the irresistible inference is drawn that this wound was inflicted by his wife whilst of unsound mind. The court finds that death took place during the night June 5/6 1947.' *Wisden* and the *Cricket Annual of South Africa* have had to amend the date accordingly after many years of misinformation.

The other who played only one Test was Glen Hall, a leg-spin-googly bowler who burst upon the scene with great brilliance in 1960–61 only to fade away before his thirtieth birthday, having taken 110 wickets in 32 first-class matches at just under 30 apiece. Born in Pretoria on May 24, 1938, Hall had an astonishing debut. Playing for South African Universities against Western Province at Cape Town, he took 4 for 24 followed by 9 for 122 when Western Province went in again, well in arrears. It was a record for a South African on debut.

Going on to play for North-East Transvaal in the Currie Cup, he took 10 more cheap wickets that season, then had three seasons with Eastern Province while studying pharmacy at Rhodes University, Grahamstown, his bowling being more expensive now. Still he earned a place in the South African Test team by taking 6 for 145 against the 1964–65 MCC touring team in their large innings against North-East Transvaal at Pretoria.

Glen Hall — brilliant beginning; lonely end.

At Newlands, Cape Town, he found Test cricket tough, managing to get only Parfitt's wicket—the England left-hander playing no stroke—for 94 runs in 31 overs. An habitual tail-ender, Glen Hall was bowled by Barrington for 0.

He spun his way to success in the following domestic season, with 27 wickets at 26, including 11 for 132 against Orange Free State, but he played his last first-class match two years later. Batsmen generally were glad to see the back of this tall cricketer who snapped his topspinners and well-disguised 'wrong'uns' down at a brisk pace, getting awkward bounce. But he was considered a loss to the game, not only for his skilful bowling but for his pleasant personality.

Life was to turn sour on him. He had married a blonde Miss South Africa, Carol Davis, in the mid-1960s, and they had had two sons. By 1980 the marriage had broken down, and there was a divorce. Glen Gordon Hall became a recluse, refusing to see his sons. His wife remarried. In 1986 his mother died, and Hall spent some time in Johannesburg, having medical treatment, before returning to his home in Ramsgate, Natal. There was subsequent talk of his being on drugs. Whatever the case, he suffered severely from loneliness, and was known as 'Ramsgate's lonely man', a 'reclusive chemist'.

LONELY BOK GLEN HALL FOUND DEAD was the sullen headline in Johannesburg's *Citizen* newspaper a few days after he had shot himself in the head in his bathroom on June 26, 1987. He was 49, and police, summoned by a neighbour, stated that he had made four previous attempts on his life. 'Mr Hall is reported to have made an effort to snap out of his self-imposed loneliness,' the paper went on. 'Twice in recent years he became engaged, but each time the marriage plans foundered.'

About a year later, in strikingly similar circumstances, Joe Partridge, one of South Africa's most successful bowlers in the 1950s and early 1960s, killed himself in a suburban Harare (formerly Salisbury) police station, having been arrested at the hotel where he lived for not paying his bill. He had been unemployed and almost destitute for some time.

Partridge was born in Bulawayo, Rhodesia (now Zimbabwe), on December 9, 1932. He began taking wickets at a steady rate for Rhodesia in the mid–1950s, but his path into the South African Test team was blocked by the faster men, Neil Adcock and Peter Heine. In 1954–55 Partridge took 8 for 124 against Border, hitting them again with 7 for 9 five years later. In 1961–62 his dipping swing bowling earned him 53 wickets at just under 14 apiece in only seven matches, Natal suffering most when he took 8 for 69 and 6 for 32 against them at Salisbury.

Even that was not his peak. In 1962–63 he broke the South African record by taking 64 wickets in the season at 16.62. He simply had to be taken to Australia and New Zealand in Trevor Goddard's 1963–64 Springbok side. The breezes and humidity suited him perfectly, particularly at Sydney, where he took nine wickets in the early New South Wales match. He had little success in his maiden Test, at Brisbane, where Ian Meckiff and the whole of Australia were stunned by the no-balling of Meckiff for throwing. In the Melbourne Test, Partridge, partnering the fiery Peter Pollock, plugged away and got five wickets. Then, back at Sydney, he took 9 for 211 in the match, off 52.3 eight-ball overs. Lawry, O'Neill, Burge, Booth (twice) and Shepherd were among his victims, and after a hard-working but almost fruitless Adelaide Test (where South Africa drew level), Partridge dramatically showed his affection again for the conditions at Sydney by taking 7 for 91 and 2 for 85 in the final Test.

He looked the bank officer that he was, in his spectacles, and the Sydney crowd took to him. He seemed inoffensive enough, alongside Pollock, and there was an absence of ostentation about him which added to his appeal. Round after round of applause greeted him as he returned to his position on the boundary after each probing over, and the third-man territory became known as 'Joe's corner'. In two Tests and a State match at the SCG, Joseph Titus Partridge had taken 27 wickets (18.67) off 148.1 enthusiastic overs. He almost became one of their own.

Joe Partridge — swing bowler who became one of drink's victims.

He had a photo taken of himself with the obligatory koala and went off with the Springboks to New Zealand, where his either-way swing won him 13 more wickets, including 6 for 86 in the Auckland Test. All the promise of those years of Currie Cup performance was pouring into prolific achievement as if to make up for lost time. On the complete Australasian tour he took 62 wickets, five ahead of the next man, Pollock.

In 1964–65 he played in three of the Tests against England (but not the one at Cape Town in which Glen Hall played). Partridge's strike-rate was but a shadow of what it had been on the Australasian tour. He was dropped after the fourth Test, never to play for South Africa again, though a trip to England in 1965 could have seen his particular skill and method richly rewarded, as it was for Bob Massie of Australia seven years later. Partridge retired from first-class cricket at the end of the 1966–67 season, when he was 34.

He worked for 10 years for Rhodesian Breweries as a sales representative, but life was all downhill after his cricket days ended. By 1988 he had been divorced for five years (he and his wife had four children), and was a very heavy drinker. He got deeply into debt, tried a number of jobs, one with a security firm where a company car was provided, but he had a couple of accidents while under the influence, and lost the car privilege. A friend recalled that Joe had become 'virtually a beggar'. Desperate friends and acquaintances knew finally that only Partridge could help himself. Booze had made him a slave.

He was staying at the George Hotel in Harare with his girlfriend, and had run up a huge account. When, fairly drunk, he caused a disturbance one evening early in June 1988, the police were called, and he was escorted to Avondale police station. After some questioning, Partridge asked if he could be taken back to the pub, where he believed (probably fancifully) that friends would have a whipround for his hotel bill. As he and the constable made to leave, Partridge pulled a pistol from the pocket of his safari suit and shot himself in the head. He was dead upon arrival at the hospital. His wife, now remarried, and the children attended the funeral.

He was 55, and had still been the mild and gentle chap—when sober—happy to reminisce about his Australian tour a quarter-century earlier. But drink transformed him, and the patience of his friends was exhausted. They could only urge him to seek help from Alcoholics Anonymous. BOWLER JOE'S FRIENDS LET HIM DOWN was a somewhat unreasonable headline, for many of his numerous pals had come to his aid financially. One may have put his finger on it when he told the reporter: 'His real tragedy was that after the glory and fame of cricket he couldn't adjust to normal life.'

It was a bad time for South African cricket-lovers. Two months after Partridge's death, one of the country's finest sportsmen, Stuart Leary, took his own life, which had become tormented and complicated beyond endurance. His story follows. But three months before Glen Hall's death, on March 29, 1987, a cabinet minister who had played university and Currie Cup cricket capitulated to intolerable pressures. John Walter Eddington Wiley was the only non-Afrikaner in the South African cabinet, an MP for 21 years who had twice switched allegiance from one party to another. From the United Party, he formed and became chairman of the South Africa Party, and then, sensing that things were changing, he joined the ruling National Party and became Minister of Environment and Water Affairs. He had beaten former South African all-rounder Eddie Barlow in a 1980 by-election.

Described in an obituary in *The Times* as 'a large, energetic man who nursed his constituency assiduously and gained respect from politicians of all persuasions', Wiley had played, as a middle-order batsman, for Western Province in 1947–48, when he was 20. From Cape Town University he went to Oxford to read law, and there played first-class cricket between 1949 and 1951, without winning a Blue, though his brother did so in 1952. Strangely, the Oxford captains in two of John Wiley's three seasons were South Africans: Clive van Ryneveld

John Wiley — Oxford cricketer and South African cabinet minister.

and Murray Hofmeyr. Wiley's highest score in his 12 first-class matches was 70 for Western Province against Rhodesia at Salisbury in 1947–48.

When John Wiley was found by his son Mark beyond a locked bedroom door in his large home near Fishhoek, south of Cape Town, he had a bullet wound in his right temple and a .32 pistol was in his hand. He was 60, and left two sons and a daughter from the first of his three marriages. He had been trying to sell some of his property investments, and was said to be suffering anxiety over his health.

A few years after Wiley's spell at Oxford University, David Millard, who had played as an all-rounder for Western Province in 1951–52 and 1954–55 and for Eastern Province in the two seasons in between, enrolled at Oxford as a mature student on a Commonwealth Scholarship and played twice for the university in 1965, having been at Cambridge 10 years earlier, winning a Rugby Blue but making little impact with his cricket. For Oxford, at the age of 34, he had no luck at all, Titmus getting him for 5 in the Middlesex match and, again at The Parks, bagging a 'pair' against Notts. He played

14 first-class matches in all, with a top score of 73 for Eastern Province against Orange Free State at Port Elizabeth in 1952–53 and best bowling figures of 6 for 68 (including Nourse and Goddard) with off-spin against Natal on the same ground in the same year. It was an irony that David Edward Shaxson Millard, who shot himself in Cape Town on January 30, 1978, when 46, had played for South African Schools back in 1950 at the expense of another brilliant schoolboy batsman Stuart Leary.

Leary, born in Cape Town on April 30, 1933, was one of the best all-round sportsmen ever produced by South Africa. Educated at Sea Point High School, he ventured to England while still in his teens, and was signed up by Charlton Athletic, where he played in the forward line alongside fellow Springbok Syd O'Linn, who was to play Test cricket for his native land. Leary's touch on the football field was such that Colin Cowdrey, watching from the directors' box, likened him to George Best, though Tony Pawson, a Kent amateur cricketer and Charlton and England footballer, felt this was slightly to exaggerate Leary's skill. He later played for Queen's Park Rangers.

As a batsman he was unorthodox, not always pleasing to the eye, but effective to the point where Kent had 16,169 runs from him between 1951 and 1971 at an average of 30.80, with 18 centuries, the highest being 158 against Northants at Kettering in 1963. His infrequent leg-spin bowling came in useful at times, and he finished with 140 wickets at reasonable cost, with a best analysis of 5 for 22 against Glamorgan at Swansea in 1961. Adding further to his worth to Kent was his fielding close to the wicket. Of his 362 catches, six came consecutively in one innings, against Cambridge University at Fenner's in 1958.

Kent were county champions once during Leary's long association with the club, and that was in his second-last year, 1970. In the team photograph Leary, seated in the front row next to his skipper Cowdrey, has his hand jokingly on Derek Underwood's knee. The previous year's team group shows Leary with his hand on Mike Denness's knee. Some

Stuart Leary —
found on Table Mountain.

of his team-mates remember Leary's concern for his appearance—the comb was always handy—but, seemingly without exception, they liked him. He was 'fun', outgoing.

Darker days followed. He returned to South Africa and did a lot of coaching, but by 1985, with Robin Jackman's appointment as Western Province's coach and manager, the scope was reduced. Leary had married a woman older than himself who was prominent in business and constantly travelling, and by 1988 Stuart Edward Leary was feeling pressures known only to the damned. According to three people who knew him, he was not only apprehensive at the nationwide investigation into juvenile vice but feared he was infected by the dreaded disease AIDS.

In August 1988 he was reported missing when his car was found abandoned near Table Mountain, Cape Town. Mists and high winds hampered the police search, but on August 23 Leary's body was found, a note nearby. He was 55, and the shock of his death reverberated through the cricket and soccer fraternities of England as well as his homeland.

And so to the story of Billy Zulch, one of the finest batsmen ever produced by South Africa. He was born in Lydenburg,

Transvaal, in January 1886 and had a college education in Cape Town. His first notable innings was 180 for Pretoria against Potchefstroom. From the Transvaal side, he was elevated into South Africa's Test team when England toured in 1909–10, and began a career of 16 Tests and 32 innings without a duck and including two centuries, four half-centuries and a small store of anecdotes.

Opening the innings against England in that first home series, John William Zulch managed a highest score of only 34 in the first four Tests. But South Africa were by then 3–1 up, and the selectors wanted to create as little disruption as possible. He had shown his worth with an innings of 176 not out for his province against this MCC side—putting on 215 with Stricker for the first wicket—and the selectors' faith was justified when he carried his bat right through South Africa's dismal innings of 103 (Blythe 7 for 46) in the fifth Test at Cape Town, making 43 not out. The match was lost, but Zulch's reputation was boosted.

He had had some difficulty against the English underarm lob bowler Simpson-Hayward, and the little Surrey wicketkeeper Herbert Strudwick told of how Zulch, when he arrived at the crease in the third Test, placed a small piece of paper on a good length just outside off stump. The keeper asked him what he was up to. 'If Mr Simpson-Hayward pitches the ball outside that piece of paper,' said Zulch, 'I shall play it with my legs.' Strudwick, normally the epitome of inoffensiveness, said, 'I can't have that. It's in my way.' And he trotted round and removed it.

A year later, Zulch was in Australia with the first Springbok side to tour that country, in 1910–11, and—aside from being run out for 99 against Queensland—he struggled with form and luck into the new year before making 105 in the third Test, at Adelaide, an innings full of strong shots, good fortune (he was missed at 12, 13, 68 and 84) and lasting just over three hours. He put on 135 with Faulkner (who scored 732 runs in the series), and with S. J. Snooke following up with a century South Africa totalled 482 and eventually won by 38 runs—their first-ever victory over Australia—Faulkner

J. W. Zulch — one of the best batsmen from South Africa; found in a pool of blood.

making a second-innings hundred after Trumper's glorious 214 not out for the home country.

In the fifth Test, Zulch excelled himself further with a resolute 150 when South Africa followed on at Sydney, having more luck in the shape of three chances, but surviving in all for five hours. His stand with the magnificent Faulkner this time amounted to 143.

Zulch played in three of the 1913–14 Tests against England, when S. F. Barnes took wickets almost at will on the matting. Zulch and Herby Taylor posted 153 for the first wicket at Johannesburg and 129 at Port Elizabeth, Zulch's contributions being 82 and 60, the former innings being cut short when a century seemed likely when Relf caught-and-bowled him. At international level, Billy Zulch was getting used to the need to fight and to the taste of defeat.

Having missed the 1912 tour of England, he was destined never to tour other than in Australia, and when the Australian Imperial Forces side called on their way back from England in 1919, Zulch was again to the fore, taking 60 and 95 off their bowling (spearheaded by Jack Gregory) for Transvaal and 135, again at Johannesburg's old Wanderers ground, when he captained South Africa in an 'unofficial Test'.

In his mid-thirties he had become one of the world's top runmakers, and in one purple patch in 1920–21, when Transvaal were on tour against other provincial sides, he scored a fast 185 and 125 against Orange Free State at Bloemfontein—the first instance of twin centuries by a South African—making, in all, four centuries in five innings which produced 681 runs.

In the following summer he was ready to take on the Australians again, and in the Durban Test he scored an 80 (highest of the innings), with 50 and 40 (both innings' top scores) in the third and final Test, at Cape Town. There was to be no more Test cricket for him, his health now beginning to crumble. But, in his second-last Test, he was the object of another curiosity when the Australian fast bowler Ted McDonald broke a piece from his bat, sending it flying into the stumps for a 'hit wicket' dismissal. Herby Collins had just made a double-century and Gregory had smashed a hundred in only 70 minutes (still a Test record). There was little play remaining that day, and when the umpire pointed out the split in Zulch's bat he decided not to bother changing it. McDonald's thunderbolt found it like a champion fighter seeking out the first sign of a cut eyebrow.

In 16 Tests Zulch had made 985 runs at 32.83, and in the few innings to come he was to take his first-class aggregate to 3558, and his Currie Cup average to just under 60, a hugely creditable figure. His bat must have been as broad as Ponsford's in its way in club cricket as well, where his highest score for the Wanderers was 206.

All those runs, all those rearguards. Then the nervous breakdown. Then the walk-out of his wife, presumably because his condition rendered him somewhere between difficult and impossible to live with. By May 1924, with the South Africans having an uphill battle on their English tour, Billy Zulch was fighting to regain his health and balance out at Umkomaas, Natal. It was there, on May 19, as the Springboks were sinking to an innings defeat at the hands of Lancashire in faraway Manchester, that Zulch cut his throat. He was 38.

He had taken his little daughter—one of four young children—with him, and it was a friend who first encountered the scene of horror, trying the door of his hotel room just after noon and then peering through the window to see Zulch lying blood-soaked on the bed. The *Natal Witness* reported that Mrs Lesbia Zulch was, at that time, on her way to see her husband, bringing with her from Johannesburg a cablegram asking him to join the South African team in England. Herby Taylor had sent for another batsman because it was feared that Susskind would not be fit for some time. A month later the Springboks were bowled out for 30 in the Edgbaston Test, 11 of the runs coming in extras. Such a morbid scoreline might have been interpreted as a memorial to Billy Zulch (whose names are shown as Johan Wilhelm on his death certificate).

The newspaper came back on the case a few days later, quoting a relative's claim that Zulch had suffered chronic headaches and abdominal pains for six years and believed them to be a legacy of his Australian tour, when he went down with sunstroke. A doctor had kept him supplied with sleeping draughts. His friend, who was sharing a room with him at the Umkomaas Hotel during those last few days, said that Billy was taking the draughts towards the end, but they were not helping his insomnia. The friend last saw him in bed, but Zulch subsequently got up, shaved and dressed, and then, according to the local doctor, 'must have been seized by a sudden brainstorm and committed the fatal act'. He was a motor auctioneer and had no financial problems. He simply could take no more ill-health. And yet if the cable had reached him, inviting him to take the ship to England, to play at Lord's and Old Trafford and The Oval . . . .

6

Tormented Genius

The appellation 'tormented genius' is David Foot's. Aided by tape-recorded outpourings and personal memories of the batsman himself in action, and haunted by Harold Gimblett's eventually successful attempt to escape his troubled world, the West Country journalist completed his book on Gimblett for publication in 1982. Apart from A. E. Stoddart and Arthur Shrewsbury, Gimblett is the only suicide among Test cricketers to have a posthumous full-scale biography written—if Stan McCabe is accepted as inadmissible. (The modest Australian maestro, frail and convalescing from serious illness, fell to his death at the rear of his Sydney harbourside home at Beauty Point, Mosman on August 25, 1968, at the age of 58. He had thrown a dead possum down the incline and probably lost his footing. Injuries to his head proved fatal, and the tufts of grass in his hands were accepted as telling evidence that he had tried to save himself; but he had been too weak. Rumours of supposed suicide circulated for years, but McCabe's biographer, Jack McHarg, probably succeeded in dispelling them in his 1987 book.)

It is apparent that in the majority of cases so far viewed cricket has been, at most, incidental in pushing those players beyond the limit. But Harold Gimblett, a kind of seminal figure, seems to have been a victim of clinical depression the underlying cause of which was the tensions of cricket. The torment of facing failure every day of his sporting life seemed not to ease, and may have had something in common with the disorder suffered by veterans of the Vietnam War and the Falklands campaign. The army psychologists refer to the condition as Post Traumatic Stress Syndrome (PTSS), and one battlefield surgeon asserts that 'the stress of battle has stayed with some'. Conflict can change a fighting man's attitude to life for the better, he pointed out, and comradeship brings mutual comfort, 'but those who left the military are in a different environment'.

Keith Miller never saw cricket as anything other than a sport to be played hard and enjoyed, for he was among those who had experienced real war. Harold Gimblett, too, had known true conflict in all its gory reality. A National Fire Service captain recalled, in 1978, Gimblett's 'magnificent and apparently fearless courage as a fireman during the Plymouth Blitz in 1941. How many lives he saved is probably not on record.' Gimblett had once said, 'I'd have sooner gone into the Air Force.' Many of his fellow firemen were killed or maimed, and although there may have been a tendency to pass decision-making to a senior officer, his men admired him greatly.

It may all have gone wrong from the beginning. Young Harold, a broad-shouldered 20-year-old farmer's son from Bicknoller in Somerset, belted a century off the famous and experienced Essex attack in 63 minutes at Frome in May 1935, having been summoned in an emergency for his first match for the county. The news flashed all over England, and a legend was launched. He had gone in at No. 8, having hitched a ride on a lorry from his village. He had out-hit the mighty Arthur Wellard, and was the new name on every cricket-lover's lips. 'I savoured the moment,' he said many years later, 'but loathed the publicity that followed.' His wife,

Harold Gimblett — cavalier opening batsman.

Rita, told David Foot: 'I kept the cuttings. Harold would have destroyed them.'

It was soon evident that he was no archetypal simple farmer's boy. His mind was volatile, complex, worrying. Through a professional career lasting to the start of the 1954 season, when he was 39 and already undergoing psychiatric treatment, he scored over 23,000 runs at 36, with 50 centuries, most of them swashbuckling and six-studded, the highest 310 against Sussex at Eastbourne in August 1948. 'Well, that's got rid of one amateur's name in our county record books,' he said to fellow pro Jim Langridge. All along the way he upset and saddened people with his bitter outbursts; and John Arlott, in his foreword to Foot's book, still had a sharp recollection of having to duck under a bat hurled by a disappointed Gimblett 'in that gloomy old pros' dressing-room at Taunton'. Arlott wrote:

> There were few sadder dual experiences in cricket than being exhilarated by a sustained innings in which Harold

> Gimblett went on and on treating good bowling with almost Jove-like contempt, and, afterwards, going in, hoping to make a small contribution of admiration to a moment of glory, only for all those with the same purpose—friends, fellow players, even relations—to meet a remark—not aimed at them but at that world which he felt he owed a grudge—of such bitterness as marred the former splendour.

Some of his retorts would have won the backing of, certainly, most full-time cricketers. Trekking back through the Long Room at Lord's after a failure, Gimblett heard a grizzled member's complaint that he had travelled a long way that day to see Gimblett bat, and was very disappointed. 'You ought to have bloody well stayed at home,' shot back the defeated batsman.

It was hard enough playing cricket for your county for a living. Representing England was a greater demand, almost too much for some to bear. Gimblett is thought by some to have batted carelessly when a touring team was about to be picked, for he feared being locked into a major representative tour and encountering a string of failures. When chosen for his first Test match, against India at Lord's in 1936, he didn't really want to know. On one of his tapes for David Foot, he recalled: 'Honestly, I didn't know enough about cricket to play for my country.' (It was only his second season in first-class cricket.)

> I can remember listening to the 12 names announced on the radio. The names were given in alphabetical order and I prayed that I wouldn't be included. Far from throwing my hat in the air, I was terrified. Suddenly I realised the fearful responsibilities resting on my shoulders. The telephone started ringing, cars arrived, the usual nonsense. I just wanted to go away and get lost. I didn't want to play for England. In desperation I jumped on my bicycle and went in search of Rita.

He opened and scored 11 in the first innings and finished off England's victory by nine wickets with the match top score, 67 not out, which *The Times* branded 'glorious'. Four successive balls from the big and very fast Mohamed Nissar went to the boundary.

When he had looked out at the ground upon arriving that first morning the 21-year-old Gimblett had seen the cause of the background buzz. There were 30,000 people gathered to watch the match, a packed full house. His instinct was to run away. But the kindly Yorkshiremen Hedley Verity and Maurice Leyland, seasoned Test players both, invited him to sit with them. 'We'll look after you.'

He was a relieved man when he was dropped after the next Test, at Manchester, after he had cover-driven two fours before Nissar sent a stump whistling at 9 in his only innings. He had also missed a catch, of which much, to his mind, was made. Rain curtailed the match, and he returned thankfully to county cricket.

He played for England once after that, at Lord's against the 1939 West Indians. He hit Hylton for six in both innings and held an astonishing running catch to dismiss 'Bam Bam' Weekes which brought special congratulation from the greatest fielder of all, Learie Constantine; but Gimblett's 22 and 20, together with his cavalier style, were not enough to hold the selectors' attention—much to his relief—though they did include him in the side due to tour India in 1939–40, a tour cancelled upon the outbreak of war.

In 1946, when first-class cricket resumed, a mature and hardened Gimblett (seven centuries) and Somerset both had fine seasons. At Taunton the church bells happened to ring as he reached his first double-century (having dished out pointed punishment to leg-spinner Walter Robins, a pet hate of Gimblett's among those opponents who irritated him). He later recalled looking at the scoreboard and saying to himself, 'Have I really done that? Did I do it myself or was there someone guiding me? It wasn't the only time I had that odd feeling. I wasn't really a churchgoer at the time . . .'

Jealousy, which cleverer men disguise, leaked out in the odd remark or gesture as Gimblett saw brilliant strokemakers join the Somerset XI and evoke not only admiration but comparisons with his own aggressive strokeplay. Maurice Tremlett was a target at times, and so was Micky Walford, who, to make matters worse, was an amateur, a schoolteacher, a triple Blue at Oxford before the war, and was to be England's hockey captain at the 1948 London Olympics. Gimblett's biographer David Foot shrewdly observes that 'jealousy is not unknown in county cricket; nor is it unreasonable in a game of internal competition, with its accompanying sense of insecurity'.

In 1949 Gimblett passed 2000 runs and made two hundreds in a match, all for the first time, and out of the blue in 1950 came an invitation to play for England again, against West Indies at Trent Bridge. It was not to be. He developed a carbuncle on the back of his neck. If some people are to be believed, and if such a thing were possible, it was a psychosomatic carbuncle. He had to withdraw. As the match loomed, the neck still throbbed. 'In any case,' said Foot, 'the head had been saying no for several days.'

He went to India that winter with a Commonwealth side led by Les Ames, and lost two stone:

> I had no energy, no spark, no conversation. I became very withdrawn. At first I wondered if I'd picked up a bug. But it was purely mental. I was sickened by the continual smell of curry and lost the will to eat.

Halfway through the 1951 season he took medical advice and had a break from the game, which seemed to have benefited him when he returned and made centuries with style. He had a benefit in 1952, and again passed 2000 runs, and came very close in 1953 too. But there were signs that he was not enjoying the game, was not at ease with himself or his surroundings. He later recalled a comment John Arlott is supposed to have made on the air while Somerset were in the field: 'And there's Harold Gimblett, studying eternity.'

'If John had only realised,' he told his biographer, 'what was going on inside the head.'

On one of his cathartic tapes to David Foot, Gimblett whispered his feelings at that time:

> I couldn't take much more. I was taking sleeping pills to make me sleep and others to wake me up. By the end of 1953 the world was closing in on me. I couldn't offer any reason why and I don't think the medical profession knew either. There were moments of the past season that I couldn't remember at all.

Electroconvulsive therapy brought some relief while he had a four-month spell in Tone Vale mental hospital, but when it was time for pre-season nets he found himself institution-bound, afraid of the outside world. 'I just knew I wouldn't complete the next season.'

He hit 97 in a friendly match against Hampshire, but in the first Championship match, against Notts at Trent Bridge

Gimblett — tormented genius.

(the ground where his carbuncle kept him from his fourth Test cap), he 'just folded up' while batting. He tried desperately to collect himself, and Reg Simpson, the Notts captain, suggested he retire to the dressing-room. 'No, I mustn't,' said Gimblett. 'If I go off, I'll never come back again.'

He scored 29 before being bowled by Arthur Jepson, and in the follow-on as Somerset sank to an innings defeat, he was caught for 5. At home at Taunton for the next match, also lost decisively, Gimblett was out to Fred Trueman in both innings, for 0 and 5. Bob Appleyard bowled Yorkshire to victory with 7 for 16 on a damp pitch: Somerset all out 48, and severely shaken, what with Gimblett's walk-out.

For weeks he stayed away from cricket, then returned, idly curious, for a peep at the Somerset v. Pakistanis match late in July. He made his way unobtrusively into the scorebox, welcomed by the county scorer, Tom Tout. The kitchen staff sent him a cup of tea and a bun—and charged him for it—and then the secretary sent for him and ordered him out of the ground. 'I was speechless,' Gimblett said, to the recording machine. 'I just turned and went back to collect my wife. That had to be the final severance with the county I had joined in 1935.'

Job-hunting was frustrating. For a while he worked in a steelworks in Ebbw Vale and made runs in the League. Sick of being caged up and of union excesses, he became a cow-herder in Abergavenny. And finally he found passing satisfaction at Millfield School, where R. J. O. Meyer installed him as a kind of 'clerk of works', working on the grounds, running the sports shop, and assisting in the cricket coaching, where his role had a 'pastoral element' as the boys, some of them, unloaded their personal problems to him. He was there for 20 years, during which time a second major breakdown hit him. This time the shock treatment did not work. He decided to retire, and he and Rita found a house in Minehead.

Soon, Gimblett, now with arthritis so acute in his left leg that he needed a walking-stick, began to find irritations in the neighbourhood, and decided to move on to Dorset, where the couple took possession of a 'mobile home'—a caravan. It was not a good move. They knew no-one in the district. Harold spent much time in the local Methodist Church affairs, and concerned himself with the welfare of the aged in the parish. He also worked for the Samaritans, effort which had conflicting results, as David Foot relates:

> His involvement with the Samaritans offered some kind of spiritual fulfilment; at the same time, the counselling stoked his own mental agony. He found himself repeatedly talking to others with suicidal tendencies, less evident than his own. Once a chirpy, even garrulous batsman, he was now the listener. The advice he gave, when asked, in that slow, morose voice of his, was invariably sound. But mainly his Samaritan role was that of a listener.
>
> He listened to dejected lovers and wretchedly lonely pensioners; to the physically and mentally sick; to the human derelicts. Then he motored home from the Bournemouth headquarters to live again the introverted agony of all those people who had cried for help. The experience exhausted him. He would lie awake at night, quietly weeping to himself.

There was still hatred within him, directed at all kinds of people and things which fell short of perfection. There was deep anxiety too, principally about the prospective security in old age of Rita and himself. He even once suggested, in full seriousness, a suicide pact, which his loving wife nervously laughed off. There was paranoia; and there was a sense of rejection, fanned to white heat when his efforts in aid of the Save Somerset appeal in 1975 were poorly rewarded, and, two years later, when he, an ex-England player, was refused entry to the Long Room at Lord's. This incident he described as 'a pinprick that festers from time to time'.

Gimblett, the greatest native-born Somerset batsman of them all, watched cricket, mainly on television, until the commentators began to irritate him beyond redemption. Batsmen who couldn't hook properly irritated him in particular.

So embittered had he become that a handsome photograph, 4 ft by 3 ft, of him going out to bat with South Australian Neil Dansie was used as a fireguard in the Minehead home—the picture facing the fire. Eric Hill, the former Somerset batsman, RAF decoration-winner and journalist, helped retrieve that fireguard after Gimblett's death. He had a penetrative view to offer on the make-up of his old team-mate: 'I've always thought, very uncharitably, that a lot of this mental trouble was self-induced in order to excuse his shortcomings.'

To return to David Foot's *Harold Gimblett: Tormented Genius of Cricket* once more—for it stands alone as a masterpiece of individual study of a cricketer's rock-strewn path—the author refers to Dr K. C. P. Smith's work on personality disorders, with special reference to the Reversal Theory:

> His theory is that the subject has a tendency to treat life as a kind of game in which he strives to reach feelings of high excitement or arousal. 'Any fall-off is felt as boredom. Some people find themselves constantly bored and frustrated, and they describe this as being depressed. They often think the remedy is tablets.' A low-key man like Gimblett, he said, needed high excitement. When he failed to reach it, he became phobic: hence talk of too much batting responsibility, ill-health, money anxieties. 'He had strong "anti" feelings of aggression. He enjoyed hitting a ball around the ground, having revenge on the world at the same time.'

Harold Gimblett's brother Dennis, a clergyman in Australia, remembered Harold once saying that every time he went out to bat he saw a great finger pointing at him, as if daring him to fail. 'National fame was certainly not good for him,' said Dennis. 'I believe he enjoyed the spotlight of publicity but it could be a great burden to him at the same time.' It is no surprise to hear the opinion that Harold was insecure, sensitive and unsure of himself, which latter failing often caused him to become aggressive. His loving brother said:

> He lacked the inner strength to resist the temptation to commit suicide. He was inclined to put himself first and God second. I have always thought his life would have been much happier and more full of contentment if he'd found a country job, out of the public eye.

The weathercock on Bicknoller church, pitted with playful shot from teenaged Harold Gimblett's gun, remains testimony to the theory. Dennis Gimblett continued:

> There was deterioration over the last two years of his life. I don't think he realised that the suicide he planned for himself would adversely affect his reputation. In one way, I feel he thought it would give him one last great stance in the public eye—a kind of enormous hit for six, that would excite everybody's attention. It did so, but not in the way he mistakenly thought it would. Perhaps, in some strange way, he was the victim of a publicity he couldn't live without.

Alan Gibson, cricket-writer for *The Times* and former commentator, conjured a typically vivid impression of Gimblett during his memorial tribute:

> If you want a picture of him to carry in your mind, think of him first not driving Larwood or Miller through the covers but chugging round Verwood, often in acute pain, taking old folk their hot lunches.

Gibson had had his own close communion with the old Somerset batsman:

> Fifteen years ago I was in a mental hospital after failing to kill myself. Many friends wrote to me, sympathising at

> that difficult time. The most understanding letter and the wisest advice came from Harold. As a result of that, we would sometimes in later years talk, not morbidly, about the problems of people such as us, beset by bouts of depression, often quite irrational. Experience of mental illness, he insisted, should be used to help others.

Gimblett's last tapes to David Foot were harrowing in their hopelessness, 'almost unbearable in their ominous intensity'. Almost inaudibly, the sufferer, now 63, talked of being in a tunnel without end and without light.

On the morning of March 31, 1978 his wife found him in his bedroom lying peacefully on his back, his glasses still on, a newspaper gripped in one hand. The room was tidy. A note was folded under his wristwatch. He listed the tablets he had taken, and requested a simple, private funeral service, with a reading from Ecclesiastes.

A memorial service was held two months later at St James's Church, close by Taunton cricket ground. That day the mighty Viv Richards was batting for Gimblett's old county, to be followed by the mighty Botham, while bowling for Gloucestershire was the mighty Procter. That proximity in itself gave satisfaction to many who came to honour the memory of Harold Gimblett of the flashing blade.

David Foot's book was published four years later. Rita Gimblett, a long-suffering wife and widow, died from cancer a week before its launching. A son, Lawrence, survived them.

When Harold and Rita Gimblett were on honeymoon in Torquay they were spotted by a friend, who called out across the street, 'Why don't you two get married!' Harold told him that they just had done. The man who had hailed them was Raymond Robertson-Glasgow.

A quarter-century after his death, from not the first overdose he had taken, Robertson-Glasgow remains the favourite cricket-writer of many, for he wrote with charm and playing knowledge and humour. It was especially the last quality which appealed during his newspaper days and through his books.

Ever since Charlie McGahey of Essex was bowled by him, couldn't grasp his polysyllabic name, and dubbed him 'Robinson Crusoe', he was known as 'Crusoe'. Tall and high-foreheaded above delicate features, he was the academic kind of fast bowler: not a fire-breather, but agile and enthusiastic, and good enough to take 9 for 38 for Somerset against Middlesex at Lord's in 1924, almost the best figures on that great ground this century. He had been educated at Charterhouse, though born in Edinburgh on July 15, 1901, and won the rare honour of four cricket Blues at Oxford from 1920 to 1923. Not that he did anything in the Varsity matches until the last one, and then unexpectedly with the bat, a half-century.

He enjoyed his cricket and had some fine moments—not least when he bowled to Jack Hobbs at Taunton when The Master equalled (and then passed in the second innings) W. G. Grace's tally of hundreds in 1925—but, as he wrote in his 1948 autobiography *46 Not Out*:

> I have never regarded cricket as a branch of religion . . . I have never believed that cricket can hold Empires together, or that cricketers chosen to represent their country in distant parts should be told, year after year, that they are ambassadors. If they are, I can think of some damned odd ones.

He fell just short of Test class as a bowler, though he took 108 wickets cheaply in 1923, and 464 (25.77) in all for Oxford and Somerset and the Free Foresters between 1920 and 1937; and he played once for the Gentlemen against the Players at Lord's, in 1924 (3 for 157 off 43 overs), and more than once at Folkestone, labouring through 53 overs in the 1933 fixture to record 3 for 207 as Ames made a double-century and Ashdown a century. There were days when he needed all his wit and good humour.

Playwright Ben Travers, who was to give the address at Robertson-Glasgow's funeral, remembered him coming in for lunch at The Oval after bowling unavailingly at Hobbs and Sandham through two sweltering hours. 'It's like bowling to God on concrete,' 'Crusoe' said. 'I can hear, as though I had been there,' wrote Travers, 'the bellow of laughter and the slap of the thigh that followed it.'

'Crusoe's' psychiatric problems reared up early. He was only 21 when, while at Oxford, during the Christmas term of 1922, he had his first breakdown. 'I went to Jersey, where, after a few weeks, I revived, took to playing badminton, and fancied myself to be in love with the leading lady player.' His condition seems to have been 'clinical'. As a young man, he seemed to have had a wide choice of pleasures and vocation in front of him. 'Only those who have suffered it know the hell of nervous illness.' This was written two further breakdowns on, in 1947, and was one of the few solemn paragraphs he ever wrote.

In 1925 he took up schoolteaching, at Hindhead, though he felt far from well at times, 'like warmed-up death'. He expanded his reading beyond the literature of Greece and Rome, tried to consort only with people who pleased him, and tried also to get in as much fresh air as he could on the cricket-field and golf-course. While his brother, Bobs, kept his Scottishness, Raymond became utterly English.

Eight years passed before his first opening into journalism came. He was asked to report the Oxford v. Cambridge golf at Sandwich for the *Morning Post*. Apprehensive at first, he liked the work. Soon he took over from P. F. Warner as the paper's cricket correspondent, at nine guineas a week. 'I had always laughed when playing cricket,' he later remarked, 'except when the slip fielders showed signs of lumbago, and I saw no reason to stop laughing when I wrote about it.'

He was soon to behold some fairly dramatic stuff, like the West Indians' bodyline onslaught on England at Old Trafford in 1933, when Hammond had his chin cut open and Jardine made as courageous a century as it would be possible to witness.

He found the press-box in the 1930s, on the whole, rather

too serious and cathedral-quiet. (He would have had no grounds for such disappointment today!) He also detected the early invasion of the 'news men', who were not there for the cricket but to stir things up—an objection which has a strangely latterday ring about it. He explained:

> In my own reports of cricket matches, I tried for naturalism. Flippancy was never far absent, because cricketers, especially bowlers, need flippancy to live and to avoid going a little queer. I was doomed, therefore, to affront those to whom cricket is a quasi-religion.

Soon, 'some of the colonels were very angry' at 'Crusoe's' 'inane asides and abominations' and demanded Warner's return!

He told gleefully of once walking through Manchester and seeing his name on his newspaper's poster. It read 'Read R. C. Robertson-Glasgow in the *Morning Post*'. Alongside was another poster: 'Read *The Times* and see what really happened'. He loved that; or at least professed to.

His essays over the years grew into something substantial and prized by connoisseurs of the recording and interpretation of cricket and cricketers. Hammond 'came from the pavilion like the *Victory* sailing to destroy Napoleon'; of Bradman, 'poetry and murder lived in him together'; O'Reilly 'came up to the wicket like a perambulating pump-handle'; Woodfull reminded him of 'a master who gets the whole school to and from a bank holiday picnic without losing his reason or a boy'; Miller's distaste for bowling reminded him of 'the executioner who claimed to prefer stamp-collecting'; Woolley 'batted as it is sometimes shown in dreams'; and Gimblett was 'too daring for those who have never known what it is to dare in cricket.'

Robertson-Glasgow was of the Cardus mould, to cricket's ongoing benefit. But it did not come easily, this craft of words, to a man whose temperament was as brittle as a teatime wafer. Another breakdown just before the Hitler war, soon after 'Crusoe's' father died, brought him and Elizabeth

Raymond Robertson-Glasgow — gusts of laughter; bouts of depression.

together, and they married in 1943. She was to love him and buoy him up through depressions for the rest of his days, riding through untold hours and days of despair.

'One thing about being ill,' he wrote of that setback. 'You get to know who are your friends, during, and immediately after.' He started again, this time at his brother's prep school near Pangbourne in Berkshire. Watching Len Hutton make his 364 in the 1938 Oval Test must have given him a renewed vision of eternity.

'Crusoe' now joined *The Observer*, which paper he was to serve for many years, and during the war he donned Home Guard uniform, to exercise in the Berkshire hills, imagination rife. Afterwards, sharing the populace's exhaustion which misted over the elation of victory, he mourned the lost England, deplored the rising egalitarianism, missed intensely the dreamy pleasures of Oxford in the 1920s and the innocent sporting joys of the 1930s as reflected in his autobiography.

He covered the 1950–51 MCC tour of Australia for *The Observer, The Times* (when its man fell ill) and various Australian papers, and he broadcast as well.

Alan Ross, who succeeded him as *The Observer*'s cricket correspondent, recalled how 'he simply got up in the press-box one afternoon, put on his old battered trilby and raincoat, and announced he was calling it a day.' He returned to his house near the Thames and apparently saw no more first-class cricket, becoming reclusive and writing more about country life.

Ross, while at school, had treasured a copy of Robertson-Glasgow's *The Brighter Side of Cricket*, little realising that its author was a manic-depressive who had more than once tried to take his own life. He later got to know him well: 'He was a large, bald man, with a deafening laugh. He talked non-stop and he had a disconcerting habit of thrusting his face right up close and then weaving away.' Fellow cricket writer E. M. Wellings thought him a genius, though he remembered his laughter as 'maniacal'. He remembers, too, seeing cut-marks on his neck.

John Woodcock, who read the lesson at 'Crusoe's' funeral, said of him: 'When in good health he was marvellously and infectiously genial; when not, he was still wonderfully good fun.' Alan Ross again: 'Underneath the raconteur and joker there was, nevertheless, a man of considerateness and charm, also of a gravity that seldom got into his writing.'

In the early spring of 1965, on March 4, unable to endure his melancholia any longer, Raymond Charles Robertson-Glasgow, 63, took his fatal dosage of barbiturates, perhaps ruminating as eternal night fell on just how close he might have come to winning a place in Arthur Gilligan's team to Australia 40 years before. And perhaps not.

'Crusoe' inevitably occupies a more prominent place in cricket history as essayist than player, and is one of three cricket-writers known to have committed suicide. Of the other two, John Gale and Berry Sarbadhikary, Gale wrote for *The Observer* in Robertson-Glasgow's time. He was the journalist who, with colleague Michael Davie, invited Groucho Marx to Lord's in the mid–1950s. The crowd was sparse, the play lacklustre, and when his escorts asked him, half-an-hour on, how he was enjoying this first game of cricket, Groucho bugled, 'Great. Just great.' And after a pause: 'When does it start?' The MCC secretary, meeting the hilarious American in the Long Room, asked, in his finely chiselled tones, 'Are you over here on holiday, Mr Marx?' The famous heavy eyebrows twitched. 'I was—until I saw *this* game,' he snapped, feeling he was being condescended to.

John Gale's excursions into cricket came as relief to much of his life as a foreign correspondent. Alan Ross recalled: 'When I first met him he looked, with his bright-eyed, joking, obtrusively physical presence, about as far removed from a candidate for breakdown as you could imagine.'

Born in Edenbridge, Kent, on September 28, 1925 and educated at Stowe, Gale batted at No. 3 for the school 'but seldom came off because I was too nervous. My bowling was more successful.' (He imitated Alf Gover's 'wound-up' bowling action.) His figures in the 1944 and 1945 *Wisdens* are anaemic. Like most schoolboy cricket-lovers he spent countless hours in the garden, often bowling alone, with his flicker of Maurice Tate as inspiration. In describing himself in adulthood, he referred to his fingers as 'long, double-jointed, and a little knobbly from catching cricket balls'. He had also long known by then that he was a manic-depressive: 'They love to label us. When I am manic I am close on six feet tall; when I am depressed I am not much over five feet ten inches.'

A teenager during the war, he was playing cricket when two Spitfires shot down a Junkers 88 overhead, and soon after being coached at Lord's, in the presence of Jim Sims and Plum Warner, he was in the army. There was no delay in the onset of dramatic events:

> On our first night at the depot there was a loud air-raid; two Grenadier corporals hanged themselves with their braces; a guardsman bayoneted a friend in the latrines; and in our hut a boy called Hubert Doggart had a screaming nightmare.

Gale's brother, Peter, was killed towards the end of the war, and soon the first-hand horrors of battle surrounded him. Then came entry into some of the German death camps; combat in Palestine; movement all around Europe; and eventually full-scale journalism. Marriage followed, and babies, and tours of duty to the world's trouble spots, his sensitivities gradually buckling under the weight of the atrocities in places like Suez and Algeria. Intermittent breakdowns occurred, the last two in America and London, the final crack-up to be recorded with brave honesty in his book *Clean Young Englishman*, an autobiography marked not only by frankness of an almost exhibitionist nature but by its staccato style, thoughts hurrying upon each other, sometimes almost before completion of registration. It ends in hope: warmed by the joy of his children, he handed in his Mauser pistol at the local police station.

During almost 20 years on the staff of *The Observer*, John Gale had travelled extensively. He also worked for a time for *Asia Magazine* in Hong Kong. He wrote a novel—*The Family Man*—and, later, *Travels with a Son*, and *Camera Man*, which was published posthumously in 1979.

John Gale — Groucho's escort to Lord's. Jane Brown

A paragraph from *Clean Young Englishman* (1965) was chosen for inclusion in *The Faber Book of Cricket*, and it reveals the strength of the spell that cricket cast over Gale: he wrote of a shot he played in a school match in 1938: 'I hit it square off the front foot past point for four: it went like butter. I have never hit a ball better. Cricket was worth playing for that shot alone.'

A lengthier piece by Gale was included in *The Observer on Cricket*, a 1955 interview with Frank Tyson's mother in Lancashire when 'Typhoon', her express-bowler son, was blasting out Australian batsmen in Sydney and Melbourne. It reads in the modern idiom 35 years on, but was of a style unusually punchy for the time, almost Americanese.

John Gale's mental disturbance was complex and became deepened beyond rescue. Not for him—or for many of us—to sneer and shrug at the world like a Groucho Marx. On February 7, 1974, the day West Indies secured victory over England in Trinidad, Gale's body was found near Red Arches, Hampstead Heath. He had taken tablets, drunk vodka, and drowned in the stream beside which he had settled for his final sleep. It was not his first attempt at ending it. He left a wife, two daughters and a son, and had packed a lot of action into his 48 troubled years.

Indian cricket was stunned a week before Christmas 1976 when the 'doyen' of the press-box, Berry Sarbadhikary, aged 72, threw himself to his death from the third-floor lodge he occupied in south Bombay. A man of vast experience, he had written books and broadcast on cricket for just on half-a-century, and had seen almost every Test his country had played since the inaugural in 1932. In 1972–73, when England toured, he celebrated his hundredth Test match covered, and as recently as 1975 he had been shown the appreciation of a touring team—this time the West Indians—by a presentation at the end of the tour. His books included a biography of C. K. Nayudu (1945), *Indian Cricket Uncovered* (same year), *My World of Cricket* (1964), various tour souvenirs, and, for several years in the 1950s, an *Indian*

Cricketer Annual. K.N. Prabhu, a journalist of equally high stature, wrote of him:

> There was an air of the beau about him. He was neat to the point of being fastidious. He loved the good things of life. He lived well and spent lavishly, with never a thought to the future.

There is no puzzle about where it all went wrong as he grew old, for he left a three-page handwritten letter to the police, whose headquarters were across the way in Bombay's Mahatma Phule market area. It was written the night before he jumped, the final act coming at six in the morning on December 19. He wrote of a straitened financial condition being even harder to bear than his ill-health. For one who had lived so long on tour in high-class hotels, he found it repugnant to have to walk a long way to toilet facilities, especially as he had a kidney complaint, as well as a heart ailment. He knew that ending it this way was an action 'which is messy, but which can't be helped', and he strangely requested that his daughter, living in Calcutta, should not be disturbed: 'Let her know from the newspapers or radio'—perhaps seeing this as a symbolism for the professional life he had led. There was no money at all on his person or among his meagre belongings. He asked for some Hindu charitable organisation to 'do my last rites'. Niran Prabhu wrote:

> Life ceased to have any meaning for Berry the moment he came up against its harsh realities: the ravages of time and the demands made on his dwindling resources of energy and money. He was an aristocrat by birth and upbringing. Though impoverished, he did not care to live on the charity of his friends.

Sarbadhikary had played cricket for Calcutta University as an opening batsman and wicketkeeper when young, but gave it up to concentrate on his sports journalism, which was carried out on a freelance basis all his life. He was the

Berry Sarbadhikary — unable to cope with the loss of the good life.

only Indian sportswriter at the early post-war Olympics, so that towards the end of his career he bore a kind of mystique. So many places had he been and so many events had he witnessed. His last overseas tour was the 1970–71 Indian tour of West Indies, when he had the pleasure of seeing Gavaskar burst on the scene with over 700 Test runs. Had he managed to visit England a few months later he would have sampled the great joy surrounding India's first Test victory on English soil.

His travels were still considerable when viewed kaleidoscopically, and Prabhu, in writing his obituary for *The Times of India*, had to cope with a cavalcade of flickering images in his mind:

> . . . of Berry in the neon-lit dusk of Kennedy Airport, sipping Manhattan cocktails and acknowledging the greetings of UN delegates who thought he was Krishna Menon, whom he greatly resembled; of long discourses in the lively company of Sir Frank and Velda Worrell at Mona University; the smoochy darkness of a Kingston nightclub,

> where Berry thought we had a fight on our hands, but eventually ended up by greeting the dawn with friends of 'James Bond'.

From all that to a squalid little room would have tested the most forebearing man.

Five years before he died he had let an Indian journalist, Subroto Sirkar, interview him on the overnight train out of Bhagalpur, where Bihar had played Orissa, the first Ranji Trophy match to be staged in the town. 'A young man like you, you shouldn't waste your life in sports journalism,' the veteran said by way of an opening remark. Sirkar concluded that such an utterance from the country's most-travelled and most famous sportswriter and commentator could only be 'the bitter reaction of a man who, for all the benefits he had enjoyed, had discovered himself to be a loser in the end'.

That night he explained how his real name, Bijon, had given way to 'Berry'. He had once organised a cricket match and, finding himself a player short, had written down 'John Berry' (Jack Hobbs's first names). When no substitute could be found, he himself played. The new name stuck.

Sirkar visited him again three years later, when he was installed in the lodgings in Bombay. 'He was really touched that someone from the Calcutta sports world had remembered him, and searched around his room for one of his books to give me.' Sarbadhikary was nostalgic, then bitter, then anxious about the future, and frequently mentioned his faraway daughter. Sirkar recalled:

> But his memory was still sharp, and he was as frank as ever. 'It's only since I came to Bombay that I've become an alcoholic.' When I took my leave, he was apologetic: 'You should have come at six. I look absolutely fresh after a bath in the evening.'

Later, his visitor recalled another of his remarks: 'When I am gone, I want just this to be said: "He was a good man; he never did anybody any harm." '

The owner of the unmistakable voice, 'gruff and old with experience' as another writer heard it, was last seen by K.N. Prabhu at the Bombay Gymkhana club:

> He kept away from the crowd. Banerjee, Nayudu, Merchant and the cricketers of his generation were all there, swapping tales at the lunch table. I would like to imagine him now in a far better world, with the lights low, in lively company, picking up from where he stopped when he last met Sir Frank Worrell.

The chapter began with Somerset cricketers, and closes with as fearful a case as could be imagined. TRAGIC DEATH OF A SOMERSET CRICKETER rang the headline in the *Taunton Mail* of March 15, 1916. P.F. HARDY COMMITS SUICIDE. His autograph reveals that he was *F.P.* Hardy, and he was, at the time of his death, a private in the 3rd City of London Yeomanry, on leave from the slaughter at Verdun. He was 35, and had a professional cricket career behind him whose length was not matched by any great distinction.

Dorset-born, in Blandford on June 26, 1880, Percy Hardy went to the College of Preceptors, Milton Abbas School and soon showed—at least by local standards—remarkable talent as a left-hand batsman and right-arm medium-pace bowler and as a footballer. Hardly out of school, he played cricket for Dorset, and later, representative soccer for Somerset. He went up to London for a trial with Surrey, and Len Braund, who left Surrey for Somerset himself in 1899, recommended Somerset. There, he received encouragement, and soon after being taken on the staff, he moved his things up to Taunton. Scores of 140 against Wandsworth and 144 not out against Mitcham Wanderers for Surrey Colts in 1901 must have boosted his confidence.

As the new century unfolded, however, Hardy, given few opportunities, struggled vainly to make an impression. There was an 82 against Worcestershire at Taunton in 1905 when Somerset were in trouble in the second innings. He batted then for two hours, and put on 125 with Braund for the fourth wicket, having batted at No. 10 in the first innings. He was clearly being used as a utility player, batting anywhere—but usually fairly low—in the order, and getting little bowling. And 1906 was scarcely better: 418 runs at 20.90, with a two-hour half-century against Warwickshire and another against Hampshire, both at Taunton. In 1907 he had a mere three innings for the county, and played in no match at all in 1908.

A few useful stands with Braund came in 1909, when the county made more use of him, and against Lancashire at Bath he had the long-awaited satisfaction of a decent double, 46 and 76. Then came twin failure against the Australians, and another season had fizzled out.

At last, in 1910, he had an extended run in Somerset's first team, and put together 700 runs (19.44) and 27 wickets. Besides Hardy, only Braund, Lewis and Robson played in all 18 of Somerset's matches. Fifteen were lost, three drawn, none won, and the printed epitaph for the summer read: 'Somerset cricket in 1910 was a thing to weep over.'

Hardy did at least make what was to be the highest score of his first-class career, 91 against Kent at Taunton in August, driving well for 11 fours and staying at the crease for just over two-and-a-half hours while D.W. Carr, the googly bowler, Fielder the fast man, and Woolley, close to being the best left-arm slow bowler at the time, did their best to shift him. Hardy had already dismissed Woolley for 102. Kent, of course, went on to win, by 47 runs, Hardy making 28 in the second innings. Somerset's team photograph was taken about this time, and there stands Percy Hardy in the back row, straw boater tilted towards the back of his head, blazer opened wide, cigarette perched on his lower lip, hands thrust nonchalantly into pockets. The Edwardian age had closed only a few weeks before with the death of the naughty, non-conformist monarch, and as his son ascended the throne, Armageddon grew ever closer.

Towards the end of that summer Hardy had another good score, 79 against Surrey, opening the innings with John Daniell at Taunton; but 1911 brought further agonising setbacks. He

Percy Hardy — throat cut at King's Cross station.

had made a pair of noughts against Sussex the previous season, Albert Relf completing the execution. Now he made four ducks in a row, George Hirst delivering him of a pair in the Yorkshire match at Headingley. He managed one half-century all season, a 62 against Worcestershire at Taunton, his next-best being 41 against All-India, also, of course, at Taunton. He made seven ducks in all. It was enough to drive a 31-year-old to drink. And it probably did.

Disasters followed one upon the other in the last few seasons before the Great War. He began the 1912 season with another duck against Kent at Gravesend, and in the following summer, when he hardly played at all, he registered another pair against Derbyshire. He had been a professional at the Imperial Tobacco Company's cricket club at Knowle, near Bristol, as it became obvious that full-time county cricket was not to be, and just before the war he obtained a position on MCC's ground staff at Lord's.

In the patriotic fervour of 1914, and 1915 until the casualty figures began to bite into national morale, it would have been a relief for many men who had failed in their everyday lives to have a fresh chance of achievement, companionship, even glory. How many hundreds of thousands of dreams were shattered?

Percy Hardy enlisted in September 1915, came home on leave, and on the morning of March 9, 1916 he was found dead on a lavatory floor at the Great Northern Railway Station, King's Cross, a bloodstained knife by his side. He had collapsed mentally at the terrifying prospect of returning to the fighting.

At the inquest at St Pancras Coroner's Court, his widow, who gave her address as 18 Magdalen Street, Taunton, said that her husband had returned home on March 4, a Saturday, around 10.30 pm. He was suffering from a bad cough, and had been drinking. The war had seemed to be preying on his mind, and though he did not say so, she thought that he dreaded going back to the Front.

He had not been of sober habits for some months before he joined the Army, she said, and on the morning of his death, when very depressed, he had told her of his intention to take his life. Her father, William Hawker, a groom, also of Taunton, said that when Hardy was 'in drink' he had often become violent, afterwards becoming very depressed. Sgt Fred Skoyles, of the City of London Yeomanry, stated that Hardy was 'a strange man', but he had never given any trouble in the regiment—although he could not say that he was abstemious.

The doctor called to the scene at King's Cross station found that Hardy had been dead at least three-quarters of an hour, with a deep gash in his throat and through the windpipe, with all the small blood vessels severed. The wound, self-inflicted in his opinion, had caused the victim to faint, and he died from shock and loss of blood. The jury returned a verdict of suicide while of unsound mind.

Private Percy Hardy, war casualty many miles from the trenches, Somerset player in 99 matches, left a widow and two children, Frederick aged 11 and Winifred, nine. It can only be surmised that the recurring frustration of his failure as a cricketer, in spite of his natural flair, led him to drink heavily. He was not alone in fearing battle. Others were shot or imprisoned for cowardice and desertion. Hardy might, in the final count, be given credit for having had the courage, in his terror-filled vision of the future, to take his exit alone and in the 'privacy' of a public cubicle. What torment might he have felt at leaving May and the children to their fate? There comes a moment in man's ferocious mental turmoil when considerations like that are blinded from view.

The Marquis de Ruvigny's military *Roll of Honour* includes an entry for Hardy, euphemistically listing him as 'died of illness'.

Percy Hardy's name thus remains inscribed on the memorial board and in the records of Somerset County Cricket Club. Of equal intensity though the terminal agony of Arthur Thomas Sanders must have been, he had nowhere near the years or the cricket experience of Hardy when he shot himself, and there is little probability that he had seen action in France or anywhere else, for he was so young. Arthur Sanders was only 19, and had played once for Somerset as an amateur, and probably as a late fill-in. He was born in London on December 21, 1900 and was educated at Harrow, playing in

Arthur Sanders — Harrow XI, and duck in only first-class innings.

the cricket XI in 1918, the final summer of the war, and top-scoring with 24 in the second innings against Eton in the one-day match at Harrow, having played against young D.R. Jardine in the Winchester match. He played his Somerset match against Essex at Leyton in July 1919, in the season when county matches were of two (long) days' duration. The Rippon twins gave Somerset an excellent start with 144, but poor Sanders, going in at No. 9, was bowled for a duck. Sixteen months later, on November 22, 1920, Sanders, a second lieutenant in the Grenadier Guards, his address given as 3 Eaton Square, shot himself in the head with a revolver and died in Millbank Military Hospital, which overlooked the Thames.

Twenty-odd years earlier, French sociologist Emil Durkheim, in a classic study of suicide, had examined the phenomenon from a social perspective and come up with the unsurprising conclusion that soldiers were more prone than civilians. He went further, to assert that Protestants had a higher suicide rate than Catholics, and Catholics higher than Jews, and unmarried higher than married, and that the rate was higher in times of economic stability than during both recessions and booms. Some of this data may have some bearing upon why all these cricketers shortened their own lives, but the part that cricket itself plays in the pattern is very—perhaps impossibly—elusive.

A successful, intense, intelligent, hard-working cricketer of modern times who has written convincingly of the strain of full-time professional cricket is Peter Roebuck of Somerset—one of the counties, as it happens, most strongly identified with fun and frolic. He was as moved as anyone else by the Gimblett biography, and believes that cricket, rather than being the blameworthy force in corroding the nerves to a point of desperation, is merely a catalyst: it tends to attract those of vulnerable personality in the first place. It becomes an ideal vehicle for those who perversely thrive on uncertainty and the mental cruelty it spasmodically (or, even worse, relentlessly) imposes.

In *It Never Rains . . .* , his highly entertaining diary of a cricketer's summer, published in 1984, the agonies of playing cricket for a living and keeping one's employers satisfied are bared on many of its pages. Roebuck writes:

> This game preys on doubts. It is a precarious game. Form, luck, confidence are transitory things. It's never easy to work out why they have so inexplicably deserted you. Inevitably you analyse, you fret, you try to understand what's happened. Why was the game so easy yesterday? Why is it so impossible today? Sometimes you condemn yourself, as if it were your fault that your drive ends up in gully's hands, that your bat will not swing through straight. Sometimes you tense yourself to try harder, sometimes you decide to relax and to go for your shots. Probably neither works. As Foot says, 'Cricket is played very much with the mind. Only the unimaginative player escapes the tension. Many, whatever their seeming unconcern, retreat into caverns of introspection.'
>
> It is a cussed game. It can show you glimpses of beauty in a stroke perfectly played, perhaps, and then it throws you back into the trough of mediocrity. Only the most phlegmatic or those who don't give a damn or those with unshakeable belief survive these upheavals easily. Gimblett must have torn himself with worry. He must have twisted himself into rejection not only of his own personality but of people around him too. He must have sensed envy and plots; suspicions of others must have burdened him as he sought some explanation for his failures. Usually the good times return—Gimblett had a magnificent career—but there is no guarantee, that is the worst of it . . . Maybe cricketers 'shouldn't take it so personal', but most of us do all the same.

Roebuck was soon to become embroiled in the bitter turmoil which rocked the club when Somerset sacked West Indians Viv Richards and Joel Garner, a decision which led to Ian Botham's resignation. Whatever the tensions of making runs for a living, the greatest heartache came in the committee room and at rallies, Roebuck, now Somerset's captain, being labelled a Judas, but riding through the upheaval and even, to all but the eyes of the unforgiving, proving his point. Without the 'superstars', the Somerset dressing-room had a more cohesive atmosphere and the vital junior-through-to-senior structure was made sounder.

Thinking of Gimblett again, and cricketers like him, Roebuck recognised certain basic truths:

> It's strange that cricket attracts so many insecure men. It is surely the very worst game for an intense character, yet it continues to find many obtuse sensitivities amongst its players. Men of imagination, men of ideals risk its harsh exposures.

The Gimblett biography had reminded him of patches of his own career which he would rather have forgotten: 'times when ill-fortune or sheer bad play caused me first to tear myself to pieces and then to turn on my undeserving friends.'

In the second half of the 1983 season Peter Roebuck was overtaken once more by despondency: difficult to interpret this time, since he was making runs. It might have had something to do with the repetition of routine, travelling, practising, eating, playing, sharing hotel accommodation with the same bunch of fellow players, 'as if we were a group of monks who eschewed the world and its people'. Away matches are worst, for at least at Taunton he could go to his own home in the evening and divert himself with music or books. After driving for two-and-a-half hours from Northampton to Manchester he searched in vain for a sense of purpose:

> I've dedicated myself to being good at cricket and simply cannot do it, which is immensely frustrating. What's more, in my efforts to succeed I become irritable and tense, characteristics I rarely show in my winter's teaching in Australia. If that is what playing cricket does to me, why

> the hell do I continue with it? I suppose it's because it's the only damned thing which means enough to me to cause frustration, irritation and gloom. It's the only thing which stretches, tantalises and tests my personality. That is why it's so bloody disappointing that I cannot crack it. I feel like admitting defeat.

The 27-year-old Somerset batsman was by now unmistakeably depressed. Like a thousand county cricketers before him, he hated the loneliness of the evenings, the repetitiveness of strolling round meaningless localities. He started to drive back to Taunton, realised the futility, and turned back to Manchester, via Cheshire, where he walked a little and sat on a bench, reflecting on it all: he had chosen to play cricket for 'noble' motives, but, to his shame, he now reasoned that he was playing not for love or enjoyment but out of habit, and 'because it pays well'. Another not particularly honourable reason, he supposed, was 'to prove my superiority over rivals'. Perhaps he ought not to have been so hard on himself, for competitive sport is based precisely on that—so long as the rivals belong to the opposing team, of course.

He was so fed up the following day that he did not even bother making a diary entry.

The decision to quit the game was made as he wandered about the hills in the evening. He wanted to start afresh at something 'less tormenting'. He also hoped, deep down, that somebody would talk him out of it. He spoke to Viv Richards, who, with typical passion, told him that there was no sense in blaming cricket. 'It is what people do to themselves that causes their turmoil.'

Richards had straightened out the young West Indian all-rounder Eldine Baptiste a few seasons earlier when Baptiste was struggling to make his presence felt on the Kent playing staff, and seemingly getting nowhere. The young man told *The Observer*:

> He kept telling me that my name was Eldine Baptiste and that I had to fight for it, and by the time he'd finished

two hours later the tears were running out of my eyes. I can cope with failure now.

The mighty West Indian batsman—who by 1990 was showing worrying signs of instability himself—had not been quite so convincing with Roebuck, who now felt that retirement was inevitable. There was one last hope. His close friend and team-mate Vic Marks would surely put his mind at rest and see the self-doubt demolished? They walked round Old Trafford, took a bench, chatted and laughed and philosophised. 'Vic was supposed to be convincing me that one must persevere. As it was, my competitive instincts were aroused and I won the debate.' It was decided they would *both* retire: a decision fortunately annulled soon afterwards. Roebuck, in a flash of revelation, saw what he had been missing: 'that sardonic sense of humour which offers a shield against the severest blows'. Soon the only thing he was worrying about was, once more, his batting average. 'This season's darkest moment has been survived—with a little help from my friends.'

If Roebuck—and all others—can continue to weather the bad spells and doubts that they bring, the only remaining hazard might well be premature retirement. Once finished, barring successful comebacks (and unsuccessful comebacks rot the soul), a cricketer lives on his memories; so the danger of leaving the game too soon is serious. You are finished forever. Many a player, though exhausted, has soldiered on, knowing that what lies ahead is meagre in attraction. There is even a theory, aired once in a while, that one of the fundamental causes of friction between players and journalists is the realisation by the former that they are the risk-takers, the performers, on a short-term lease, while the latter have a lifetime tenure on their jobs, enjoying travel comforts, financial security, and the advantage of being able to change direction with the wind editorially. It is therefore amusing to contemplate the shift in behaviour which often occurs when former players take up positions in the broadcasting-booth and press-box.

Before the examination of other cricket suicides, there is one further case of a cricketer of our time warding off the worst consequences of the strain of top-level competition. Sir Richard Hadlee, the great New Zealand fast-medium bowler, the first man to claim 400 Test wickets, may have learned to adopt the 'sardonic sense of humour' which abounds in county dressing-rooms during his decade with Notts, but it was not enough to save him from breakdown in 1983, when his commitments to the New Zealand Test side and to the frantic needs of his various business and promotional activities had drained him dangerously. It was one of the most triumphant periods for New Zealand cricket, thanks to Hadlee as much as anyone, but he was experiencing physical and mental depression, blurred vision, excruciating headaches, chest pains and a preoccupation with death. He felt he would never be able to play cricket again. Playing at Rotorua in a festival match, he had to leave the field, 'in a daze, wondering what the hell was happening to me. I couldn't see properly and my head was splitting.'

He admits to having become neurotic. Always fastidious anyway, he was now upset by the slightest thing: pictures hanging not quite straight, dead flies by the skirting-board, cricket trophies that needed polishing. He could not even seek the escape of running in the park, for his legs did not want to carry him.

Unlike Roebuck, Hadlee is married, and Karen, a top cricketer herself, stepped in with some positive action. She arranged a holiday in Raratonga, an idyllic spot in the Cook Islands. When a sportswriter tracked him down with a phone call, Hadlee gave him an earful he will never forget.

On top of his self-doubt, this serious man developed a conviction that he had a suspect heart. What would happen to his family if he stopped producing the goods? Then there was his fierce pride. What if he lost his premier position among New Zealand's cricketers? When Karen allowed a phone call through from Hadlee's Notts team-mate, Clive Rice, the South African hardly recognised his voice: 'It was as though he didn't even have the confidence to talk.'

Into his life then walked a 'motivation expert' named Grahame Felton from the Institute of Management in Christchurch. He was to achieve for Hadlee what the doctors had been unable. Hadlee was convinced now that the only way ahead was to have goals in life which would be approached in unwavering fashion. Such credos as 'Fear is negative' and 'Self-esteem: know your own worth/ability/value' and 'Never get tired—just pleasantly weary' were inculcated into the troubled sportsman's mind, and eventually written, with other ego-supportive slogans, onto a card which Richard Hadlee has kept on view in his cricket bag ever since. The only doubts since then seem to have been whether or not to retire before his powers showed signs of waning. Notices of retirement were issued, then, to the horror of opposing batsmen, countermanded. Hadlee's physical attributes, allied to his uncompromising mental approach to the task of overthrowing the opposition in the field, remain, despite the crisis of 1983–84, one of the most dominant forces that international cricket has ever known.

Once he had regained his poise and was back on cricket's treadmill, some thought that it might have been better for him to have released his emotions more readily on the field of play. But that would not have been him, any more than it would have been Hadlee senior, for father Walter Hadlee, a New Zealand captain in the immediate post-war years, was a man of unusual dignity. In any case, the game has quite enough of the 'ebullient' type already, exhibitionists and intimidators who wave arms, cry out, and hug and kiss. If they are not manic-depressives, the signs of hysteria are certainly there.

During much of Hadlee's Test career, Bob Willis—and Dennis Amiss a few years earlier—were among the most phlegmatic of cricketers, and both had hypnosis. Dr Arthur Jackson counselled them and provided soothing self-hypnosis tapes which could be listened to anywhere in the world when the stress level rose. Hadlee might have been spared the worst of his problems with this preventative. The comfort which Roebuck sought in vain while ruminating on a bench might easily have come from music earphones. Greg Matthews, the ‘punkish’ Australian all-rounder, wore his ’phones, taking in the inspiration and pacification of his favourite group Midnight Oil right up to the moment when it was his turn to bat. If he was soon back in the dressing-room, the music came once more to his rescue in his moment of failure.

7

More Victorians

The Victorian age, with its dark images of poverty and desperation, may perhaps justifiably be linked to a more serious intensity of alcoholism (often a disguised form of suicide) and overt self-destruction. Anybody who has taken an interest in nineteenth-century cricket is likely to have been left with the impression that suicide then was much more common than of late. Among the cricketers who played last century, well known or otherwise, some died before the century was out, while others, such as A. E. Stoddart and Cyril Bland, already dealt with, were casualties of later decades.

An extensive scan has spotlighted a number of little-knowns whose deaths diminished mankind but caused barely a ripple in the world of big-time cricket. There was James Maurice Quinton, who played for Oxford University 1895–96 and as an amateur for Hampshire in four matches between 1895 and 1899. Educated at Cheltenham College, where he captained the XI, he was a middle-order batsman (highest in first-class cricket a modest 22) and fast bowler who finished with 1 for 111. He was, besides, a good Rugby footballer, athlete and rackets player. Three days before Christmas 1922, when he was 48, he got on an express train on the Great

Western Railway and, when the train was near Reading, shot himself. The given reason was 'unnecessary worry', though it was not made clear whether over financial, medical or other matters. His brother, Brigadier General F. W. D. Quinton, played 45 matches for Hampshire, with some success, between 1895 and 1900.

Another Cheltenham pupil of former years, Thomas Moore, also an Oxford University player, though not a Blue either, fell to his death from Black Rock, Brighton, in the spring of 1925, when he was in his late sixties. He had been suffering from a 'painful disease'. A local fisherman told the inquest jury that he had seen Moore sitting at the top of the cliff before lowering himself over the edge until he was hanging by his hands. He then seemed to change his mind, and clung desperately to the edge, but it did not hold him, and he plunged to his doom. A verdict of 'suicide while temporarily insane' was returned. It would seem that he had not pursued his cricket at any notable level after having been good enough as a schoolboy to score 51 and 48 in Cheltenham's 1876 match against Marlborough and to play for the freshmen and the seniors at Oxford. He was a barrister by profession.

Cecil Patteson Nickalls, who won the DSO while serving in the Royal Field Artillery in the Great War, rising to lieutenant colonel, shot himself at his residence, Stanford

C. P. Nickalls — brilliant school batsman, gallant soldier.

Park, Rugby, on April 7, 1925, a few weeks before Moore's death. They were probably unfamiliar with each other, Nickalls being younger at 48, and having made his name as a schoolboy cricketer while at Rugby in the 1890s. He scored 109 at Lord's against Marlborough in 1894, hitting powerfully through the covers and putting on 207 with John Stanning (who was to die in a motor accident in 1929) for the second wicket in only 100 minutes. In 1895 Nickalls made 97 in the corresponding match, but apart from some cricket with Kent 2nd XI he concentrated on other sports, missing a Rugby Blue at Oxford only through injury, but representing England at polo against the United States in 1902 and Ireland in 1905 and 1911. At the time of his death he was manager of Rugby Polo Club.

George Harwood Ashley Arlington, who played in 29 matches as an amateur for Sussex between 1894 and 1898, scripted for himself one of the more curious demises by walking off into the Australian bush in 1940, when he was 68. As a young man he had been a power in club cricket on England's south coast. Born in Dover on May 28, 1872, he was educated at Brighton Grammar School, and went on to make over 100 centuries, the highest being a gigantic 309 for Sheffield Park against Nutley in 1897. *Lillywhite's* said of him that year: 'A fine hard-hitting batsman; a good field, but apt to

George Arlington — off into the bush to die.

be careless; can keep wicket.' In 1898 he hit 224 not out for Lewes Priory against Seaford and 182 not out for Hastings against Brighton Brunswick. But county cricket he found much harder, making only 615 runs in 50 innings, with a highest of 73 against Cambridge; he held 13 catches and took one wicket for 36—though Arlington did have a great day behind the stumps at Hove in 1896, stumping Abel and Lockwood and catching Brockwell, Hayward and Walter Read in Surrey's innings. What distorted visions floated through George Arlington's mind as he wandered off in search of nirvana in the Australian wilderness all those years later will never be known; but they might have included odd glimpses of green English fields and an umpire sweeping his arm back and forth to signal yet another boundary. It was a self-sacrifice in the face of apparent hopelessness to warrant comparison with that hero of the Antarctic, Captain Oates.

During the last year of the Great War, Charles Henry Benton, who had played for Lancashire 29 times as an amateur between 1892 and 1901, took his own life at The Terrace, Knutsford, Cheshire, shocking his friends. He was a civil engineer—'of independent means' at the end—Harrow-educated, a mere 5 ft 5 ins tall and weighing 10 st 10 lbs in his playing days. He played also for Cheshire, and served on the MCC committee at Lord's. In August 1899 he got to within three runs of a triple-century for Gentlemen of Cheshire against the luckless Ludlow bowlers. In first-class cricket his best performances were on a rather lower scale: 68 for Lancashire against Oxford University at Old Trafford in 1893, 51 not out against Kent at Tonbridge, and 60 against Warwickshire at Edgbaston, both in 1895. When Archie MacLaren scored his towering record 424 that year, for Lancashire against Somerset at Taunton, Benton made 43 in a fourth-wicket stand of 107 in an hour, his dismissal being doubly painful as he deflected the ball against his mouth and was caught by the bowler. He sat proudly beside MacLaren in the Lancashire team photograph that year. Benton bowled left-arm, and fielded at third man or mid-on. Having been born in the Manchester suburb of Old Trafford on January 8,

Charles Benton — a partner during MacLaren's 424.

1869, he must have felt that cricket was in his blood, a blood which ceased to flow on May 19, 1918. He was only 49. The Cheshire coroner luridly defined cause of death as 'complete extravasation of the brain caused by shooting himself with a gun whilst temporarily of unsound mind'.

A few months before the start of the war, another cricketer's suicide was registered in Cheshire. Robert Wickstead Ethelstone, a retired captain in the Royal Welsh Fusiliers, shot himself on April 27, 1914, at Malpas, 15 days after his fifty-fourth birthday. He had been an MCC member for 26 years, but his impact on the game could hardly have been slighter. Playing for Winchester against Eton in June 1877, batting at No. 11, his scores read: c & b Smith 1, and b. Ridley 0. The strong Eton side, which included the Hon. Ivo Bligh and the three Studd brothers, won by an innings. Ethelstone became a renowned huntsman and owned steeplechase horses. Montague Druitt, the Jack the Ripper suspect referred to in Chapter 2, played for Winchester in the season prior to Ethelstone.

Twelve days after Ethelstone's death, Reginald Jaffray Lucas, a distinguished Etonian who had battled with ill-health all his life, shot himself at his residence at The Albany, Piccadilly, on May 9, 1914. He was 48. He played in the Eton XI from 1881 to 1884, twice as captain, and though hampered by

R. J. Lucas — Member of Parliament, dogged by tuberculosis.

a 'delicate constitution and a weak arm' (he looks a swarthy and fairly sturdy figure in the four Eton group photographs) he made some useful little scores in the school's low-scoring matches. He went up to Trinity College, Cambridge, and top-scored with 82 in the 1885 freshmen's match but failed to make the trials for the Varsity XI. He was elected a member of MCC that year, and went on playing also for I Zingari and Quidnuncs. London-born, Lucas entered a successful career in politics, becoming Conservative MP for Portsmouth (1900–06) and writing several works of fiction. The motive for his suicide was the intolerable pain he was suffering from tuberculosis, and his final note explained that he did not wish to be a burden.

Failing health accounted also for a keen Yorkshire amateur, Charles Edward Wheatley Hallas, on the evening of August 20, 1909, when he shot himself in London's Imperial Hotel. He was only 32. A slow left-arm bowler—a highly respected breed in Yorkshire—he had captained Huddersfield and played for Yorkshire Colts and Yorkshire 2nd XI. In a 1903 Colts match against Notts he had taken 4 for 16. Suffering from insomnia and depression, he had taken a holiday in South

Africa. But the future remained bleak, and he could no longer make do—if he ever read it—with the verdict of existentialist, pioneer Nazi and probable 'nut case' Nietzsche that 'the thought of suicide is a great consolation; with its help you can go through many a bad night'.

That same year saw the end of Hume Francis Meeking, land agent at Birdsall, Yorkshire (though 'no occupation' is written on his death certificate), who shot himself on June 14, 1909, at Havering Park, near Romford, Essex. Down at Lord's, that same day, England, with Bert Relf in the side, began an unavailing fight to hold Australia at bay in the Test match. Meeking was another Etonian, an opening batsman in 1893, scorer of the only fifty in the match against Harrow (for whom R. F. Vibart opened: his story follows) at Lord's. A colonel's son, Meeking looks none too robust in the 1893 Eton team group, but the talent must have been there. He was a patient player, strong off his pads, and also a good wicketkeeper, who added four catches and a stumping in Harrow's second innings to his half-century. A year later, in 1894, he played in the freshmen's match at Cambridge but failed to win a Blue. Born on September 15, 1874, Hume Meeking was 34 at the time of his death.

H. F. Meeking — Eton batsman-wicketkeeper.

A man whose proposal for changing the law governing declarations was to have repercussions in a Test match shot himself at his home, Old Malt House, Hurley, Marlow, Buckinghamshire, on June 1, 1907. Frank Boyd May had just been declared a defaulter on the Stock Exchange. He was 44, and left a widow and two daughters. May had been an MCC member since 1888, and had played seven first-class innings for the club for 12 runs, averaging 2, a record about which he would have needed to have been grittily philosophical. He played also for Free Foresters and for his old school side, Old Cliftonians. At MCC's annual general meeting of 1906, Frank May, who was born in London on October 24, 1862, proposed a resolution:

> That in a two-day match, the captain of the batting side has power to declare his innings closed at any time, but such declaration may not be made on the first day later than one hour and forty minutes before the hour of drawing stumps.

After some discussion, the resolution was carried, to become, 14 years later, the cause of a Test match controversy at Old Trafford, where, having batted on the second scheduled day of a three-day Test, the first day having been washed out, the Honourable Lionel Tennyson, England's captain, attempted to declare at 341 for 4 at 10 minutes to six, hoping to have half-an-hour at Australia's batsmen that evening. The elephantine Australian skipper, Warwick Armstrong, strode from the field and disputed the declaration with Tennyson, Australia's Yorkshire-born wicketkeeper 'Sammy' Carter having been fully acquainted with the playing conditions. Tennyson, now realising the match was subject to the regulations of a two-day match, acknowledged his mistake, but by now the Australians had left the field, and the crowd was in uproar. By the time the England captain and the umpires had explained to them the cause of the hold-up, 25 minutes had been lost, and in the confusion nobody noticed that the bowling was resumed by Armstrong—

who had delivered the last over before the hiatus. Surely Frank May chuckled from his Heavenly perch—if suicides are allowed into Heaven, that is.

On October 16, 1904, the body of Richard William Kentfield, accountant, was retrieved from the River Ouse, at Goldington, Bedford. He was 41, a left-arm medium-pacer who had been born in Bognor, Sussex, but made his debut as an amateur for Lancashire in 1888, taking only two Oxford wickets in his three appearances (one of which was the Roses match)—though they were blue-blooded victims: Lord George Scott and the Hon. F. J. N. Thesiger (later Lord Chelmsford). Kentfield's 18 in Lancashire's second innings, when they were still in arrears at the fall of the eighth wicket, having followed on, helped set up a victory target of 63 for Oxford, a target they failed to achieve. Kentfield's next taste of first-class cricket was for Sussex six years later, in 1894, when he took 6 for 45 and 1 for 49 against Middlesex at Lord's, dismissing Stoddart in both innings on a rain-dampened pitch. George Arlington, previously mentioned, played in this match, scoring another of his ducks in the first innings and 20, top score in Sussex's total of 65 in the second. Yet another two years passed before Kentfield, who captained Rusholme for several seasons, was called into the Sussex team (on a birth qualification) at Old Trafford in May 1896 when C. B. Fry was late in arriving. Kentfield took 1 for 44 and scored 0 and 4. It had been a curious career, and the penetrative analysis at Lord's in 1894 left the question hanging in suspense of how good a bowler he really was.

Moving back into the Victorian era proper, Alan Rotherham, famed as an England Rugby player with 12 caps variously against Scotland, Ireland and Wales between 1883 and 1887 as a half-back (and member of England's first-ever Triple Crown team in 1883), was also a very fine cricketer. Born in Coventry on July 21, 1862 and educated at Uppingham, where he captained the XI in 1881, he played county cricket for Warwickshire in 1883 and 1884, before the club was granted first-class status. Rotherham was

Alan Rotherham — England Rugby half-back and talented cricketer.

described as an above-average batsman, slow bowler, and 'capital' field. In 1888 he was admitted as a barrister at Lincoln's Inn, but 10 years on, when he was 36 and secretary to Watney's Brewery, life had gone bad. He killed himself on August 30, 1898, at 15 Adam Street, off Portman Square, in London, cause of death: 'shock due to destruction of brain from injury by gunshot wounds'.

Five years earlier, tragedy struck one of the better-known cricket club secretaries, Frederick Goodall, who, at the age of 36, had reasons which may never be known now for firing a revolver through the roof of his mouth. He was honorary secretary of Sudbury Cricket Club in Suffolk, and his death ocurred on July 8, 1893, the day before William Scotton cut his throat.

Moving forward again to 1914, the rare *World of Cricket* magazine, edited by A. C. MacLaren, reported half-a-year after the event that Charles Alured Lambert Swale, captain of the Yorkshire club Settle, and well-known member of the Yorkshire Gentlemen CC, had drowned himself on November 26, 1913. Swale, of Ingfield Hall, Settle, was 43. No cause for his action was given.

Albert Beresford Horsley, who won his cricket colours at The Leys School in 1896, had one first-class match, for W. G. Grace's London County in 1904, scoring 24 and taking no wicket for 22, before having his best season for his native county, Durham, making 285 runs at an average of 25.90 in 1905, with a career-highest of 98 against Glamorgan. That year he took up the secretaryship of Durham County Cricket Club, a position he held until 1920, when ill-health forced him to retire. He was born in 1880 in Hartlepool, and it was there, on November 19, 1923, that his body was found, cause of death 'asphyxia by coal gas, self-administered; temporary insanity'. He was 44, and described on his death certificate as 'timber merchant'. He was a justice of the peace, and had been awarded the CBE. His son, Rupert Harry Horsley, then 18 and at Winchester College, was to play three first-class matches for Oxford in 1927.

Born into the Victorian age (on September 18, 1881), Hubert McLean Greenhill, a Dorset amateur who played twice for Hampshire in 1901, taking three wickets with left-arm medium-pace but realising nothing with the bat, was found dead in woods at Bockhampton, near Dorchester, on January 22, 1926—which happened to be the twenty-fifth anniversary of Queen Victoria's death. Greenhill was a product of Wimborne Grammar School and Sherborne, where he showed style as a batsman and took a lot of wickets, as he was to do in regimental cricket. He rose to major in the Dorsetshire Regiment. 'While in a state of temporary insanity caused by mental depression the result of financial worry and bad health' Major Greenhill shot himself.

All the foregoing 16 were keen amateurs—'gentlemen' players. But another whose destiny it had seemed to have been as a lifetime 'gentleman' shocked his class by being 'forced to make a living as a professional at a number of schools and clubs in the West Country'. This was Ronald Frank Vibart, born in Sidmouth, Devon, on April 5, 1879. His father, a major in the Royal Artillery, had died before Ronald started at Harrow School, and his mother had remarried. The boy immediately showed sporting promise, the seeds of future degeneracy as yet still hidden. He played in the football XI and the cricket XI, taking part in the showpiece match against Eton at Lord's in the four seasons to 1896 (he was only 14 in 1893). In that last year he captained Harrow, a 'neat' even 'pretty' batsman who, in 1896, showed an appetite for staying in. He scored 161 against the Household Brigade and 201 not out for Colbeck's against Welldon's in the Cock-House match. He won his school's prize for batting in those Eton matches on two occasions and for fielding in three.

He also, in 1896, became Public Schools heavyweight boxing champion, having taken on the best that Rugby, St Pauls, Charterhouse, Radley, and Bedford could offer all in one day at Aldershot. He was expected to be a huge credit to the school when he went up to Cambridge.

But Vibart's stay at Trinity Hall was brief. He left in a hurry, having taken the first clumsy steps down a long, spiral decline. By 1898 he was in South America, away from the gaze of family and associates, spending almost 10 years there, a period from which only fragments of data emerge. One fact was that he took 9 for 111 in the important South *v.* North match in Argentina, on the Palermo ground in 1898, and another was that he married. By 1908 he was back in England, but since his wife was not willing to sail with him, he left her there. Undaunted, he married again, a son of the union later reaching high rank at Scotland Yard and featuring in the Great Train Robbery investigation in the 1960s. His father, R. F. Vibart, 40 years earlier, was to remain on the same side of the law as Ronald Biggs.

From his scheming address-book Vibart began to look for helpful contacts, and in the years that followed he became cricket professional at Truro School and to the Camborne and Falmouth clubs in Cornwall up to 1914. Bristol cricket researcher Jack Burrell, who dug up a lot of material on Vibart for *The Cricket Statistician* (the journal of the Association of Cricket Statisticians), traced scores of 149 for Falmouth (where he was on £18 a year) against St Veryan in 1913, a knock which included nine sixes, and in Minor County cricket for Cornwall, 149 against Berkshire at Reading in 1911 and an unbeaten 125 against Devon at Camborne in 1913. Vibart was easily stirred. When his wicketkeeping proved fallible to the tune of four byes, and his captain made a sarcastic remark, Vibart tossed aside his gauntlets and kept for the rest of the innings with bare hands. The skipper was lucky the pugilist in Vibart didn't get the better of him.

His turn came to fight legitimately when the First World War broke out. He enlisted in the Public School Battalion of the Middlesex Regiment, and when it was all over he had little before him but more work as a cricket professional, joining Exmouth for two years in the early 1920s, playing for Devon, and taking part in country-house matches where, the imagination dictates temptingly, he would have been a slightly less genteel Raffles kind of figure.

Another useful contact—or did he apply some kind of pressure of his own?—found him employment in Cumberland,

Ronald Vibart — batsman, boxer, bigamist, boozer.

at Heversham School, where he became known as 'Roving Ronald'. Someone who knew him then described him as 'a rather mysterious, well-spoken man, grey-faced, broad-shouldered and rather morose, but when he found a cricket bat in his hand a different, happy light shone in his eyes'. Occasionally he would turn up at net practice slightly unsteady for drink, place half-crowns on the stumps, and say, 'Now, young gen'l'men, just you try to bowl me out. If you do, you get the money.' He had little enough of it to give away, so it was an offer he would hardly have been likely to have made had he been sober. When he was not in search of a pint, he was looking for easy prey for a small loan. Nevertheless, most of the boys were in awe of him and would listen wide-eyed to his stories as he sat on the roller, his work on the ground done. He even told of a fight with Winston Churchill at Harrow, though that may have been stretching things a trifle, England's future saviour being five years his junior.

This school posting eventually led to an appointment with the North Lancashire & District League club Haverigg in 1926, for £4 a week. He was now 47, but still the best wicketkeeper in the league—though Haverigg finished bottom. Once, his domestic landlord, missing him for lunch on a Saturday before a match, tracked him down to the Rising Sun pub, where the distraught publican, probably too apprehensive to halt the alcoholic flow to the stocky Vibart, announced that he had drunk 20 pints and hadn't yet paid a penny. Vibart was already banned at the Blue Bell.

He was chosen to play for the Northern Counties XI against the 1926 Australian touring team at Carlisle in mid-September, but failed to turn up. It can only be supposed that somewhere between Heversham and Carlisle there was a pub . . . .

By the late 1920s Vibart was back in the West Country. Nobody in the village of Heversham was game any longer to give him lodgings. He grew familiar with the inside of courtrooms after drunken brawls outside pubs late at night, and money worries preyed on his mind. A photograph of him in these later years shows a fat, bloated, surly man, as Jack Burrell observes, 'with his life of violence, dishonesty and wastefulness gradually ebbing to its tragic end'.

That end came in Taunton on July 30, 1934 when, at a self-abused 55 years of age, he drank hydrochloric acid and breathed his last in Taunton & Somerset Hospital. His death certificate describes him as 'picture repairer of Devonia, Victoria Street, Taunton'. His own life had long since been beyond repair.

A few other professionals from the period who were minor figures in cricket's vast landscape have ended their own lives, the reasons varying widely. Thomas Attenborough, a 73-year-old former Derbyshire and Lincolnshire batsman, slow left-arm bowler and fine slip fielder, and now a cattle-dealer, found the death of the great Nottinghamshire bowler Alfred Shaw too much to bear. Shaw died in January 1907, and five days later, on January 21 at 246 Nottingham Road, Ilkeston, Attenborough followed him, cutting his throat with a carving knife. He had been depressed, but Shaw's death was decisive, prompting what the Japanese would describe as Junshi: suicide after the death of one's lord and master, or in this case, revered hero and old friend. Attenborough's career in first-class cricket did not weigh a lot, though he did once, in 1870, take 4 for 8 at Lord's for Derbyshire against MCC, and he had the distinction of playing for the All-England XI. His brother William was a good cricketer too.

Another Midlander, William Underwood, a lightly-built 5 ft 8 ins, who played merely one game for Notts as a professional in 1881 (scoring 10), and also represented Devon (scoring 124 for the county against MCC in 1883), shot himself on May 8, 1914 at Bradmore, Nottingham. He was 61, and had been professional to Rock Ferry, Edinburgh Collegiate, and HMS *Britannia* at Dartmouth after his promising days as a colt cricketer had failed to launch him to the top.

David Whittaker was a Lancastrian, left-handed as batsman and medium-pace bowler, a solidly-built 5 ft 5 ins, who played in nine matches for Lancashire as a pro between 1884 and

1888, managing a top score of only 26 and one solitary wicket. In the Surrey match at Old Trafford in 1888, when he took the absent Eccles's place at the last minute, he made two ducks and dropped an important catch as his county (35 and 63) sank to an innings defeat in one day (Lohmann 8 for 13 and 5 for 38).

Whittaker was a stalwart of club cricket, playing for Rishton (Viv Richards's club a century later) for 10 seasons and for Enfield and Ramsbottom for seven each. Born in Church in 1857, he was found drowned in the Leeds & Liverpool Canal, near the Britannia Mill, Rishton, on December 17, 1901, aged 44. His death certificate described him as 'professional cricketer of 19 Burton Street, Rishton'.

In October 1899, one of Yorkshire's leading club cricketers, George Cort, 33, Doncaster Town's professional for several seasons, and a gasfitter by trade, killed himself by taking chloride of zinc. No reason for his suicide is now known.

Across the seas, and across the decades either side of the turn of the century, there were incidences of amateur cricketers' suicides, some not reported as such at the time. In January 1898, in Rangoon, Burma, H. R. Troup, a young officer who had been the finest batsman in recent Madras Presidency matches in India, put a gun to his mouth and extinguished his life, this only days after scoring 132 for the Military against the Civil. Oddly, a player in the Civil team, Arthur Gwynn, who also made a century in that two-day match, and caught Troup, died the following month from septicaemia stemming from a tooth abscess.

Over in America later that same year, on September 26, 1898, one of his country's finest cricketers, Sutherland Law, jumped (unless he fell, perchance) from a window in his room on the fourth floor of the Colonnade Hotel in Philadelphia. He was 45, and had toured England in 1884 with the Gentlemen of Philadelphia team, making a top score of 55 but managing only 15 wickets against the all-amateur opposition. Strongly built at 11 st 6 lb and 5 ft 7½ ins, Law bowled fast and with stamina, and was a steady bat and very competent fielder. He scored Merion CC's first century—

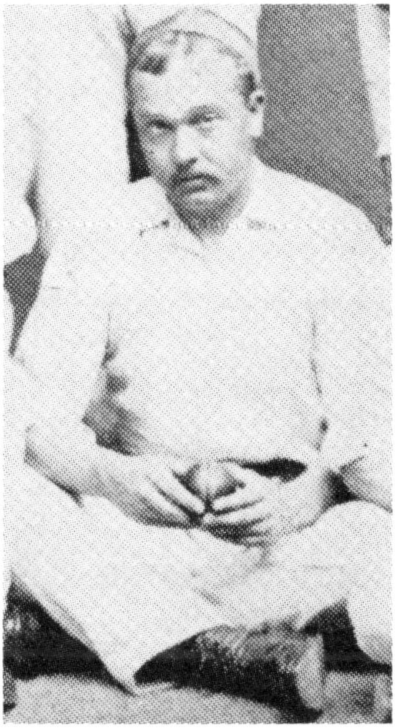

Sutherland Law — did he jump or fall?

103 in 1876—and also played for Germantown, going on to represent the United States seven times against Canada between 1880 and 1891, the oldest of international cricket contests. In the 1884 fixture, at Nicetown, he took 5 for 21 in Canada's second innings, and took in all 26 wickets at a puny 5.69 in the series. He won the Childs Cup for the best batting average (43.20) in Halifax Cup matches in 1891, the year he captained Philadelphia Zingari on tour in Bermuda. Only a year before his death he recorded his highest score, 146 not out for University of Pennsylvania Past against Merion Veterans at Haverford. If he did project himself from that window, might it have been, partly at least, because he feared his considerable powers as a cricketer were waning?

In Australia, the deaths of two relatively obscure cricketers in the last quarter of the nineteenth century are no less poignant for their humble achievements on the cricket field. George Morgan was 53 when, on July 17, 1896, he walked onto the expanse known as The Domain, in Sydney, where the earliest intercolonial and English touring matches had been held, and shot himself for reasons unrevealed. He had been born in Bathurst, New South Wales, in 1843. A member of the famous Albert Club, he played one match for the State in 1874–75, at Melbourne right after Christmas, and failed to score in his one innings, Sam Cosstick bowling him as he batted at the not very inspirational position of No. 10. It was a distinguished New South Wales side, with Charlie Bannerman making 81 and 32 not out and Spofforth taking three wickets in each Victorian innings. Morgan at least had the satisfaction of being on the winning side in his sole first-class appearance—and that against the 'hated' southern enemy.

Two years earlier, in the 1872–73 season, in a rare first-class match featuring Tasmania, William Anthony Collins, Launceston-born and now 35, played and scored 16 runs in his two innings. That was all the first-class cricket he was to play, but Tasmania eventually owed him a considerable debt for his work as treasurer of the Launceston club, whose ground he rehabilitated, using the immense sum of £300 of his own money, rendering facilities to such an acceptable standard that W. G. Grace's 1873–74 touring team agreed to play there. Shortly afterwards Collins was so disenchanted by circumstances that he resigned from Launceston Cricket Club, but his sporting interest was sustained through the secretaryship of the Tasmanian Turf Club.

His money problems, however, became acute, despite his solicitor's practice, and on January 12, 1876, after he had been noticeably glum for at least two weeks, he took strychnine. He had bought several items at Hatton & Laws, adding a shilling's worth of strychnine, which prompted the shop assistant to query Collins's purpose. He explained that the rats were bad again. Just before noon, Henry Turner, who worked in the office next to Collins's, in St John's Street, Launceston, answered his call for help, and found Collins on his knees near the door, crying for a doctor and saying he had taken strychnine half-an-hour before. Turner ran to find Dr Maddox, alerting Holmes, the shop assistant who had served Collins that morning. He rushed morphia to Collins as an antidote, and found him lying by the doorway. He gave him the morphia, then went back to the shop to search for an emetic and some mustard and water. When he reached Collins again he found him in convulsions, his clenched teeth forbidding further treatment. Dr Maddox then arrived but was unable to make use of the stomach pump or to administer chloroform. Collins repeated his agonised pleas to be saved, but it was hopeless. Another doctor arrived just as he died, the convulsions continuing to the end. He left a widow and two young children, to whom the *Launceston Examiner* extended sympathy in the stilted manner of the time: 'It may be easily imagined how widespread was the regret that pecuniary embarrassments should have so preyed his mind as to make it for a moment lose its balance.'

In Limerick, Ireland, on August 1, 1881, Nathaniel Thomas Hone—a distinguished family name in Irish cricket circles—a wicketkeeper educated at Rugby and a Blue at Cambridge in the summer of his death, expired after drinking carbolic acid 'in error', though such a grievous mistake cannot have been easy to carry out. Hone, born in Monkstown, County Dublin on June 21, 1861, was a few weeks beyond his twentieth birthday, and left a record of two runs, six catches and two stumpings in three first-class matches.

Jack Usher, a proven suicide, had only the one first-class match, but his story is unusual: pathetic and amusing at the same time. He was born in Staincliffe, Yorkshire, on February 26, 1859, and developed into a valuable slow left-arm bowler and left-hand batsman. It is not unusual for professionals to move around the league clubs, but Usher was more peripatetic than most. He served, from 1886 until the time of his death in 1905, Heckmondwike, Holmbeck, Holmfirth, and Wortley in Yorkshire, and Bacup, Rishton, Haslingden in the Lancashire League, Whalley in the Ribblesdale League, and finally Crompton in the Central Lancashire League. He was also looked at by Yorkshire, but played in only one first-class match for his native county, against MCC at Lord's in 1888. Scotton was one of his two wickets, and Scotton caught him in the first of his two single-figure innings. It was a tantalisingly short flirtation with big cricket, but at least he had gone all the way down to the capital for it.

He did the hat-trick against 22 Yorkshire Colts, but is best remembered for his wonderful season of 1900, when he helped convey Haslingden to their first championship by taking 143 wickets at 6.03, a league record until West Indian Charlie Griffith took 144 wickets for Burnley 64 years later. Usher's nine wickets in the extra match—a two-innings final—actually left him with a dazzling 152.

In August 1905 Usher drowned himself in the mill reservoir at Haslingden, the cause apparently being financial ruin. An unconfirmed narrative has it that he took to taking bets on the horses, setting up his position in a pub at Helmshore. What he never suspected—at least until it was too late and he was penniless—was that the local rogues had set up a system whereby the race results were signalled secretly by telegraph via the railway signal-box within view of the pub. Usher would take bets some time after the scheduled start of a race, believing that it would take a considerable time for the results to come through. The punters were many minutes ahead of the poor man (for that is what he became). He was 46 when he died in despair, leaving a widow and seven small children.

One final minor cricketing figure born into the Victorian era was Arthur Povey, Staffordshire-born in 1886, and a professional wicketkeeper for Kent in five matches in 1921 and 1922 when Hubble was injured. Povey held five catches and made a stumping, and had a highest score of 21 not out. Later he became a coach at Tonbridge School, where the young prodigy Colin Cowdrey enrolled in 1946 at the age of 13. It was early that year, on February 13, that 59-year-old Povey hanged himself in an outbuilding near the school's cricket pavilion.

8

Essex Grief

Essex became a first-class county in 1894, as the so-called Golden Age of Cricket was gathering pace in popularity and elan. Not for 85 years, however, was the county to win a title, and then, mainly under Keith Fletcher's captaincy, they kept on winning, creating a golden age in every sense. The earlier period, despite the exhilaration of the rise to the uppermost level of competition, had several chilling shadows cast across it.

First, in 1892, came the suicide of the young captain, C.D. Buxton. There was no covering-up. *Cricket* gave the raw details. He had returned home to the family spread at Knighton in Woodford on Monday evening, May 9, and was found next morning, dead with a gun by his side. A hastily scrawled note to his parents bade them goodbye, explaining that he had felt something was going to happen. The customary jury verdict incorporating the expression 'while of unsound mind' was tendered.

Cyril Digby Buxton died virtually at his birthplace. He came into this world, to a locally distinguished family, on June 25, 1865 and was educated firstly at Elstree then at Harrow,

Cyril Buxton — popular Essex captain at 24.

where he starred as a batsman and fielder, before continuing his progress at Trinity College, Cambridge. At the university he was a Blue four years running (having been given his first colours by the future Lord Hawke), captaining the Light Blues in the last, 1888, by which time he was already an experienced county cricketer—amateur—with his native county (having begun with a pair of noughts). He was an accomplished rackets and tennis player, and was soon earmarked for leadership. By 1889, when he was only 24, he was Essex captain.

He played some club cricket for Elstree, and his Essex cricket was all non-first-class, but for Cambridge he displayed his talent with regularity, a 57 in the first first-class match at Leyton, against the Australians for Cambridge Past and Present 1886, being one of his more notable achievements, and 30 and 40 against the dreaded Turner and Ferris of the 1888 touring team being another. His only first-class century came in 1889, when he made 108 not out for MCC against his old university, showing the good taste and judgment of performing this deed not only at Lord's but with W.G. Grace as his captain. It would have been the brightest of memories to sustain him when depression stalked. And yet the finest of Buxton's innings from a technical point of view was probably 79 in 130 minutes against Surrey (with Lohmann) at The Oval in July 1887, when Essex were bowled out for 121. Those runs were first-class in quality if not by definition. At times, too, he would chip in his round-arm medium-pace bowling, and once took 5 for 16. With his 1213 first-class runs (18.95) were bracketed 60 wickets at 25.36.

But Cyril Buxton, though standing over 6 ft tall, was not in full health. A bout of influenza was followed by congestion of the liver, and he was stricken by 'great nervous prostration and accompanying depression of spirits'. While he loved walking the dogs, he was equally keen on hunting, and several falls did him no good at all. Although his father, E. N. Buxton, ran the brewing business which bore his name (it later merged with Trumans), it appears that son Cyril did not see work as part of his obligation in life: and therefore lacked it as a distraction when brooding came upon him.

Early on the morning of his death he told the nurse, who slept in an adjoining room, that he was going downstairs. There, by manipulating a double-barrelled shotgun with a handkerchief and a poker, he blew out his brains. His youthfulness and good nature magnified the shock felt by the neighbourhood and the world of cricket. Essex's captain was mourned by *Cricket* as a young man who 'won golden opinions from all manners of men. Modest and unassuming in himself, he was the first to admit merit of any kind in others.'

At Harrow, his old school, a memorial plaque was placed on the arch of the chancel of the chapel, and down at the lower cricket ground some friends erected a small pavilion in his memory.

We move on 15 years, to 1907, when an Essex professional who had served the county loyally and well between 1881 and 1897 now found himself, at the age of 45, close to penniless, with a wife and several children to support. The weight of despair cracked him. On September 27 Harry Pickett disappeared from his home and walked into the sea off Aberavon. His body was found on October 3 but not identified until the end of December, some articles in his clothes proving his identity.

Pickett had been born in Stratford, Essex, on March 16 (some records state 26), 1862, and, having proved very destructive with the ball in local club cricket, played as a young professional in Liverpool before joining the MCC ground staff in 1884. His attachment to Essex marked the start of an exemplary service as he bowled and bowled for a county often outclassed but game to the end. Pickett was a strong light-heavyweight and seemingly tireless as he held one end tight for hour after hour, bowling honest fast-medium, trying always to keep things well in control.

In 1884, playing for MCC against Forest School at Walthamstow, he had bowled all 10 batsmen out in the first innings, following this with five wickets in the second. In club matches he had some dramatic returns and was obviously a bowler who belonged in a higher sphere. Essex became his

Harry Pickett —
all 10 wickets in 1895.

niche, and his sweat was rewarded sweetly at times: 12 for 78 in the match against Surrey at Leyton in 1889 (for which he received a collection of £26, made up to £31 by Cyril Buxton); 76 wickets in 1890 (his best season); a hat-trick against Warwickshire at Leyton in 1890, the year he took 12 for 162 against Surrey on the same ground; and, most famously, all 10 Leicestershire wickets for 32—at Leyton of course—in 1895 (Essex's maiden summer of Championship cricket), for which the collection amounted to something just under £20. This remains an Essex innings bowling record, only Trevor Bailey, in 1949, having taken 10 wickets in an innings besides. (Bailey, incidentally, lost his brother Basil, 73, in 1986 when, in hospital care after attempting to shoot himself, he threw himself from a fourth-floor hospital window.)

Harry Pickett was perhaps unduly modest about his hat-trick:

> It was the luckiest hat-trick on record. The first ball got Shilton caught, but the catch was taken so low down that only the umpire knew whether the man was out or not. I bowled Joe Cresswell with the next ball, and then Harry Pallett received the third. It was not straight, and would not have bowled him, but it knocked his legs from under him and as he fell he trod on his wicket.

Pickett was a typical tailend hitter, capable of awkward defence when needed, which was often; and he once amazed everyone, himself included, by belting 114 against Hampshire at Southampton, in 1891, putting on 244 for the eighth wicket with Charles Kortright (158).

His benefit came in August 1897—by which time his weight was burgeoning and his powers diminishing—and the Hampshire match at Leyton returned him only £150. Rain fell, the opposition were weak, and the beneficiary himself did not play. A penny subscription among the schoolboys of Essex went towards a handsome timepiece, while a halfpenny collection among the kids of West Ham, Leyton, and thereabouts was converted lovingly into a silver-and-gold miniature of stumps, bats and ball. They probably all had to be pawned in the years ahead.

He was not without shrewdness. In an interview for *The Cricket Field* in 1895 he said:

> I work well within myself. I only take about eight yards' run and twelve short strides. An amateur can manage to take a long run without hurting himself, but a professional who has to bowl day after day at the nets as well as in matches is likely to wear himself out very soon if he takes a very long run.

Pickett was complimentary towards his captains, and sad about C.D. Buxton: 'Mr Buxton was a grand captain; he used to make us play up so well. It was the greatest loss that Essex ever had when he died.'

Pickett had nearly gone to join his uncle in America when still in his teens, but the offer to play for Beckton came along. It is pointless to speculate on how the course of his life would have changed had he emigrated. Suffice to note that in this 1895 interview, although he was in his thirty-fourth year and knew his county days were almost over, he still regarded Essex as 'the best little county in the world to play for'. From county cricket he went to Clifton College as cricket coach. And from there he went to oblivion. His wife died less than a year after him, on March 24, 1908, the children unprovided for. If ever the Cricketers' Fund Friendly Society were needed it was then.

Two-and-a-half years later the sea claimed another Essex cricketer as a deliberate victim. Frederick George Bull, an amateur, born in Hackney on April 2, 1875, and having elicited no interest from Kent, played in 88 matches for Essex between 1895 and 1900, taking 416 wickets in all first-class cricket at 21.74 with a strange off-break action which caused suspicion over a period of years and eventually had him 'listed' in 1900 when the authorities decided to crack down on illegal bowling. He had attempted to change his style, but lost his effectiveness as a result, and Essex dispensed with his services as 'unpaid' cricketer and club assistant secretary.

C.B. Fry, who himself was no-balled for throwing his fast stuff, wrote in complimentary terms of Bull, having reservations only about his throwing-in from the outfield: 'a peculiar return that much resembles weight-putting'. Otherwise, he saw the young slow bowler as having 'all the requisites—a natural spin, a mastery of length, and a long repertoire of tricks'. He was quick to spot a batsman's weakness, and would play on it subtly. The off-spinner was his stock ball, but he mixed in the quicker one, the straight one, and one which twisted from leg. With these wiles he harvested 85 wickets in his second season, 1896, his best figures being 8 for 44 against Yorkshire at Bradford and 8 for 94 for the Gentlemen against the Players at The Oval. Better followed in 1897, with 9 for 93 against Surrey at The Oval, and match figures of 13 for 156 against Derbyshire and 14 for 176 against Lancashire, both at Leyton.

There was an unholy row in this last match. The follow-on was not optional in those days, and Lancashire were about to fall short of the target. The Essex batsmen did not fancy batting fourth on that pitch and felt it would be better to let Lancashire steer clear of the follow-on, allowing Essex to bat third and build upon their lead. So Bull, needing no prompting, bowled a deliberate wide ball which went for four. Detecting the ruse, Arthur Mold then knocked his own wicket over, and Lancashire had third use of the pitch after all. It availed them little. Essex won by six wickets.

Bull took 120 wickets that summer, and went off to America on P.F. Warner's tour and took most wickets (43). Warner considered him the best of slow bowlers at that time. Another 101 wickets followed in 1898, but suddenly it was all over.

That odd action condemned him in the eyes of opponents and administrators, and even today the action photograph defies easy explanation. With the arm still horizontal behind him, the shirt-sleeve loose around the elbow, his chest is already well on the way to full exposure to the batsman.

Fred Bull —
brilliant career cut short.

At an age when many a spin bowler was starting to make an impact, Fred Bull already had his great days behind him and was out of work. His often lethal partnership with Essex's terrifying fast bowler Kortright was at an end.

Bull came close to starting again with Surrey, but the stigma attaching to his suspect bowling action probably scuttled any conclusive thoughts about engaging him at The Oval. Notions of his joining the Stock Exchange evaporated. He went north.

The bowler who had taken all 10 Saffrons wickets (eight bowled) for 16 while playing for Granville (Lee) at Eastbourne in 1894, and for whom *Wisden* had predicted a brilliant future when he was one of the Five Cricketers of 1898, was back to part-time cricket again. With a job in Blackburn, he joined East Lancashire for the 1904 season and took 91 cheap wickets. The next two summers he 'embraced professionalism' for Perthshire, taking 167 wickets overall and representing Scotland against the 1905 Australians (taking eight wickets, though not Trumper's). In the two after that, 1907 and 1908,

Bull was back with East Lancashire, as a pro, with 111 wickets at 8.81 in 1907, sustaining his reputation as one of the more feared bowlers in league cricket. He moved on in 1909 to Rishton and took 61 wickets at 12.21, but by the following autumn his disillusionment and anxiety had grown intense. In Blackpool in search of employment for the coming winter, he reached the end of his tether.

He was found washed up in a sea pool at St Anne's on September 16, 1910, with stones weighing down the pockets of his trousers and Norfolk jacket, and a 7-lb stone tied up in a handkerchief around his neck. He had clearly been determined not to surface once the waters of the Irish Sea had closed over him. He had thoughtfully sent the key of his room back to his landlady via a messenger, and on his body were found only another key, a penknife and a leather purse, which was empty. An inquest returned a verdict of suicide, for once sparing the public any reference to insanity or 'unsound mind'. There had simply been 'no evidence as to the state of his mind'.

Fred Bull was only 35, a victim of gross disappointment. Had an umpire had the courage to no-ball him for throwing at the start of his first-class career he might have found another pathway through life. But after several summers of success and acclamation, the sudden reservations in high places about the legitimacy of his bowling would have had a crushing effect. The substitute pleasures of success in the northern leagues were never to suffice and the old problem of winter employment for professional cricketers proved cruelly decisive. A spectator in the good Essex days had seen a photograph of Bull's bowling action as that of 'a gallant soldier' who had just taken a bullet in the chest and was staggering back with upthrown arm. Had Bull made it as far as the Great War, with what must have become a death wish, that image could well have turned to reality.

9

Who Ever Hoped?

'Who ever hoped like a cricketer?' Robertson-Glasgow once wrote. Who, indeed, when the pads were on, bat in the hands, the sun above.

But when all hope is gone? In cricket it often merely seems that way. Then all of a sudden things click right, luck changes, everything's fine. In real life, something only sometimes turns up, and sometimes it doesn't.

In 1870 a conspicuous talent emerged into the Surrey ranks. He was 21, fielded beautifully, and batted with a polished and correct style that suggested a Harrow background. But Richard Humphrey, a 'natural', was a product of the famous cricketing village of Mitcham, brother of John, Tom and William Humphrey. Tom, 'the Pocket Hercules', had risen already to great heights as a professional with Surrey, forming an opening partnership with Harry Jupp from Dorking which ranked in terms of awesome reputation with that of Hobbs and Sandham of later years at The Oval.

Richard Humphrey won what in cricketing terms was a royal accolade in his first match for the county, against Gloucestershire at Durdham Down in 1870. Mrs Martha

Grace, mother of W. G., told him: 'You haven't made many, but some day you will get a lot. A good field like you is bound to get runs.' With which the grand dame gave him half-a-sovereign.

Humphrey was soon making runs for Surrey: an 82 against Cambridge University at The Oval that seemed 'almost perfect', and 116 not out in his second year, against Kent at Maidstone, to go with an 80 against Yorkshire and a 70 against Mrs Grace's county. The third season, 1872, found him compiling 1072 runs (23.82), an exceptional aggregate in those low-scoring times on poor-quality pitches. He carried his bat for 30 not out in Surrey's innings of 60 against Notts at The Oval, making a further 52 runs in the second innings; again on his home ground, he scored 70 in each innings against the powerful Yorkshire attack, a double considered the best feat of his career; but the 96 he made for the Players against the Gentlemen, also at The Oval, could not have been much inferior. The Gentlemen v. Players match was the showpiece match of the times, as sharp a trial of ability as was known in the days before Test cricket.

Humphrey was celebrated as one of the best batsmen in England, and he was still only 23. A year later, however, his form fell away, and as failures succeeded each other, he knew of no way to cope. A measure of his struggle can be seen in the scores which followed his 96 for the Players. In Gentlemen v. Players matches at The Oval, Lord's and Prince's up to the point in 1874 when those responsible lost interest in choosing him, Humphrey scored 5, 4, 5, 4, 0, 1, 4, 1, 12, 10 and 4. This would have demoralised even the most resilient soul, and although he made the odd half-century in the seasons that followed, and toured Australia (with little success) with W. G. Grace's side in 1873–74, Dick Humphrey, though still a young man, was regarded as a 'has-been' already, a bright flower which wilted in late spring. The plumber-turned-professional cricketer, 5 ft 6½ ins and 10 st 10 lbs, subsided into the ranks of the ordinary, and played his last match for Surrey in 1881, when he was 32.

Richard Humphrey — past his peak at 24. His body was found near Waterloo Bridge.

In 1879, the year following brother Tom's death at 39 in Brookwood Asylum, Humphrey had gone into business in City Road as a tobacconist, but by 1883 he was taking up a post as coach at Clifton College, having had a ganglion operation at St Bartholomew's. At the college he not only coached the boys but ran a cricket outfitters, and life must have presented a fairly serene picture after all when Surrey informed him that they would be staging a benefit for him in 1885.

It was a failure. Total receipts were £180.19.6 and expenses were £99.10.0, leaving the 36-year-old former player with £81.9.6. He carried on at Clifton, doubtless hearing a few months later, to his chagrin, that Walter Read, the Surrey amateur, had been given £250 and a clock worth £16 by the Surrey committee on the occasion of his wedding. The club's donation to Humphrey's fund had been 20 guineas.

His health deteriorated over the next few years, and he was forced to resign his position at Clifton College in 1889. While being cared for in Bristol Infirmary in April 1891 he endured a 14-hour epileptic attack, but by 1892 he was well enough to take up a coaching appointment at Bedford

Grammar School. Surrey County Cricket Club had dished out some helpings of aid to him and his wife: a sum of £10 in November 1890, and a six-shilling weekly payment from August 1891 until October 1894, when, although the club had a tidy £10,000 invested in stocks, the grant to its old opening batsman ceased.

In 1900 the club made another small payment to Mrs Humphrey when she was in 'great distress' after her husband had left her for some days and had not been heard of, but by 1904 things had steadied to the point where Richard Humphrey found employment—and gave satisfaction—as an umpire in Minor County cricket. But two seasons seems to have been the limit.

On February 24, 1906, the body of Richard Humphrey, 'a professional cricketer of 3 New North Street, Theobalds Road', was found by Waterloo Pier. He had drowned himself in the Thames. He was 57.

The old Surrey stumper, Ted Pooley, who was to die in Lambeth Workhouse a year later, told an interviewer that, for himself, it had been 'the workhouse or the river'. His team-mate of over 25 years earlier had taken the other option.

Wisden lamented that Humphrey 'did not accomplish half of what was expected from him', and *Cricket* said:

> . . . He was born before his time, and if it had been his fate to play in the later years when wickets were vastly improved, he would have gone from success to success, and would then have had no occasion to be disheartened by a few failures, for he had many fine strokes which would have told well in modern days.

He was buried at St Pancras Cemetery, East Finchley, a few days later.

Another whose hopes died, though not until a good and full cricket career had run its course, was Arthur Woodcock, who, in the straining eyes of some batsmen, was the fastest bowler in England in the mid-1890s, Kortright notwithstanding.

Woodcock was a striking figure, 5 ft 10 ins and 13 stone, a modest and good-tempered man, born in Northampton on September 23, 1865 and removed to the Leicestershire village of Billesdon while still a baby. It was there that he was to die almost 45 years later.

At 21 he had secured a coaching engagement at Mitcham, where he not only took 75 wickets at less than five runs apiece in 1887, scattering apprehensive batsmen in all directions, but began a friendship with Tom Richardson, then a teenager, born in a gipsy caravan in Byfleet in 1870 and destined to become, in today's vernacular, the 'role model' for all honest, tireless, chivalrous fast bowlers. Woodcock did a lot towards developing his talent. Their methods were not dissimilar, Woodcock, from the start, relying on pace and variation of pace to overthrow the batsman—and also 'by bumping the ball up a bit'. History may never offer a full explanation as to why Richardson heroically went on to take 88 wickets for England in 14 Tests while Woodcock and Kortright between them played in not one single Test match.

The Mitcham contract, through Surrey secretary C. W. Alcock's good offices, led to Woodcock's engagement to coach at Haverford College in Philadelphia, where for seven seasons from 1888 he spent the winters encouraging American youngsters, many of whom had never seen a cricket bat before, to practise hard—usually in a large shed adapted for the purpose—until some of them were close to first-class standard. He was optimistic—as are most missionaries in the game's outposts— about the United States' future as a cricket nation.

During those years, from 1889, Woodcock joined Leicestershire in June and played for the rest of the summer, his career as a professional extending to 1903, when, at 37, he found his knee injury too severe to allow daily poundings. He had been universally respected for his skill and demeanour, and, naturally, his reputation was built on some spectacular performances. In 1894, against Notts, on the Grace Road ground, he took 8 for 67 in the first innings and 7 for 69 in the second after some rain, shouldering the extra burden of Dick Pougher's absence from the Leicester attack. In 1895

Arthur Woodcock — devastating fast bowler who poisoned himself.

he took 8 for 111 against Warwickshire. In 1897 he played ducks and drakes with MCC, taking 8 for 66 and 5 for 66 *for* the Marylebone club, against Kent, at Lord's, and, a few days later, playing for Leicestershire, 6 for 66 and 7 for 59 *against* MCC at Lord's, where he was on the ground staff from 1895 until his death.

Lord's saw some more of his thunderous stuff in 1899 when, back in Leicestershire colours, he demolished MCC with 9 for 28 (14 for 72 in the match). But 1895 remained his best season: 102 wickets at just over 19 apiece. In Leicestershire's match against the illustrious 1902 Australian side, Woodcock had Duff, Hill and Gregory out with his first seven balls.

In all first-class cricket he yorked and bounced his way to 548 wickets at 22.28, and when his county days were over he continued to play as much as possible, having the pace even in 1908, when he was 42, to send a bail six inches short of 50 yards, over the boundary wall, when bowling a batsman at Lewes, Sussex, while playing for MCC. Ten years earlier, when he must have been a few miles-per-hour quicker, he sent a Hampshire batsman's bail 58 yards. In minor cricket he caused terror: six wickets in six balls for Hungerton against Keyham in his early days of village cricket, and, in 1894, for Uppingham against The President's XI of Past and Present, he took all 10 wickets in the innings.

He was generous in attitude towards other cricketers, and particularly admired courage in his opponents. In an interview with *The Cricket Field* in 1895 he singled out C. D. Buxton of Essex (who had shot himself three years earlier) as one who had played him particularly well.

Cricket recorded his death, without comment as to his circumstances or state of mind, in its May 19, 1910 edition:

> Death has been busy among Leicestershire cricketers during the present month, Charles Randon, William Tomlin and Arthur Woodcock all passing away—the last-named as the result of poison self-administered—within a fortnight. Woodcock returned to his home at Billesdon late on Saturday night and asked his sister to kiss him, saying that he had come home to die. Shortly afterwards he became unconscious, and, although the doctors did everything possible to save his life, he passed away at three o'clock on Sunday morning.

Only a few days previously he had been at the practice nets at Leicester, perhaps watching the youngsters bounding in, and wishing he could still measure out his long run-up and roar in with all the might of his frame to dispatch a ball that would have the batsman ducking hurriedly or, better still, shatter his stumps. Age had seen to it that all hope was gone.

10

Australia's Sons

William Bruce, 61-year-old solicitor and former Test cricketer, kissed his wife goodbye one August morning in Melbourne in 1925. 'Will you be home for dinner, dear?' she asked. 'I'm not quite sure,' he replied. It was 10.15 am. She was never to see him alive again.

Billy Bruce once held the Australian record for the highest score at any level of cricket. In a district match in 1883–84, when he was 19 years of age, the left-hander made an undefeated 328 for Melbourne against Hotham. He was soon to become a Victorian State cricketer, and then to represent Australia, making his debut on his home ground at Melbourne on New Year's Day 1885, opening the bowling, and claiming the wretched Scotton as the first of his three wickets. Scotton avenged himself on the fourth day by hitting (or probably tapping) England's winning run off Bruce's bowling.

Bruce owed his selection, at 20, to the need for an entirely new Australian XI after a dispute had caused the team from the opening Test of the series to be sacked. They had demanded 50 per cent of the gate takings.

He batted at No. 10 in his first Test innings, but top-scored with 45 when Tom Horan sent him in first in the second innings, hitting freely in the manner which had established his reputation in the first place, 6000 spectators giving him every encouragement.

With the big guns returning, there was no room for Billy Bruce in the Australian side for the next Test, in Sydney, six weeks later, won by six runs, or the next, also at Sydney, where Australia drew level, 2–2. But for the decider, at Melbourne, he was included, and opened the batting (in the first innings only, with Alick Bannerman, the stonewaller) and the bowling. It seemed that luck was with him. In the second over he touched one from Ulyett to wicketkeeper Joe Hunter, and the bowler's fellow-Yorkshireman dropped it. Two overs later, with Bannerman refusing a call, Bruce was stranded—but the English fieldsmen collided and he got back to safety. Soon his fine strokeplay was on show: until Peel deceived him.

Bruce took 3 for 99 (including Scotton again) with his left-arm slow-mediums in England's tall score of 386, and made 35, top score again, at No. 6, in difficult conditions as Australia slid to an innings defeat. His name would therefore have been among the first written down when the team for the 1886 tour of England was being organised by Melbourne Cricket Club, a campaign which remains one of the most disastrous on record. Australia lost all three Tests, and Bruce played in the first and third, at Old Trafford and The Oval, with 22 runs and no wickets to show for the experience. In all matches on the tour he scored 780 runs in 50 innings, average 16.44, with one century, 106 against C. I. Thornton's XI at Chiswick Park in July, a powerful effort admired by at least one of his opponents, Drewy Stoddart, who was about to hit 485 for Hampstead, a world record, a month later.

It was unlikely that Billy Bruce would have failed to enjoy the experience of touring England, even though he took a mere 13 wickets to go with his modest quantity of runs. But he had the pleasure of featuring in a full-length interview in *Cricket* soon after the ship berthed which itemised his education at Melbourne's Scotch College and the fact that he stood '5 ft 10 ½ ins in his stockings', a 'good specimen

Billy Bruce —
kissed his wife goodbye.

of the native Victorian'. Currently articled to a leading firm of solicitors in Melbourne, he already had a cache of trophies in his cabinet, one for taking 8 for 9 and top-scoring in each innings of a recent Melbourne match against Richmond. Scotton was quoted as saying that Bruce can get him at any time. 'A great favourite' in Australia, Bruce was expected to do well in England.

He did not tour England again until 1893, though he played with considerable success against the side captained by W. G. Grace that toured Australia in 1891–92. His scores of 57 and 40 at Melbourne and 72 at Sydney had much to do with Australia's two victories, and although the third match, at Adelaide, was lost, he top-scored with 37 in the second innings. England was glad to see him again in the spring of

1893, and anticipated better this time, for he was at the height of his batting powers, while his fielding, at least, was remembered from 1886 with huge satisfaction, the slim figure with the sloping shoulders having true authority stamped on it.

He sailed, with Hugh Trumble, ahead of the main party and got in a fortnight's sightseeing before the serious business got under way. Bruce bobbed along nicely in the lead-up to the Test series, enchanting with his style, and sometimes impressing with his power, as when he lifted a ball from Bobby Peel clean out of Trent Bridge in the Australians' match against Shrewsbury's XI. Then came a dreadful run preceding the first Test: 0 and 1, 1, 6, 1 and 4, and then 1 (stumped off the underarm guile of Humphreys of Sussex). Had there been a bigger tour party, Bruce might have missed the Lord's Test, though his 6 for 29 against Yorkshire helped his cause. But he played, took three wickets, and scored 23 batting at No. 8. in a drawn match.

A duck, 12 and 5 followed, and his spirits must have been dragging the floor until his 60 saved the innings against Surrey. With that, and a 37 in the second innings, his luck swung. In the next match, against Oxford and Cambridge Past and Present, at Portsmouth, he made what was to be the highest score of his first-class career, 191 in 220 minutes, out stumped. Alick Bannerman and Trumble made centuries too, and the Australians ran up a total of 843.

In the second Test, at The Oval, England thrashed Blackham's team by an innings, and once again Bruce was up and down the batting order like mercury in a thermometer: 10 not out at No. 7 in what was really a strong batting line-up (Australia fell to Lockwood and Briggs for 91 in high heat on a fine pitch) and 22 in the second innings, when he opened with Bannerman and helped put up 50 in half-an-hour.

Back in the middle order for the last Test, at Manchester, he top-scored in the first innings with 68 against the demanding bowling of Mold, Richardson and Briggs (Bruce hit him for 16 off one over), and was second-top in the second with 36 (four fours and a two off a Briggs over this time), having had the great delight of bowling Grace (off his pad) as well as catching Shrewsbury. It was turning out to be quite a tour for him after all.

In fact he finished at the top of the Australian Test batting averages with 159 runs at 39.75, a signal honour well recognised at the time, though almost 100 years later few people have heard of him.

His remaining four Test matches happened to be the last four of the extraordinary 1894–95 Ashes series, with George Giffen as his Australian captain against Stoddart's star-studded English team. England had won the opening encounter, at Sydney, by 10 runs after having followed on. Now, with Bruce back in the side, Australia bounced back by dismissing the tourists for 75 at Melbourne. Bruce opened in each innings, making 4 and 54, and his side lost after England's stout second innings, mounted on Stoddart's 173, reached 475.

Then came the fightback. Australia, introducing Albert Trott, who turned in sensational performances first with bat, then ball, then bat again, and whose story follows, won at Adelaide and Sydney to draw level, Bruce scoring 11 and 80 in the former Test.

That 80 was the highest of all his Test innings, a typically stylish performance, with occasional overs that thrilled the huge crowd: 13 runs off one by fast-medium bowler Brockwell, and two boundaries and a three off the wily fast man Lockwood. It ended when he hit an alluring ball from Briggs into Brockwell's eager hands at square leg.

The deciding Test of the '94–95 series, at Melbourne, became famous for its dramatic script, which included a hurricane 140 from J. T. Brown of Yorkshire (his 50 in a Test record time of 28 minutes) which won the match, against the odds, for England. For Billy Bruce, it was a final appearance for his country and he scored 22 and (in almost an hour as Australia fought to set too tall a target) 11. He had hurried down from his legal duties at North Melbourne police court for the start of the match. Now he could make his way slowly into the remainder of his life. In 14 Tests he had scored 702 runs at the respectable average of 29.25, taken 12 wickets at 36.67, and held 12 catches. He did not tour England again, though his final match for Victoria was as late as 1903–04, when he was in his fortieth year. In 117 innings for his State he made only one century, and averaged 25.21; and he took 69 wickets, with a conspicuous best of 7 for 72. As the years passed he enjoyed coaching the younger players, particularly left-handers, and numbered the future Test batsman Vernon Ransford among his 'pupils'.

As the hair turned grey and the spine became less flexible, Bruce had his legal work to absorb him, and if he reflected at all on his days out on the cricket field, with no bowler hat upon his head and no necktie to half-halter him, he had his Tests and tours and Sheffield Shield contests to choose from—or the 260 he slammed in December 1892 for Melbourne against St Kilda; or the 131 he made in company with England's Arthur Shrewsbury (236) back in '86–87 for the Non-Smokers against the Smokers at East Melbourne, their opening stand amounting to 196. This innings had prompted the English magazine *Cricket* to declare that 'Bruce is probably now the best batsman in Australia'.

All so long ago as he left Majestic Mansions in Fitzroy Street, St Kilda, on that early-spring morning in 1925. Some hours later his body was found in the sea at Point Ormond. The inquisition taken at the Melbourne morgue found that William Bruce died from 'suffocation by drowning by his own act'. His name was visible on his shirt and singlet, and in his pockets were found 7/6d in cash, a pocketknife and a lead pencil. Tied to the railings of Elwood Pier, six feet below the level of the pier flooring and 400 yards away from the body, his overcoat was found, his hat tied to it with his scarf. His spectacles, in a case with his name in it (and the addresses 360 Collins Street and 191/5 Queen Street), were in the overcoat pocket. His face was badly bruised, for there were rocks by the pier, but no other marks were found.

His brother-in-law, Frank Gibbs, testified that Bruce had been 'low-spirited' during the past 12 months, since he had suffered a bad attack of influenza. He said his brother-in-law had nerve trouble; that he was a reserved man, who said little about his complaint: 'He never at any time led me to believe that he would take his own life.'

Gibbs had lived next door. He sensed that Bruce may have had a worry of some sort: he could be moody, depressed. 'He used to take a drink or two, but he didn't show it.'

The surgeon gave evidence that the body was of an elderly, rather stoutly-built man before the widow, Florence Grace Bruce, told of her husband's departure that awful morning. She felt he was probably worried over business matters, and said he did not confide in anyone; he was very reticent. He once had a good legal practice, but it had 'fallen off'. She asserted that he was a sober man, though lately he may have been a 'regular drinker'. She observed that he used to read a great deal.

Thus ended the life of a man who was once Australia's foremost batsman, the reasons for his suicide indistinct. Just over half-a-century earlier another Melbourne Cricket Club batsman, Richard Wilson Wardill, had drowned himself by jumping into the Yarra River. There was no great mystification about his motive. He had embezzled £7000 (probably close to half-a-million in 1990 terms) over a five-year period from the Victoria Sugar Company, who employed him as their accountant, and he knew he had no future.

Wardill, too, could once reasonably have been regarded as the best batsman in Australia. He certainly recorded the first century in Australian first-class cricket, 110 for Victoria against New South Wales at the Melbourne Cricket Ground on Boxing Day 1867 (followed by 45 not out in the second innings). He also featured in the first century partnership.

Dick Wardill had been born near Liverpool, in England, in 1835 and took a sailing ship to Australia when in his early twenties. His brother Ben followed later, around 1862. Six or seven years younger, Ben was to make a great success of his life in the New World, attaining the rank of major, achieving some distinction as a wicketkeeper, though much the lesser cricketer when compared with his elder brother, and becoming a prominent figure in the world of rifle-shooting. He was very much a man about town in young Melbourne.

Dick Wardill — embezzler who scored the first century in Australian first-class cricket.

From 1878 he was secretary to Melbourne Cricket Club, a prime position he held for 32 years until his health began to fade, and he could look back with pride upon three Test tours of England in which he was manager, 1886, 1899, and 1902, the first of them, of which Billy Bruce was a part, one of the most difficult of all tours in that harmony between many of the Australian players was glaringly absent.

So much for the successful and respected brother. The name of the other, Dick, remains cloaked in shame. He played for Victoria in eight first-class matches between 1861–62 and 1872–73, scoring 348 runs at the contemporarily high average of 31.63. He captained the State side and was a selector. He was captain and secretary to Melbourne Cricket Club. He was co-founder and treasurer of the first Victorian Cricket Association. And he played for the Victorian XVIII against the very first English XI to play in Australia, in their opening match, at Melbourne Cricket Ground early in January 1862. He was run out without scoring, and in the second innings he made 18 before being caught off the bowling of George Griffith (who hanged himself in 1879).

Wardill played in front of another huge crowd—10,000—in the match against the Aboriginal XI in 1866, and his liking for the big occasion—and undoubtedly for the rewards inherent—must have inspired him to arrange the preliminary meetings in Melbourne to plan a tour in the 1873–74 season by an English team with W. G. Grace at its helm. The embezzled money may have been intended, some of it at least, for investment in the tour.

At last the fraud came to light, and Wardill was challenged by the company's directors. He owned up and agreed to go with them to the police station. They accepted his plea to be allowed first to call at his home in Punt Road, South Yarra, to explain to his family. At the house, he suddenly slipped through the rear entrance and made for the banks of the River Yarra, there to throw himself in, seeking oblivion.

It was three days before his body was recovered, and relatives then had to endure the further anguish of meeting rivermen's demands for £10 before they handed over the body. Greed, which had destroyed a life, was mockingly evident to the bitter end.

Tom Wills, like Dick Wardill, was born in 1835, though half a world away, in Molongolo Plains, near where Canberra was later built. He also played in the match when Wardill scored Australia's first first-class century. A third-generation Australian, Wills also played cricket on many a farflung patch. He was sent to England for his education, and appeared at Lord's for his school, Rugby (where he captained the XI and the football team, and was school dux), in 1852, when he was only 16, and took five wickets in MCC's first innings and seven in the second.

Thomas Wentworth Spencer Wills turned into a fair figure of a man, 5 ft 10 ½ ins and 11 st 2 lb at his peak, a good batsman and fast round-arm bowler—sometimes chucking the ball and sometimes bowling underhand lobs—and a fine fielder. *Scores & Biographies* found his batting style curious: 'scarcely moving his bat at all, unless the ball is well pitched up to him, when he hits hard'. In 1855 he played twice for Kent, and once again the following year, when he played for MCC and—although not a resident at any of the colleges—for

Cambridge against Oxford in the Varsity match at Lord's. He was clearly popular and in demand. In 1855, at Hove, he played for the Gentlemen of Kent and scored 56 against the Gentlemen of Sussex, and took nine wickets in an innings in the return match at Gravesend. Later in his career he took 13 for 92 for Victoria against XVI of Tasmania at Launceston in 1870, having returned to Australia in 1856, with some imported innovations, such as the toss for innings, now accepted as an improvement on the Australian custom of allowing the visiting team to have the choice.

Wills is a major part of Australia's early cricket history. Playing with great success for Victoria in the early intercolonial matches and serving as Melbourne Cricket Club's secretary were important in themselves. But in 1871 he compiled *The Australian Cricketers' Guide*, a 120–page rarity. And he was one of the inventors of Australian Rules football in 1858, a wild amalgam of Rugby and Gaelic football. He and his cousin, Henry Harrison, saw it as a means of keeping cricketers fit during winter, and the cricket influence was obvious in the concept itself, the ground being a complete oval rather than marked-out oblong. The first recognised match, at the Melbourne Cricket Ground on August 7, 1858, between Scotch College and Melbourne Church of England Grammar School, featured 40 players on each side, with the goalposts almost half-a-mile apart. By 1866 there was a clear need for the new game to undergo some sort of sophistication, and Wills sat down with Harrison, Will Hammersley and J. B. Thompson, and they moulded what would be instantly recognisable to the legions of Aussie Rules fans of today.

But beyond all this, even, Wills's contribution to Australian sport continued through the pioneer encouragement of Aborigines to play cricket. He had fostered interest among the labourers on his father's sheep station and eventually, as coach of the Aboriginal cricketers at Edenhope, Victoria, he planned a tour in 1867, the eventual collapse of which cost him a lot of money. A year later a tour did get off the ground when Charles Lawrence, formerly of Surrey and All-England, led an Aboriginal side to England, but for all

Tom Wills — a great figure in Australia's sporting history.

the efforts of Wills, Lawrence and others, it has to be accepted that Australia's indigenous people have either failed to rise to cricket eminence—apart from fast bowlers Marsh and Henry and Eddie Gilbert—or have been denied the kind of patient encouragement given them by Tom Wills.

The appalling irony was that Wills, whose kindness and consideration towards the Aborigines were notable, had had to absorb the slaughter of his own father and two brothers in a massacre on his father's station, Cullinlaringo, by the Nogoa River in the Springsure district, 200 miles from Rockhampton, Queensland. Tom had been an articled clerk to a solicitor, residing in Collingwood, Melbourne, in 1859, when his father had been all the way up to inspect the area soon after Queensland had been declared a separate colony.

Now, friends gave 26-year-old Tom a cricket bat with an inscribed gold plate affixed to it as a farewell souvenir of Melbourne. He and his father and several of their employees then set out from Geelong, bought equipment in Ipswich, and took possession of 10,000 sheep in the Darling Downs before eventually reaching Nogoa months later, in October 1861.

The local Aborigines were known to be hostile, but Wills senior was confident he could handle them. Young Tom had told a friend that, despite their familiarity with the Victorian natives, he always carried a pair of six-shooters with him. The father, though, was completely trusting, and when a party of warriors came to inspect the new arrivals Horatio Wills was chiefly concerned with persuading their giant leader that they ought to cover up their nakedness.

Within the fortnight 19 of the settlers were dead, killed in a savage slaughter, which was soon avenged more then threefold when around 60 Aborigines were tracked down and killed by a posse of police. Wills's father was among those slain, together with George Elliott, the brother of the Victorian cricketer Gideon, and some women and children. It was the worst outrage in terms of the killing of whites by blacks in Australia's history. But fate had spared Tom Wills. He and two others had been disappointed when their wagons broke down, on the two-day journey back from collecting stores, but the overnight delay saved their lives.

For a couple of years Tom kept the property going, against the odds. During that time he wrote to a friend:

> I have now to watch sheep at night—having only three hours' sleep—and attend from daylight to dark in the shed. If I were to leave at present, the station would simply go to 'blazes'; in fact, after the murder, shepherds cannot be got, and most likely, with all other troubles, I shall have to take a flock out myself.

Like many another in grief and turmoil, Wills turned to cricket and found relief. He went back to Melbourne in 1863 and attached himself to George Parr's team, the second English side to tour Australia. He played against them to strengthen several opposing teams, and even escorted them across to New Zealand.

In 1866 came his devoted association with the Aboriginal cricketers in Victoria, when an indication of the respect and admiration shared between white coach and black learners came in the remark of one of the Aborigines, Jellico, when someone suggested he ought to get Wills to teach him to read and write in English: 'What's usy Wills? He too much along of us. He speak nothing now but blackfella talk.'

Wills's cricket talent had not left him, as was shown in his performances with the Aboriginal team, but he and his young partner W. R. Hayman were too trusting of a con man 'promoter' and also ran into difficulties in the new year with the Central Board for the Protection of Aborigines. Enterprise abandoned.

Wills returned to Melbourne Cricket Club as 'cricket tutor', less than pleased at seeing the Aboriginal side reorganised and shipped off to England for the 1868 tour under the leadership of former Surrey player Charles Lawrence.

It is clear, however, that by now Tom Wills was a heavy drinker, and not the best of influences on his black cricket pupils. For that matter, his young charges at Melbourne CC may have been at some risk of 'contamination'. Wills continued to play for Victoria, and reserved his lifetime best for the 1869 match against New South Wales, when he took 7 for 44. But the downhill slide had begun. The haunting memories of the Cullinlaringo horror must always have been somewhere in his mind. The bottle brought a kind of short-term solace. Soon he was a complete and dangerous and apparently incurable alcoholic, and detention in Kew Asylum became essential.

He was let out, but there was no dramatic recovery. Instead, on May 2, 1880, in a fit of depression, he stabbed himself fatally with a bayonet at his home in Heidelberg. He was 44, and his death might just have been an illustration of Freud's early theory that suicide is transposed murder, an act of hostility redirected from the original object back into oneself.

Tommy Wills had his idiosyncrasies, but he was proudly revered by the sporting fraternity of Victoria and of Australia at large, while friends in England from 20-odd years earlier were equally saddened by his passing. From the youngster who had struggled to show his worth at 15 when he played against the mighty Melbourne club and dropped a catch, scored a 'pair', and earned a black eye, to the much-travelled veteran who, 27 years later, supported the prospect of an epoch-making inaugural white Australian tour of England, Wills had enormous impact on Australian cricket in its formative years.

His friend William Hammersley wrote of him that 'a finer young fellow never donned the flannels'. He described him as 'a very peculiar man, rather taciturn, but very good-natured and a very general favourite'. He remembered him as a disorganised secretary at Melbourne CC:

> When he left office everything was in a muddle—club papers, books, cricket balls, cricket guides, Zingari flannels, cigars, spiked boots—everything one can conceive stuffed together in the large tin box of the club. A most untidy mortal he was, and quite unfit for such work. The cricket field was his place, and I don't think Tommy ever gave a thought to anything but cricket in his life.

Hammersley's account, in the *Sydney Mail*, of Wills's end varies slightly from the others:

> He was attacked with softening of the brain, induced by his not taking that care of himself which he should have done, and gradually became irresponsible for his actions, and in a fit of frenzy stabbed himself in the left side with a pair of scissors he snatched from the table. He sleeps quietly in the cemetery at Heidelberg, about eight miles from Melbourne.

Nine weeks after Wills's death, John Alexander Cuffe was born in Toowoomba, Queensland, on June 26, 1880. Opportunities in that State were severely restricted, with entry into full-scale interstate cricket decades away, but the youngster, at 17, got his name into *Wisden* by taking four wickets on his hometown's matting-over-concrete pitch against Stoddart's 1897–98 side. 'J. Cuffe, a left-handed medium-pace bowler, showed great promise' remarked the good book. The Englishmen messed about with their batting order, Hayward and Wainwright later saving the innings; but XVIII of Toowoomba still delighted the townsfolk by taking a lead in a drawn two-day match.

It would have thrilled the colt to have seen what Ranjitsinhji wrote about him in his book on the tour:

> Cuffe is a medium-pace left hand bowler, keeps an accurate length, and makes the ball on the matting wicket come back either way. The balls with which he dismissed Storer both times, and Wainwright in the first innings, being beauties. He bowled any number of good balls besides, and beat several of our best batsmen.

Jack Cuffe's ambition ignited, off he soon went to Sydney, where he eventually won selection in the New South Wales side, for one match, before the appeal of cricket every day of the season lured him to England, where he set about qualifying for Worcestershire, part of a medium-sized influx of Australians. Between 1903 and 1914 the county really got its money's worth.

They already had Ted Arnold, one of the most effective all-rounders of the Edwardian age. Cuffe, though, soon began to play a major role in sustaining the fortunes of a club which was emphatically outside the big league of Gloucestershire, Kent, Lancashire, Middlesex, Notts, Surrey, Sussex and Yorkshire. Cuffe took 716 wickets for Worcestershire at 25.52, bagging five or more in an innings 31 times, and in his 215 matches he scored 7404 runs at 22.78, with four centuries,

Jack Cuffe — from Queensland to Worcester to make his name.

the highest being 145 against Hampshire at Bournemouth in 1905 (he batted right-hand).

His slow-medium swervers harvested 9 for 38 against Yorkshire at Bradford in 1907, the team group photograph for that season showing Cuffe standing with protective scarf and coat, beneath straw boater at a happy angle. That same summer, having taken five wickets in each innings at Gloucester (as did Arnold), in the return match at Worcester, Cuffe featured in a stand which was still a Worcestershire record over 80 years later.

Their first three wickets fell for 20, before the classical batsmanship of R. E. Foster put the Gloucestershire bowling well and truly to the sword. His 144 came in almost even time, but just when the visitors must have felt they were working their way through the order, Cuffe (81 not out in two hours) and Dick Burrows (making his first major century) put on 181 for the ninth wicket.

In 1910 Cuffe not only took a hat-trick against Hampshire at Bournemouth, but returned 9 for 5 against Glamorgan in a match not granted first-class status. There was rain about at Cardiff, and Cuffe was not close to unplayable so much as untouchable. Eight of his victims were bowled, the other stumped by the deliciously named Worcestershire wicketkeeper Gaukrodger. The Welsh county were all out for 36, and the Australian would hardly have raised a sweat, having needed no more than 49 balls to carry out his demolition work.

He did the double the following season, 1911, making 1054 runs and trapping 110 wickets, 14 of them against suffering Gloucestershire again, this time at Dudley, staging its first county match. He got Jessop cheaply twice, and finished with 8 for 41 in the second innings, this on a surface good enough three years later to serve as a platform for Frank Foster's triple-century. Cuffe's superb all-round efforts that summer helped Worcestershire to rise from fourteenth to second in the County Championship, their best until 1964. But still they struggled financially, and it was only a grand bazaar that saved them from extinction before the 1912 season began.

The team photo for 1911 shows Jack Cuffe looking somewhat less suave than before, in cap and turtleneck sweater, the heavy garment flapping loosely halfway down his thighs. The 1914 group, however, had him restored to immaculate smartness, seated in the front now as senior professional, striped blazer neat as a uniform. That winter, the 1914–18 war having broken out like a hideous thunderstorm, Cuffe played the last of his 10 seasons of football for Glossop, during which time he had played in 279 matches. His county cricket was finished, too, the war having cut it short when he was 34 and still playing well enough to head the Worcestershire bowling averages, the club once again having avoided financial extinction only narrowly.

League cricket followed for Jack Cuffe, and then, at 44, he donned the umpire's white coat from 1925 to 1927. By 1931 life looked very different for him. He was 50, and his achievements on the cricket field were already not only a generation behind, but somehow sealed off by the dreadful years of war. All those hard-won honours—the century at Lord's for Worcestershire against MCC in 1908 perhaps in a sense the proudest of them all—were almost forgotten except unto himself and ardent Worcester spectators.

On April 30, 1931 the popular and rumbustious Somerset Australian Sammy Woods died in Taunton of cancer. Sixteen days later, on May 16, Jack Cuffe's body was found in the River Trent at Burton-on-Trent. Twelve days earlier he had taken up the position of coach at Repton School, where J. H. Human was the captain and star batsman. Fred Tate, the old Sussex and England player, took Cuffe's place.

The obituaries were not over-indulgent, which may have had something to do with the fact that he was Australian, a player with unglamorous Worcestershire, and a suicide. There was no real attempt to cover it up. Some references used the favourite and foggy stock phrase 'tragic circumstances', but the death certificate verifies the fact: 'John Alexander Cuffe, of No. 23 Victory Road, Little Lever, near Bolton, Lancashire, professional cricketer: drowning due to throwing himself into a river—suicide whilst temporarily insane. No post mortem.' He had been a very competent cricketer, and Queensland, at least, will have shed a tear.

At least two other Queensland cricketers took their own lives. A couple of years after Cuffe drowned himself, Bruce Vincent Suche, a Sydney-born left-hand batsman and right-arm fast-medium bowler, killed himself by taking poison in Townsville, the northern coastal town where he lived and played cricket. He was only 27.

Suche had done well in the selection matches, Country v. Metropolitan, in 1931 (5 for 62) and 1932 (5 for 45 and 30 not out in Country's all-out 82: teenage legspin/googly bowler Jack Govan taking 8 for 20 and 8 for 30 in the match), and in the Easter 1931 match against Kippax's all-star team his bowling had earned praise from the New South Wales skipper.

Suche played twice for Queensland, his debut coming in November 1931 in the famous match at Brisbane in which Aboriginal Eddie Gilbert bowled like lightning (he was no-balled for throwing in the next match) to dismiss New South Wales batsmen Wendell Bill and Don Bradman for ducks and Alan Fairfax for 5, and with Alan Kippax removed to hospital after being hit on the head by 'Pud' Thurlow, the visitors were staggering in their reply to Queensland's impoverished 109 (Suche, batting at No. 9, caught by Bradman for 6). Stan McCabe then embarked on what he always regarded as his best innings, an unbeaten 229 which ranked with his three sparkling Test innings for Australia in subsequent years at Sydney, Johannesburg and Trent Bridge. Jack Fingleton made 93, New South Wales totalled 432 (Suche 0 for 50 off 14 eight-ball overs), and Queensland were routed again, this time for 85 (Suche c & b Bill Hunt for 12, third-top score) to lose by an innings.

In Suche's other match for Queensland, a year later, things hardly improved. This time New South Wales had first use of the Brisbane pitch and amassed 602, McCabe making 91, Kippax 179, Bill 80, Hird 106, Oldfield 46. Opening the bowling with Thurlow, Suche toiled through 26 eight-ball overs and took 1 for 133. Batting at No. 9 again, he was caught by Fingleton off the irresistible O'Reilly for 15, and was there at the end with 6 not out in the follow-on as New South Wales tied up another innings victory.

Not everyone can claim to have played in just two first-class matches and lost them both by an innings. Poor Suche died five months later, on Easter Monday, April 14, 1933, six weeks after Hammond had dispatched the final ball of the turbulent Bodyline Test series for six.

Nine months later, as fate would have it, was born Barry Fisher, destined to be the most successful of the hundreds of young fast bowlers in the late 1940s and early 1950s who passionately imitated the powerful, rolling, accelerating, round-arm, pinpoint fast-bowling action of Ray Lindwall. Fisher, born in Brisbane on January 20, 1934, was the son of a Sheffield Shield cricketer, his father, Alec (1908–1968), playing for Queensland three times soon after the birth of his son. Barry, who played variously for Western Suburbs, South Brisbane, and Colts, won his first Queensland cap on New Year's Day 1955, at Sydney, just short of his twenty-first birthday, and took 8 for 128 in the match. His opportunity had come through Lindwall's absence, playing for Australia against England in the Melbourne Test. It was the great fast bowler's first season with his adopted State, Queensland.

Fisher lost his place when Lindwall returned, and played in only the opening fixture in 1955–56, at the Gabba, taking 0 for 50 against New South Wales and falling lbw to Benaud for a duck. He didn't play for Queensland at all in 1956–57, and must have wondered at his prospects, but he forced his way back the following season, and though his captain, Lindwall, and Jim Bratchford took the new ball, Fisher was usually first change, and came out on top of his State's Shield bowling with 18 wickets at 23.27, a few points above his hero. He also helped cement his place in the side by scoring 103 from the No. 9 berth in Queensland's hopeless second innings against Victoria at Melbourne. Life was looking up.

In 1958–59 Barry Fisher's promise was recognised by selection in an Australian XI to play Peter May's MCC side at Sydney, and he hung some distinguished names to his honours board by getting the wickets of Peter Richardson, Raman Subba Row, Jim Laker, and, in the second innings, May himself just after he'd posted his second century of the match. But Australia was too well stocked with fast bowlers—some of them with not the purest of actions, though Lindwall, 37, was still around—to call Fisher up for Test cricket, though had he done something exceptional in the Queensland v. MCC match which followed, he might just have been lucky.

The closest he was to get was the Australian '2nd XI' which toured New Zealand in February/March 1960, under Ian Craig's leadership. Fisher played in the first and fourth representative matches, taking 3 for 54 at Wellington, where he captured the illustrious wicket of Bert Sutcliffe.

In 1960–61 he paid over 50 for each of his 19 wickets, but had an innings of 81 to compensate; yet the following

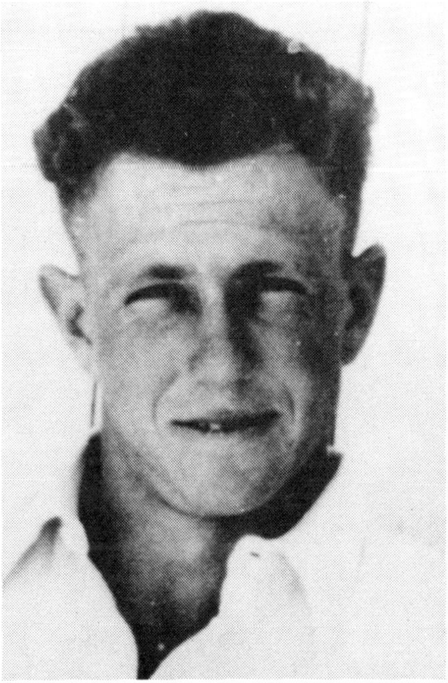

Barry Fisher —
in Lindwall's shadow.

year brought an uplift in form, and he began taking wickets again, beating with swing and pace men of the calibre of Harvey, Lawry, Booth, Favell, Davidson, Benaud and Barry Shepherd, perhaps inspired at sharing the new ball now not with Lindwall but with another great fast bowler in Wes Hall, the West Indian.

Fisher's team-mates thought him 'strange' in some ways. While he took his lean times with fair stoicism, he never got excited about success. A session producing three wickets for him would find him calmly sitting down and unlacing his boots. Jack McLaughlin said, years later, that he only ever sensed Barry Fisher upset or disturbed once, and that was when he failed to win the captaincy of Queensland.

He continued to make useful runs at No.7 or 8, and in 1962–63 he took 5 for 18 (4 for 1 in a spell) at Sydney to dismiss New South Wales for the record low score of 82. In the next match he could manage no better than 1 for

105; such is the game's treachery to the spirit. Then came the wickets of Garry Sobers and Ian Chappell, and at Perth he blasted through Western Australia's line-up with 6 for 41, which were to remain the best figures of his career. At Melbourne, on the way back, he took no wicket for 93 as Victoria piled up 633 for 4, Redpath 261, Cowper 141 not out. Hall's figures of 1 for 158 must have comforted him. A little bit of history came Fisher's way when he ended Doug Walters' first innings in first-class cricket, bowling the 17-year-old for 1.

And that was the end of Fisher's big cricket . . . until, five seasons later, when Queensland called him up again at the age of almost 34, to play against the traditional enemy, New South Wales, home and away. In the Brisbane match he made a satisfying 37 not out and took the hard-to-come-by wicket of Bob Simpson, but at Sydney he finished with 0 for 111, Simpson this time making 277.

Barry Fisher had played 50 times for his State, giving a ghostly impression of the rhythmic Lindwall action several years after the master bowler had disappeared from view, and trying like mad with ball and bat—despite recurring shoulder problems—for a Queensland side which invariably finished low in the Shield table. He finished with 126 wickets at 32.15 in his 56 first-class matches, and made 1369 runs at 21.06, with that solitary early century.

He moved down to the northern rivers area of New South Wales to run a pub. He had a conspicuously attractive wife and three or four children. Soon after the marriage broke up, Barry Fisher shot himself. His death occurred on April 6, 1980, in Inverell. He was 46. Perhaps because of the absence of an immediate announcement, he did not make it into *Wisden*'s obituary section.

Queensland team-mate Ern Toovey compares Fisher in size with modern-day Australian fast bowler Greg Campbell, and goes on to say:

> It's difficult to describe Barry. I personally liked him. He was a very competitive player. I like this in a person as

it means one always gives one's best. Having been an opponent of Barry's at club level and a team-mate at Shield level, this was most evident. At the same time, he was not a demonstrative player. When he took those eight wickets in his first Shield match he took his success calmly. He seemed surprised at our congratulations. Personally I think he was hurt in his early years when his father and mother's marriage broke up. Naturally, when history repeated itself with his marriage I think life must have lost some of its drive.

11

Across the Tasman

At least two New Zealand Test cricketers have committed suicide. On January 10, 1966, Fen Cresswell, who played in three Test matches against England, was found dead at his home in Blenheim, a town at the top of the south island, a shotgun at his side. Fifty years old, he had been suffering from a 'severe illness' for some time.

He was an extremely popular man, a late discovery in cricket terms, having surfaced with enough wickets and a strong enough pattern of accuracy in the pre-tour trials to win a place on New Zealand's 1949 tour of England. His brother Arthur, a Wellington fast-medium bowler, who had been regarded as a certainty to tour, was not invited.

George Fenwick Cresswell, born at Wanganui, on the north island, on March 22, 1915, was thus already 34 when the English venture got under way. For years he had been a success at minor level, starting at Marlborough College and then playing for Marlborough province, in the Hawke Cup, building a reputation for his medium-pace to slow inswing bowling and steady length. He had the shortest of run-ups and bowled chest-on to the batsman, left arm playing no part, cutting rather than spinning the ball, bowling just fast enough to deter any but the fleetest-footed of batsmen from going down the pitch to him. His accuracy and 'unflappability' were a form of torture, though he smiled readily with twinkling eyes and probably had the perfect bowler's temperament.

Some of his friends called him The Ferret because his batting ability was so woeful that he went in after any rabbits. Others called him 'Fritz' for his habit of standing to attention, like some Prussian guard, before trotting in to bowl.

His maiden first-class match was the tour trial at Christchurch, and though he did little there, he had already impressed with his bowling in the earlier trials, and was soon embarking ship for England, the souvenir booklet listing him as 'electrical hardware merchant'.

He had a good tour, taking second-most wickets (62) at the second-lowest average (26.10), that tally being exactly half of his eventual total of first-class wickets, 124. He picked up 21 wickets (including Gimblett's) before the first Test, but New Zealand's bowling in the first three Tests was carried by Cowie, Cave, Burtt and Rabone.

As July turned to August it was not only Cresswell's infectious laughter that reminded Walter Hadlee and the rest

Fenwick Cresswell — 'I bowled him!' when he dismissed Compton.

of the team that he was still around. Against Yorkshire, at Bramall Lane, he took 5 for 30, and at St Helen's his inswingers and leg-cutters accounted for six Glamorgan wickets for 21. With Rabone unable to bowl, Cresswell was called up for his Test debut at The Oval in the fourth and final three-day Test match, all of which, to New Zealand's immense satisfaction, were to be drawn.

Going in last, as was normal, Fen Cresswell, left-handed as a batsman, made 12 not out, which was to be his career-highest (he scored 89 runs in his brief first-class career and took 124 wickets). Bert Sutcliffe (88) and Verdun Scott (60) had made 121 for the first wicket, and with Merv Wallace scoring 55 and valuable contributions down the order, the Kiwis reached 345. Cresswell now took the new ball with Jack Cowie and plugged away for 41.2 overs mainly at the leg stump—slipping in the odd leg-roller—to take the wickets of Hutton (206 in five hours), Simpson (68), Edrich (100), Compton (13), Brown (21) and Wright (0)—6 for 168. For what it was worth—and he would have laughed about it—it placed Fen Cresswell at the top of New Zealand's bowling averages for the series.

He had enjoyed the tour, and had emerged as one of its popular participants, radiating his obvious pleasure, tall (5 ft 10 ins), with dark, glossy hair, parted near the centre, peculiar of bowling action in a Lala Amarnath sort of way, an elusive 'ferret', cheating the bowlers on all but four of the 15 occasions on which he went to the crease. Against Gloucestershire, he and Martin Donnelly put on 45 runs for the tenth wicket, the graceful left-handed Donnelly making 44 of them, the other a leg-bye.

Back in New Zealand, his ripe form continued. In what may be referred to loosely as an 'unofficial Test' against Australia at Dunedin, in March 1950, he took 8 for 100 in the Australians' innings of 299, starting with the wicket of Jim Burke, and numbering Bill Brown and the young Alan Davidson among his tally. He also had Don Tallon caught—after the wicketkeeper had smashed 116 to give his side a lead of 68.

Davidson, Len Johnson and Jack Iverson then used the conditions well to confound the New Zealanders, who found themselves nine down for 67, still a run behind, with nine minutes remaining, and Cresswell going in as last man—no doubt with a smile on his face. His 2 not out to save the match probably gave him as much pleasure as his eight wickets.

That 1949–50 season saw him playing for Wellington in the Plunket Shield, and winning the coveted Winsor Cup for bowling, but the following season found him with Central Districts, for whom he took 32 wickets at only 15.93. He also played in two more Tests, against Freddie Brown's Englishmen. Even more success came his way.

In the first, at Christchurch, after a Sutcliffe century had set up an imposing 417 for 8, New Zealand had to field out to an England innings of 550, with Washbrook, Simpson, Compton and Brown making half-centuries, Trevor Bailey his only Test century, and Doug Wright recording his highest Test score of 45. The innings lasted over 12 hours, into which 221.3 overs were fed, 43 from Hayes, 56.3 from leg-spinner Moir, 49 from left-armer Burtt, and 34 from Cresswell, who finished with 2 for 75.

And yet the most famous ball in that match was delivered by Cresswell to Cyril Washbrook, hit him on the pad, and gave rise to an appeal which umpire Tonkinson granted. New Zealand captain Walter Hadlee, however, asked him to alter his decision and call Washbrook back, for the ball had fairly obviously touched the bat first. Washbrook was duly recalled, and all kinds of recriminations flew. Hadlee was 'misguided'; Washbrook was wrong to show dissent; the umpire was incompetent. Had not Cresswell been such a popular fellow, he too undoubtedly would have copped some of the blame for an incident which exploded with unexpected nastiness out of innocently Corinthian motives. Alex Bannister wrote that only one lbw appeal out of 14 had been upheld in New Zealand's innings, whereas matters were rather different when England batted: 'The first appeal from New Zealand brought an unhesitating response, although it was clear Washbrook had hit the ball hard. It was high and outside the leg stump.'

He further cited an earlier run-out appeal when Statham's throw broke the wicket with Hadlee's bat in the air and still a yard from the crease. Bannister proclaimed it one of the 'most lamentable' days of Test cricket he had seen.

The match was drawn, but in a low-scoring second Test at Wellington, England won by six wickets. Still, Cresswell was successful. He took three tailend wickets for 18 off 15 overs in the first innings and dismissed Hutton and Compton for 31 off 18 overs in the second. It was in this Test that Alex Moir deliberately bowled consecutive overs, unbeknown to opponents or umpires, before and after the tea interval. Cresswell, in his final afternoon in Test cricket, having bowled the great Compton, completely forgot himself. New Zealand's veteran cricket-writer Dick Brittenden remembered the incident:

> Propriety probably demanded—from a New Zealander—that after such a success he should gaze modestly at the sky, or the turf. Cresswell went hopping down the pitch on one foot, saying, 'I bowled him! I bowled him!' in a voice which startled senior government servants in their distant offices into a panic of activity.

Fen Cresswell finished with a creditable 13 Test wickets at 22.46 against strong opposition. But at 36, being a late discovery, and carrying a back problem, there was little cricket left for him. He was to play only three further matches for Central Districts. Brittenden comments:

> It was sad that he had so little first-class cricket after so long a wait for recognition. For he loved the game. Just a year or so ago (this written in 1961) he went to play in a friendly match in Hawke's Bay but said he could not bowl: his back still worries him, it seems. However, he was prevailed upon to have an over, and finished by bowling three. His lively account of the occasion was given with an infectious enthusiasm—how the cutter 'still worked', how he had advised second slip he was about to bowl it,

> how the ball cut back across the batsman, how second slip dropped the catch. It all delighted him, and that was his way. An unforgettable character, with unforgettable and utterly captivating attributes.

How similarly that tale compares with the one concerning Aubrey Faulkner when he too found cricket in later life too painful—but irresistible.

Whatever the unhappy, even derogatory, opinions which have to be recorded at the end of Noel Harford's story, the recollection of an Indian cricket enthusiast shows, at least, what once had been. Writing in Calcutta-based *Sportsworld* magazine in 1988, Raju Mukherji remembered an apparently trivial incident in the Calcutta Test match, India v. New Zealand, of late December 1955. Mukherji was then only four years old:

> To the man in cream flannels on the boundary, I offered a piece of gum. The handsome face eased into a smile and ruffled my hair. Noel Harford may not be among the greatest of international cricketers but, without an iota of doubt, one of cricket's outstanding ambassadors, with an appropriate gesture, he converted a tot's interest into a lifelong passion.

Much is revealed in the way cricketers treat youngsters. Harford that day was evidently feeling at ease with the world. It was good to be back in the New Zealand Test team for his fourth Test after a chapter of extremes in the first three on this 1955–56 tour of Pakistan and India. He had scored 93 at the Bagh-i-Jinnah ground, Lahore, in his maiden Test innings, fighting for almost two hours for his first 50 on the turf pitch in, for a 25-year-old newcomer, the strangest of circumstances. Then, after fielding out to a massive Pakistan innings of 561, during which his medium-pace bowling was not called upon by skipper Harry Cave, Harford, going in second time round at No. 7, one position down, completed a distinguished first Test by scoring 64 and helping set up a teasing target. Pakistan reached it—116 in 110 minutes—only because Cave kept up the tempo of overs (27 were bowled), the crowd appreciating the rejection of negative tactics. The story shames many a modern Test captain.

Noel Harford's satisfaction was soon overtaken by dismal failure: 0 and 1 on coir matting in the Dacca Test, and 4—lbw to the leg-spinning wizard Gupte—when the Indian series began at Hyderabad. For all his ability to drive and pull, Harford often floundered in defence against the spun slow ball.

He was dropped for the Bombay and Delhi Tests but restored for the fourth, at Eden Gardens, where his chance encounter with the tiny Raju Mukherji warmed both their hearts. Harford made only 25 and 1 in that Calcutta Test, when New Zealand's first-innings lead of 204 was buried by an Indian second innings of 438 for 7, and the visitors ended up fighting for survival at 75 for 6. He sat out the final Test, at Madras,

Noel Harford — 'ambassador' whose life turned sour.

when Mankad and Roy started off with 413 for India's first wicket, and must have subscribed as heartily as any of the other players to Cave's end-of-tour summary: 'I think we have now learned how to play big cricket rather than Saturday-afternoon cricket.'

Had his luck and form held up, Harford might have been part of New Zealand's first-ever Test victory, against West Indies at Auckland in March 1956, but the remainder of his eight-Test career followed over two years later, when he was selected to tour England with John Reid's New Zealand squad. It was a disaster. The first four Tests were lost, three of them by innings margins, and the fifth was a merciful draw only through serious interference by rain.

Noel Sherwin Harford, born in Winton, Southland, on August 20, 1930 (11 days before Faulkner died in London), was 27 at the start of the tour, and at his peak as a batsman. Although it was only a social kind of one-day match, the first venture to the middle, at The Oval on April 17, gave him a reassuring launching with an innings of 105 in 72 minutes, during which he hit three successive balls from former Kiwi leg-spinner Bill Merritt (then in his fiftieth year) for six. A pair of fifties in the MCC match at Lord's and he reached his maiden first-class century against Oxford University, 158 in three-and-three-quarter hours. Going in now at No. 3, he was a certainty for the first Test at Edgbaston. He made only 9 and 23 in a defeat which drew sympathy from the English press and public. England were enjoying one of their most fruitful periods, and the conditions, for most of the summer as it turned out, perfectly suited their attack—bowlers such as Lock (34 wickets in the series—bent arm and all—at a ridiculous 7.47), Laker (17 wickets at 10.18), Trueman (15 at 17.07), Bailey, Statham and Loader.

New Zealand were rolled over for 47 and 74 in the Lord's Test, Harford contributing nothing in the first innings, falling to Laker, and 3 in the second, caught off Lock. It was even worse at Headingley. He bagged a pair. As his side made a pathetic 67 and 129, Harford was caught by Cowdrey off Laker and lbw to Lock without a run. At Old Trafford in the fourth Test he made only 2 and 4, having notched 49 against Middlesex at Lord's between Tests, and although he came back to life again with a 54 against a Lock-less Surrey and 127 against a fairly strong Glamorgan attack at Swansea, he was left out of the final Test, at The Oval, a decision which must have been seen as humane. He had lost any chance of elevating the grim series record of 41 runs in eight Test innings, but the prospect of no more humiliation before the England bowling must have been a great relief. The nightmare—and, as it happened, his Test career—was over.

He completed his 1000 runs on the tour, a reassuring achievement aided towards the end by an 80 against a top-line A. E. R. Gilligan's XI, including George Tribe (8 for 75), at Hastings, and he finished fourth in the tour averages with 26.02. But the 'stock auctioneer' chosen by the *Cricket Almanack of New Zealand* as its Batsman of the Year at the end of the English expedition had seen his Test average eroded from 27 to 15. Best, perhaps, to dwell for the rest of his life, if dwell he must, on that wonderful Test debut at Lahore, and his 157 runs in that match.

Harford had only one further season with Central Districts, but, continuing to play meanwhile for Manawatu, he reappeared in Auckland's colours in 1963–64, last playing for that province in 1966–67, when he was 36. In 74 first-class matches he had scored 3149 runs at an average of 27.62, with three centuries, and he held 39 catches and took 18 wickets.

He had always spread his sporting talents. He played indoor basketball for New Zealand, touring Australia, and he had had to seek clearance before undertaking the cricket tour of Pakistan and India. He was also good at snooker.

Later years saw vast changes in the man. He lost the sight of an eye when a beer-bottle top flew up into it. When conversation turned to his cricket career, a bitterness emerged, aimed chiefly at those who were responsible for what he saw as erratic selection policies. A friend said, many years later, that Harford was seen, without question, as an attractive batsman—'but you wondered about his guts'.

He became part of a school of hard drinkers. His weight reared up to 16 stone. There were rumours that his attractive wife suffered violently at his hands. There were financial problems. He misappropriated funds from the company, and was sacked in disgrace. When he lost his place as a radio and television commentator he took it very badly.

On March 30, 1981, Noel Harford secured a hosepipe from the exhaust of his car, switched on the engine, and let the carbon monoxide fumes kill him. He was 50. A week later his son was married, saying, 'Dad would have wanted it.'

The little boy from Calcutta, now grown to manhood, may not have reconciled matters quite so easily.

A promising New Zealander was lost in July 1952 when John Edgar Hollywood, having failed his exams in veterinary science, threw himself under a tram in Sydney. He was only 26, and had played six times for Auckland in first-class cricket in 1947–48 and 1948–49, also playing against the visiting Fijians, and taking 11 wickets in the latter season, a modest tally which still happened to be the record for the province at that time, shared with Jack Cowie. Hollywood, born in Auckland on May 23, 1926, was a giant, 6 ft 5 ins, with a high arm action which gave his fast-medium deliveries awkward bounce. When he took off to take a caught-and-bowled off the bat of Stewart Dempster the veteran batting ace could only gasp 'I don't believe it!' Hollywood held the ball at least 9 ft above the ground. His cricket lapsed when his studies began, and with the strong ambition to become a vet, John Hollywood entered Sydney University, hopes high. The inner soul was fragile. Failure was crippling. Perhaps feeling himself isolated, hurt, unable to confide, he died in one tragic, impulsive moment.

Yet another New Zealander, John Arthur Rawdon Blandford, of an earlier generation, destroyed himself by jumping from the window of his flat in Auckland on Christmas Eve 1954, having got himself into desperate straits through gambling. Born in Dunedin on January 31, 1913, he went on to play 15 first-class matches as a wicketkeeper and attractive middle-order batsman, though his debut for Wellington in 1932–33 had been as an opening bat, Ken James, New Zealand's wicketkeeper, being in the side. In his second big match Blandford made a pair of noughts. In this match, at Eden Park, Wellington actually had three New Zealand representative wicketkeepers in the team, for Eric Tindill, soon to earn Test honours, and Blandford and James were in the side. Blandford played for his country in 1935–36 against the MCC touring team. These were not official Test matches, but all who played were gratified to a high degree, with Jack Blandford, filling in for Tindill (who was in England with the All-Black Rugby side), having earned a place in the national team with a 62 and two catches and three stumpings in Wellington's match against Canterbury, won by two runs at the Basin Reserve.

Against MCC at Wellington he scored an important 40 in 90 minutes in an eighth-wicket stand of 104 in a drawn match, later catching Mitchell-Innes and stumping Jim Sims, and in the Auckland international he had another useful knock of 36, caught the MCC skipper Errol Holmes, and kept byes down to eight in an innings of 435. Like the other three matches in the series, it was drawn, but Blandford was replaced for the final match.

His opportunities continued to be limited by Tindill's presence, but the occasional representative match came his way, and he seldom failed, meanwhile keeping his dominant form in club cricket. He switched to Auckland in the first two seasons of wartime cricket, and before making five dismissals against Wellington, his old province, in his last first-class match, in 1940–41, he had contributed 58 not out, a year earlier, towards Auckland's record 693 for 9 against Canterbury at Eden Park, putting on 143 for the eighth wicket with Verdun Scott. Off he went to the war, playing cricket in Egypt, again with success, and left to reflect for the rest of his life how opportunities had been in such short ration. Yet he had seldom let himself or his side down. In Blandford's five seasons of first-class cricket spread over eight years he had averaged 20.47 with the bat and secured 17 catches and 12 stumpings.

New Zealand seems to have had more than its fair ration of suicides. Noel Vincent Burtt, brother of Test left-arm slow bowler Tom Burtt, was yet another. It happened just after the funeral of Tom's wife, and was the act of a man doomed by illness. Noel, also prominent in hockey and bowls, was a leg-spinner who played nine times for Canterbury either side of the war during a span of 12 seasons, and finished his first-class career in the trial match for the 1949 tour of England—upon which brother Tom was to be a considerable success. Shortly before he killed himself with car exhaust fumes in his garage, Noel Burtt, now 71, said to his old friend Walter Hadlee, 'I'm not a quitter, am I, Had?' He was given due reassurance. He died on February 27, 1983.

A few years earlier, also in Christchurch, on February 12, 1965, a tragic tale culminated in the suicide of William David Frame, a 32-year-old former Otago medium-pace bowler who had played in seven first-class matches in the two seasons 1955–56, and 1957–58, taking 26 wickets at only 15.92.

William David Frame — triple killer and suicide.

Geoff Wright, father of New Zealand Test captain John, remembered somewhat hazily in 1990 that Frame 'murdered somebody, committed suicide—and I caught him once in a match in Dunedin!' Further investigation was called for, and duly carried out, and it emerged that Frame had killed his 24-year-old girlfriend Marlene Parker and both her parents at their Papanui home around half-past-two in the morning on February 12, 1965. He had bought a .303 rifle in Christchurch the previous day, and had gone to the house in the early hours, firing seven shots through the window of Marlene's bedroom before bashing his way into the house, splitting the butt of the rifle in the process. There he found Harold Parker, 56, in the hall trying to telephone the police. Frame shot him, and then his wife Patricia, and, satisfied that Marlene (an identical twin) was dead, turned the gun on himself and shot himself through the head. Neighbours had alerted the police, who found a most gruesome scene awaiting them.

Several years on, in the early 1970s, cricket lost another identity in Christchurch when cricket commentator Jim Reid drove his car over a cliff. He had flown in RAF Lancasters during the war, and had recovered from serious head wounds to pursue a new life in New Zealand, where he was a car dealer whose Scottish voice became familiar to Kiwi radio listeners. Reid's death created an opening for a young broadcaster, Peter Williams, who was to become the face of New Zealand cricket on television from the 1980s.

12

Mysteries and Certainties

'A few of our batsmen committed suicide out there today,' lamented India's manager Bishan Bedi after his side's defeat by Australia in a one-day match at Christchurch, New Zealand, in March 1990, 'and if they want to go out and commit suicide tonight, I'm not going to stop them!'

The gregarious Sikh, most artistic of slow bowlers in the 1970s, was not being serious. His charm had been swamped by frustration and anger several times in the past. Had this tongue-in-cheek remark been acted upon by any of his players he would probably have taken the field himself in the next match—assuming trousers large enough to fit the middle-aged left-armer could have been found.

No West Indians (apart from one mentioned provisionally at the end of this chapter), no Pakistanis, and no Sri Lankans feature in this thesis; and the only Indian Test cricketers are misted by uncertainty. Baqa Jilani, for instance, has long been regarded as a suicide, but the great Vijay Merchant told statistician Anandji Dossa, who told young writer Mudar Patherya, who told the author that Jilani had suffered an epileptic fit, lost his balance on the verandah of his house in Jullundur, and fallen to his death. He was an uncle of Imran Khan.

Mohammad Baqa Khan Jilani played in only one Test match, the final Test of India's 1936 tour of England, at The Oval, when his medium-pace leg-cutters ran hard up against a Hammond double-century and 128 from Stan Worthington. The pair made 266 for England's fourth wicket. Baqa Jilani's 15 wicketless overs cost 55 runs, and he scored 4 not out at No. 10 and 12 batting at No. 5 in the second innings. It is suggested in Edward Docker's *History of Indian Cricket* that Jilani, who was one of the anti-Nayudu faction in the tour party, earned his place in the Oval Test side by insulting Nayudu at breakfast in front of the rest of the team.

He did little of note in the tour overall, apart from 113, the only first-class century of his career, against Leicestershire. That promising innings, in May, was followed by 24 not out in the second innings and then 0 and 4 against Middlesex, 4 and 0 against Essex, 2 and 2 against Yorkshire, and 0 against Notts, with only one wicket from his limited bowling in these matches, which would all have rendered him one of the unhappiest members of an unhappy, divided team.

Baqa Jilani, a Punjab University product, played for Northern India between 1934–35 (in which season he performed a hat-trick against Southern Punjab at Amritsar,

Baqa Jilani —
was it an epileptic fit?

the first in the Ranji Trophy competition) and 1938–39, averaging 18.28 with the bat in all first-class cricket and taking 81 wickets at 19.57. His best figures were 7 for 37, and there should be no doubting his class: Macartney called him a 'champion'.

His end came on July 2, 1941—18 days short of this thirtieth birthday—and may forever be shrouded in mystery. It would have heaped sadness upon sadness for India's cricket-lovers during wartime, for the fast bowler and big-hitter Amar Singh had died only the year before, also aged 29.

Cotar Ramaswami, another 1936 England tourist, decided, as he approached the age of 90, that he was too much of a burden on his family, and tried several times to end his life in the early 1980s. In letters to his grandchildren and nephews he told of attempts at drowning near his home at Adyar, South Madras, and swallowing tablets. India's oldest surviving Test cricketer finally walked off on the evening of October 14, 1985, wearing white shorts, blue T-shirt and slippers, seemingly never to return. Depressed at the gradual loss of hearing and the inability to live the kind of life he had known and enjoyed for so many decades, the old man vanished, doubtless caring little whether he would succumb to the deprivations confronting an aged wanderer, and even wishing it upon himself.

But four years later no body had yet been found, and police maintained that he must still be alive. There had been reported sightings in Ootacamund, in the Nilgiri Hills, and in Tiruvannamalai, 100 miles south of Madras, and those who have to attend to such matters were still unable to enter a death date for a very fine sportsman of the earlier years of the century.

Ramaswami remains the only man to have played Test cricket and Davis Cup tennis. A left-hander, he played in two Davis Cup ties for India in 1922, and his cricket peak was reached when he was 40 (protesting that he was lucky to have been chosen, being too bulky and slow) when he made the 1936 tour of England. There he played in the Old

Cotar Ramaswami — Test cricketer and Davis Cup tennis player.

Trafford and Oval Tests and did remarkably well. Against an attack containing Gubby Allen, Alf Gover, Hammond, Robins and Verity he scored 40 and 60 at Manchester (after Merchant and Mushtaq Ali had opened with 203). In the Oval Test, Ramaswami made 29 and 41 not out, which took him to the top of India's Test batting for the series: 170 runs at 56.67. He had scored 127 not out against Lancashire at Old Trafford, and finished with 737 runs on the tour at a respectable 30.71, having learned during that summer to curb his wilder instincts during his first few overs at the crease.

It was not his first taste of England. Born in Madras on June 16, 1896, he had gone on to Cambridge after having played his first Indian first-class match in 1915–16. A 92 for Indians against Europeans in the Madras Presidency had signalled his cricket talent at 21, and his sporting passions must have been stirred when, in 1919, he found himself at Pembroke College alongside two future England cricket captains—and good fellows—in Arthur Gilligan and Percy Chapman.

Tennis won Ramaswami's full attention during his Cambridge summers, and he became a popular and successful figure on the English circuit. His Davis Cup appearances came at Beckenham, against Romania, and Bristol, against Spain, in 1922. A year later he won the South of England Grass Court Championship at Eastbourne.

When, approaching 40, he continued to show his worth as a batsman for Madras, he secured his place on the English tour, and went on to play domestic first-class cricket until he was 44. He also became his State's Deputy Director of Agriculture. Cricket administration followed: Test selector, manager of India's team in West Indies in 1952–53. He had a wealth of sporting tensions and pleasure behind him when he sat down to write *Ramblings of a Games Addict*, published in 1966.

Cotar Ramaswami was erect still and firm of handshake at 89, and only a month before his disappearance he had been seen chatting and joking with other cricket veterans at a Tamil Nadu Cricket Association function. There the memories must have swilled around at flood level, and he was happy, after a poignant fashion. At home, though, he felt ancient and useless, on a different wavelength to that of his son. He was in the proverbial position of a batsman who tries to get out, lofting the ball all over the field, but finding only empty spaces.

The Baroda dynasty is one of India's most prominent. Three of the 'clan' have played for India, H. G. Gaekwad in one Test, D. K. Gaekwad as captain, and A. D. Gaekwad, his son, in 40 Tests—scoring the then slowest double-century in first-class cricket with a 671-minute epic 201 against Pakistan at Jullundur in 1983. Lieutenant-Colonel Fatesingrao Gaekwad, as the Maharajah of Baroda ('Jackie' to his friends), was manager of the 1959 Indian team in England and two later teams in Pakistan. He had played Ranji Trophy cricket for Baroda as a 16-year-old, with 99 his highest score. Also a broadcaster, president of the Board of Control for Cricket in India, he was a member of the Indian parliament and gave much effort to the World Wildlife Fund. He also claimed membership of the 'Mile-High Club'. These are the better-known cricketing Gaekwads. On May 8, 1985, Prince Sayajirao

Pratapsinha Gaekwad of Baroda, youngest son of the last ruling maharajah, was found with his throat cut, apparently having committed suicide, at his villa in Cagnes-sur-Mer, in the south of France. He was 40.

The only other known casualty of this nature among Indian cricketers was Dorab E. Mody, brother of the top Parsee fast bowler R. E. Mody. Dorab himself was good enough to play regularly for the Parsees from colts level in 1892 onwards, and scored a plucky 36 and 39 against Lord Hawke's somewhat awesome team of amateur gentlemen at Bombay in December 1892 in a match gladly won by the Parsees, thanks also to the bowling of M. E. Pavri. Dorab Mody went on to enjoy his cricket for many a season, rising to the captaincy of the Parsees in 1911, when Dr Pavri and Dr Ranga were both unavailable. *Cricket* described his style as 'steady and careful, if somewhat cramped', with an effective scoring shot over cover point's head! He was 'energetic' in the field, said *Wisden*. He was 39 when, in May 1913, depressed beyond endurance by heavy financial losses in his business as a timber merchant, he threw himself out of a second-floor window.

Goodbye notes are usually proof enough; coroners' verdicts equally so. Doubt sometimes clouds the facts, however, as with the 'accidental death' returned on Ian Akers-Douglas, the stylish Kent amateur of the 1930s. Born in Kensington on November 16, 1909, and educated at Eton, he scored 158 against Harrow at Lord's when 18, and made plenty of runs at Oxford, yet missing a Blue. In 1933 he was British Open Rackets champion, by which time he had started contributing some attractive runs to Kent's wonderful batting line-up. The first of his two centuries was 123 against Hampshire at Portsmouth, but the second one, in 1934, was as spectacular as anything ever seen at Taunton, 100 in only 65 minutes off Somerset's despairing bowling. In 1936 he became Kent's vice-captain under Percy Chapman.

On December 16, 1952, Captain Akers-Douglas, 43, returned to his home in Frant, near Tunbridge Wells, and died in his garage from shotgun wounds. His son, now a film-maker but then only a boy, remembers hearing a loud bang and thinking it must have been a car backfiring. There was a second shot soon afterwards, and he has wondered ever since whether a man could shoot himself deliberately with a shotgun, and whether his father had tried to do so all the same, but succeeded only in disfiguring himself. Might his mother, who had rushed to the garage, have put her husband out of his terrifying misery? It remained a question which tormented him still, and though he wanted to know the truth, his aged mother would not talk about it. He believed his father was not the sort to commit suicide. Of so many who did so *without* shadow of doubt, this has been said.

Only the production of an official death certificate could convince former Oxford and Surrey cricketer and cricket-writer E. M. (Lyn) Wellings that, almost half-a-century earlier, L. P. Hedges had died from 'streptococial septicaemia' combined with 'influenza' in Cheltenham on January 12, 1933, and apparently was not a suicide. A junior schoolmaster at Cheltenham College, Lionel Hedges, only 32 at the time of his death (when Wellings was 23), had been a brilliant schoolboy batsman, with scores of 193, 176 and 163 while at Tonbridge. He made less of an impact at Oxford, but went on to play in 52 matches for Kent between 1919 and 1924, and then 30 times for Gloucestershire while teaching at Cheltenham, between 1926 and 1929. There was no comparison between his school average in his final year—86.50—and his later first-class average of 22.20, but he had four first-class centuries to his credit, and his fielding had been a joy to behold. Perhaps it was because of his relatively tender years at the time of his death and an occasionally perceived sense of let-down over the promise of youth having failed to blossom into adult cricket success on quite the expected scale that rendered it easy for his pupils and contemporaries, Wellings among them, to suppose—or even to be utterly convinced by the swell of rumour, aided by juvenile morbid romanticism—that Hedges took his own life. The certificate would seem to refute the suspicion; unless doctors can be wrong.

Rumours also ensued after the death of Raymond William George Emery, which was belatedly reported. A popular man of great local eminence in Auckland, his hometown, he had flown in the Battle of Britain and contributed much to New Zealand aviation, helping set up Auckland's international airport and having a roadway named after him. Ray Emery's two Test appearances came when he was 36, against the 1951–52 West Indians, and he failed to reach double figures in three of his four innings, all as opener, though he scored 28 in the second innings at Christchurch. In the second Test, at Auckland, he was given a bowl during West Indies' innings of 546 for 6, and got both Worrell and Walcott out soon after each had reached 100. Emery was playing for Canterbury at this stage, and enjoying his best season (433 runs at 72.16 in the Plunket Shield). He had made his first-class debut for Auckland before the war, and during the conflict, between sorties, he played at Lord's, one appearance being for the RAF. In all first-class cricket between 1936–37 and 1953–54 Ray Emery made 1177 runs at 29.43 and took 22 wickets, and when he died in Auckland on December 18, 1982 he was 67.

Also unproven, but freely suspected as suicidal, was the death of Pakistan radio commentator Nadir Hussain in his Karachi flat in 1988. A bachelor in his early fifties, he was a heavy drinker and suspected of being on drugs too. A friend would say no more than that he 'had a disturbed life'.

One Yorkshire player of the 1890s may have been a suicide, having fallen from an express train near Hull. Benjamin Charles Bolton played as an amateur, a fast bowler, in four first-class matches in 1890 and 1891, and was no journeyman in that he took 5 for 40 against Sussex at Hove in 1890, having earlier taken 4 for 85 at Derby, and, before that, 8 for 26 in a non-first-class match against Warwickshire at Halifax. Limited opportunities, maximum return. Born in Cottingham in 1862, Bolton met his death in November 1910, when he was 48. The question lingers: how difficult is it to avoid accidental death while travelling in an express train?

In much more recent times, Tom Hall, whose death is

classified as 'accidental' on his death certificate, is thought by several of those who knew him to the last to have taken his own life. At the age of 53, this fast-medium bowler for Combined Services, Derbyshire, Somerset, MCC, and Norfolk, died after a fall from a moving train at Arlesey, Bedfordshire, on April 21, 1984. The certificate gives as cause of death 'multiple injuries' and 'hypertension', and two inquests were held.

Hall, who had a boat-building business at Rockland St Mary, Norfolk, had certainly had big financial worries just before his death. He had started his working life on the railways at Derby, shovelling coal into the locomotives as an engineering apprentice, and amazing his friends by turning up at the hunt ball a few hours later resplendent in white tie and tails. He had been born in Durham on August 19, 1930, was educated at Uppingham, and played for Derbyshire as an amateur, a useful fast bowler who enjoyed his cricket, as Donald Carr recalls, and was always keen to do well. Between

Tom Hall — a case of 'hypertension'.

1949 and 1952 he was chosen 28 times for Derbyshire and took 70 wickets at 26.89, with 5 for 57 his best figures.

With so much high-class seam bowling at Derbyshire, Thomas Auckland Hall moved over to Somerset, who were glad of his services in 21 Championship matches in 1953 during which he took 56 wickets at 32.05 and pushed his highest score up to 69 not out. But he was hardly called upon in 1954, when Somerset were bottom again. While with the West Country club he also met and married the stepdaughter of the secretary. When they settled in Norwich, Hall played for Norfolk. In 1955 he had returned his best figures in first-class cricket, 5 for 50 for MCC against Yorkshire at Scarborough. He and Trueman got each other out in that game. Hall also played once for the Gentlemen against the Players, in 1951 at Scarborough, and had the supreme pleasure, less than three weeks after his twenty-first birthday, of claiming Len Hutton's wicket in both innings. His final first-class match was for Free Foresters against Oxford University, and he took eight wickets in it.

Tom Hall was a well-liked man, and his funeral was heavily attended.

The list grows, but perhaps it begins to reveal that, much as cricket means to some men, there is a multiplicity of reasons for self-murder. The earliest, in the cricket context, to be recorded is that of Thomas Ballard in 1787. The cause remains a mystery. He was a butcher in Pluckley, west of Ashford in Kent, and in that year of the foundation of MCC he killed himself in his slaughterhouse after 'being at cricket the same evening'.

Surely that man's passion for his team's success could not even be measured against that of an American football fan 202 years later, who delayed reporting his wife Mary's death until he had seen the Superbowl final on television at his mother-in-law's house. Mary Holloway had shot herself in the head after she and husband Gary had had an argument. So important was the football match to him that it was several hours before he felt the need to report the shooting to the police. Chief investigator Jim Mabe could only shrug and say quietly, 'I can't explain this wild story. That game was so boring.'

One does not have to be a full-time professional cricketer to have the game flowing through the bloodstream, and therefore of capital importance. For Desmond Donnelly, MP, it was food and drink. Like so many men of eminence, all his aspirations would gladly have been wrapped up and tossed into a furnace had he been given the talent to bat in a Test match and display skill of the highest category before a massive crowd of doting spectators. Donnelly, though, was a duffer at cricket.

Cricket's debt to him springs from his enthusiasm and energy, which saw the establishment of the British Empire XI, a huge fund-raiser during the Second World War. His contemporary, journalist Reg Hayter, says, 'Desmond was *not* a cricketer. He couldn't bat or bowl. But he was a walking *Wisden*, and he had the cheek of a highwayman.'

Born in India in 1920, the son of a tea-planter of Irish ancestry, Donnelly was educated at Bembridge School, Isle of Wight. He was no more than 20 when he began raising

Desmond Donnelly — cricket was food and drink.

sides to play in the charity fixtures during the grim first summer of the war. He rang the Press Association for some help in raising sides, and soon the Hammonds and Comptons—and Robertson-Glasgow too—were persuaded to play on club grounds all over the home counties. The first match, at Rosslyn Park, was played with a barrel of beer as a sidestake. By the end of 1940, the Empire XI had raised £1200 for the Red Cross, and by the end of the war £15,000 had been generated from 243 matches. That was the extent of cricket's power for patriotic good and of Desmond Donnelly's ingenuity.

Long before peacetime Donnelly had gone off to join the RAF, his parting message in *The Cricketer* being one of optimism. He hoped that the sum raised in 1940 would be doubled next summer. His summary of that first summer ended with a peculiar piece of vernacular, viewed in today's idiom:

> It is calculated that over 80,000 people saw us in action last season. During one of the darkest periods in our history, the sound of bat on ball and the sight of white-clad figures in sunlit fields provided a very welcome relaxation from the sweat and toil of war. Whatever may lie ahead, the Empire XI will always have in mind its duty to help keep the people of this island fortress 'grim and gay'.

Donnelly had risen to flight-lieutenant by his discharge in 1946, and went head-first into politics, starting his volatile parliamentary career as MP for Pembroke between 1950 and 1968. He denounced the concept of the Campaign for Nuclear Disarmament as vehemently as he supported the vision of a European Common Market, and became very close to Aneurin Bevan before breaking with the fiery Welshman and drawing near Hugh Gaitskell. When Harold Wilson succeeded as Labour Party leader upon Gaitskell's death, Donnelly aired fairly persistent criticism. He was full of ideas still: he favoured a return of national service and wanted to see the welfare state abolished. He was eventually expelled by the Labour Party, sat briefly as an Independent, started his own new

Democratic Party, and then abandoned it to join the Conservatives.

Desmond Louis Donnelly was found dead in a hotel room in West Drayton, Middlesex, on April 4, 1974, a day before England were to pull off the last victory in West Indies—or against West Indies—for 16 years. Tablets and empty bottles lay near him. He left a widow, Rosemary Taggart, a son and two daughters.

'Likable and persuasive,' recalled an old friend, 'but he lived on his nerves.'

That description could have applied equally well to Ted Moult, farmer, TV celebrity, occasional cricketer, and Lord's Taverner, to whom cricket also meant a very great deal. Described in *County Champions* (1982) as 'broadcaster, raconteur and Derbyshire farmer', Moult wrote conscientiously and lovingly of his county and its cricketers, recalling his first summer at the county ground, 1936, when he was 10, and used to walk along the canal path under the trees in the company of his grandfather. It happened to be the year that Derbyshire won the County Championship for the very first—and still only—time. He wrote fondly of his long-ago heroes before coming up to date, and thinking about the 1981 season, and pondering the weather: 'If any batsman makes a thousand runs in May, it usually means a poor lookout for my barley.' And with a farmer's sound commonsense, he observed the lbw law: 'It doesn't seem to make much sense that batsmen are now given out lbw when the ball pitches outside the off stump, but not when it's on the leg stump.'

When Ted Moult's Derbyshire made it to the final at Lord's of the NatWest Trophy, 'you couldn't get a ticket for ten crates of blood-oranges' down in the Derby Wholesale Fruit Market. He followed his team's progress that day and evening through radio and television, the media which had made his homely, half-asleep face and mournful, ready-to-chuckle voice a part of Britain's consciousness: the solid country man who never flaps. Derbyshire's thrilling last-ball victory that

September evening in 1981 left not only Derbyshire supporters in a lather of excitement. Ted Moult, two of whose sentences appear in the *Wisden Book of Cricket Quotations*, summed it all up through a quote from Snoopy, the cartoon character he counted as his favourite philosopher: 'It doesn't matter whether you win or lose . . . until you lose.'

Five years almost to the day after Derbyshire's Lord's triumph, Ted Moult shot himself. He had been having psychiatric help for depression, though keeping up a cheerful front to outsiders. He had worried about the strawberry crop and about a forthcoming appearance in pantomime, as Captain Babble in *Robinson Crusoe* in Cambridge. His nerves were in shreds. The 60-year-old former Brain of Britain, the kind and friendly neighbour to all in Ticknall, TV panellist and one-time star of *The Archers*, was dead. His son, who found him, kissed him and spoke to him, but he knew he was dead.

Ted Moult's love of cricket and the affection towards him felt by the cricket fraternity was shown at the memorial service at Derby Cathedral, where England cricketers and many Lord's Taverners joined his widow and six children.

The love of the game can sustain men through stresses and setbacks, even imprisonment, as was the case with many a captive of the Germans and the Japanese during the 1939–45 war. But, plainly enough, even a pseudo-religious feeling about cricket cannot provide infinite insulation to anxiety and despair. Such circumstances surrounded schoolmaster and sometime cricket author John Finch, a 50-year-old bachelor, who died from an overdose on January 7, 1990. He had taught French and German at Uppingham School for half his life, but was forced to retire through failing sight. In 1984 he had written *Game in Season*, a happy romp through a county cricket season as seen and enjoyed by Finch and two other schoolmasters. There he stands in a frontispiece photograph, a chunky figure in sunhat, spectacles, shorts and black shoes, bearded, plastic bag in hand, like some oddly-dressed Henry VIII perched eagerly on the threshold of a new day. The handwriting in his letter is curiously boyish, unsophisticated, the contents polite, almost apologetic. Five years later, under the imprint of a pukka publisher, came *Three Men at the Match*, a book of equally joyous self-indulgence and cricket-bench chatter. When Leicestershire and England fast bowler Jonathan Agnew, a former pupil at Uppingham, heard the news of Finch's death, he cried his eyes out: 'He was a lovely bloke.' He had a ferocious temper, but his natural charm usually put the fire out fairly swiftly.

Only a few days earlier, on Christmas Day 1989, another cricket 'fanatic' demonstrated that the powers of comfort and absorption of this game have their limits. Ian Hamilton-Wood, chairman of the South African Cricket Society and a former Johannesburg league cricketer, in his mid-forties, shot himself in his car. His love for the game was a huge influence in his life, but that love was swept aside by an insuperable force.

Willie Llewelyn would not have found inclusion in this catalogue of regret but for the investigative work of Andrew Hignell. For years Llewelyn's death was classified 'accidental', but enquiries, especially among descendants, point quite unarguably to suicide. Llewelyn was the son of the founding father of Glamorgan County Cricket Club, J. T. D Llewelyn (later a baronet and Mayor of Swansea), who was squire of Penllergaer, near Swansea, and was coached by his doting father before going off to Eton in 1882, when he was 14. By 1886 he was in the XI and scoring an impressive 44 at Lord's as his side forged victory over Harrow, and innings of 124 and 41 not out against Winchester and 78 not out against an MCC team which had several hardened professional bowlers in its ranks suggested that young Willie was made of the right stuff.

Enrolling at New College, Oxford in 1887, he did little on the cricket field for two seasons, but in 1890 he earned the first of two Blues, opening the innings and becoming one of the many double failures as Cambridge demolished Oxford for 42 and 108 after rain. The unquestionable highlight of that summer, though, was his showing for his college against

Willie Llewelyn — dead a month after scoring a century.

Oriel, when he scored 107 in the first innings and 115 in the second. In the following summer he was again part of a losing Oxford side in the Varsity match, though he had the satisfaction of making top score, 38, out of 108 as Sammy Woods again tore the heart out of the Dark Blues' innings. This time the 'London critics' had a more reliable view of the promising batsman from South Wales, now 23 and standing 5 ft 10 ins, with a solid weight of around 11 stone. An all-round sports-lover, he had been a fine rackets player at Eton and partook, with equal ease, of Rugby and soccer. Life must surely have seemed good for William Dillwyn Llewelyn that summer of 1891 as he stroked 126 for I Zingari against Worcester.

His style was described as 'stooping rather than upright', but he was still a prize asset to Glamorgan, who were still some way from first-class status, and he had a proud first-class century in his locker. It came in 1890, at Oxford, for the University against Gentlemen of England, when he opened the innings and made 116 with the high proportion of 20 fours. For Glamorgan his highest score was to remain a poignant 99 against Monmouthshire in June 1893, two months before his death. A month later he hit 113 not out for Eton Ramblers against Old Wykehamists, and all around him would have supposed that he had everything to live for, particularly as he was engaged to the daughter of Lord Dynevor, the Hon. Gladys Rice.

Llewelyn had taken on the office of treasurer to Glamorgan (like Dyson 'Brock' Williams in later years: his story follows), and with his cricket talent, his distinguished family background, and the prospect of marriage later that year, he seemed to have more about which to feel satisfied than the average 25-year-old. He stayed with his bride-to-be at Dynevor Castle, Llandeilo, on the eve of his brother Charles's wedding. On the morning after the wedding, August 24, 1893 (when the Old Trafford Test began, featuring Stoddart, Shrewsbury and Bruce), Willie Llewelyn returned home to Penllergaer and quickly went off into the grounds of the estate, barely speaking to anybody. He had taken his fishing tackle and double-barrelled shotgun. A few hours later his body was found in a glade by one of the lakes. He had been shot through the chest.

Modern belief is that scandal was avoided at the inquest by the assertion that he had used the butt of his gun to push back some bushes. A thick twig probably became caught against the trigger and detonated the cartridge. The tragic 'accident' left the family name unbesmirched, the interpretation seeming more plausible than that a young man with so much apparently going in his favour should have chosen to end it all. But there are too many blanks unfilled, and the belief that Llewelyn did take his own life surfaces a few generations later in the family, the years having softened reality. The father, Sir John Llewelyn, lived on until 1927, by which time he was 91.

It is often impossible to determine, in a case of a motoring death, whether it was an accident or suicide, though relatives and close friends often have instinctive opinions based on circumstances and late conversation. When former Cambridge and Hampshire batsman, the Reverend John Richard Bridger, died in a car accident at Burley on July 14, 1986, when he was 66, there was a whisper that he might have ended his own life deliberately. The same was said after New Zealander Ian Cromb ran his car over a cliff-edge on March 6, 1984, when he was 78 and known to be doomed by illness. 'Cranky' Cromb, an all-rounder, had toured England with the 1931 Kiwis, and played in five Tests in all, winning praise for his fast-medium bowling, and averaging (in first-class cricket) 29.04 with the bat. A strong-willed individual, he had played major cricket over 17 years from his 1929–30 debut, and was a legend in club cricket. A good golfer, he also became Bob Charles's mentor, financing his first American tour. Auckland cricketers recall the time Cromb decided to resurface Lancaster Park, Christchurch with a load of new soil. It proved to be not the easiest of pitches upon which to play cricket, for it finished up 'like a carpet not properly stretched'. A man who knew his own mind, I. B. Cromb, and who, according to several old friends, might well have decided to take positive action when he knew his innings was close to termination.

Another New Zealander reckoned by friends to have taken his own life (on November 1, 1978, when he was 63) was Lankford Smith, a former Otago captain, a left-handed all-rounder who played 58 matches for his province between 1934 and 1957. He later became a selector and a broadcaster, but he never got over the tragedy of the drowning of a boy under his care during a school outing at Karatane beach, north of Dunedin.

The tales of two solicitors, separated by many years, several intervening counties and by completely diverse touches of involvement, remain linked yet by the common thread of cricket. One played and served as administrator; the other saw in the game the chance to make money—at somebody else's expense.

Dyson 'Brock' Williams, born near Swansea in 1877, was a reluctant first-class cricketer who made himself available to Glamorgan only if they were desperately short. He first played for the county in 1901, when he was 24, and, though his name appears often enough in *Wisden's* Second-Class Counties averages up to the First World War, his only first-class appearance was in 1921, when he was 44. It was the Welsh county's first year in the County Championship, and Williams came in for the last home match, against Hampshire at Cardiff. Alec Kennedy (8 for 11) bowled Glamorgan out for 37 and in the second innings they managed 114. Williams scored 5 and 9, and the match was lost. Glamorgan finished bottom of the table in their first year, and the deficit in financial terms deepened, placing more reliance than ever on the club's patrons. Brock Williams had been Glamorgan's honorary treasurer since 1913, and the worries seemed to be piling up all around him. When his mother died in the autumn of 1921, bachelor Williams was plunged into deep depression.

The Great War had already changed him irrevocably from the carefree solicitor who loved to play 'social' cricket, particularly for the Public School Nondescripts (he had been

Brock Williams — Glamorgan faithful, shattered by war.

educated at Malvern) at his family's home at Killay, where amateur theatricals were also all the rage. War saw his enlistment in the Swansea Battalion of the Welsh Regiment, and he was to experience some of the worst carnage in the attack on Mametz Wood in 1916, the Battle of Ypres and the horrors of the Somme, where he won the DSO, and was wounded in a lung. Williams, now a lieutenant-colonel, led his men triumphantly back into the city of Swansea, regimental colours flying, but his life, had he but known it (and he must have had suspicions), reshaped for the worst. A fellow Glamorgan player, T. A. L. Whittington, spoke of his friend's character as having been shattered by his wartime experiences.

Another problem faced him immediately. His solicitor's practice had been run down while he and his brother were at the Front. He then lost a lot of his money in a Welsh aviation project which failed. His gambling added to his losses. Cricket brought occasional happiness, as did a satisfying partnership with a boxing promoter. His nightmares of war were also partially held at bay by his love of music, and the man's versatility expressed itself in some compositions, all written under the nom de plume 'Florian Brock'.

Cricket researcher Bob Harragan has uncovered a song jointly written by Brock Williams and the French boxer Georges Carpentier, entitled *Vagabond Philosophy*. The second verse suggested an upturn in optimism and mood:

And so in life you'll get
A regular knockout blow.
Don't lie and grouse, but try to smile
And have the pluck to cry.
The mud and dust will soon rub off.
I'll be all right by and by.

Shortly after his mother's death in 1921, Williams, telling a friend he felt 'desolate', was soon bankrupt, explaining that he had not only business losses, interest on loans and gambling reversals but inadequate army pay. He vanished after the bankruptcy hearing.

His brother managed to find him—'he was rather down and out'—and gave him shelter in his Maidenhead home. Soon Williams was working with his old boxing-promoter friend Major Arnold Wilson, a battlefield colleague, in his London office in St Martin's Court. The Carpentier-Lewis fight was coming up as Major Wilson went off to Woking for the Easter break.

Brock Williams' behaviour now suffered another relapse. Cheques bounced as he resumed gambling, and he deceived the proprietor of a bar into giving him the enormous sum of £200 for a cheque, which bounced.

The bachelor in the panama hat, covering his baldness, sailed to Belgium and began to play the casinos, successfully too, as revealed in a letter to Wilson: 'I have at last struck a bit of luck, just when apparently things were hopeless. I shall be able to pay you back what you have let me have.' Wilson received that letter on April 19, 1922, the day after Dyson 'Brock' Williams ended it all. Historian Bob Harragan, who uncovered so much about this sad Glamorgan identity, has recorded how a charlady went to clean the London office and found the room filled with gas and Williams's body slumped on the floor. Two gas jets on the stove were fully on. The coroner returned a verdict of 'suicide while of unsound mind'. The eminent Bransby Williams family had a further skeleton to conceal in the cupboard. The 45-year-old solicitor-soldier-cricketer was yet another belated victim of the horrendous European warfare. Major Wilson said afterwards: 'He was highly strung with a nervous temperament, and the war used him up more than it did men of a quieter disposition.'

Williams's illegal manipulation of money was insignificant in scale against that undertaken by solicitor Hugh Simmonds in the 1980s. Simmonds becomes part of this work through his record-breaking performance in the saleroom when early *Wisdens* were on offer. The prices he paid at Phillips' London auction in June 1986 brought gasps from the hundred or so in attendance, not one of whom could have guessed that they were in the presence of the perpetrator of 'the biggest solicitor's swindle ever in the UK'—sums amounting to £10 million were estimated.

Simmonds was, among other things, a former mayor of Beaconsfield, Bucks, a member of the Conservative Party and speech-writer for Prime Minister Margaret Thatcher (work which earned him the CBE), solicitor to, among others, some senior members of the Tory party, a three-times failed parliamentary candidate himself, and a director of 14 companies. Beyond all this, he was a philanderer, father of a 'love child', and also active as a homosexual. One of his lovers told *Bucks Free Press* that 'Hugh liked to have mental control over another person, and he would find a way to get that if he could'.

No-one doubted, in that saleroom, that the Mr Simmonds—previously unobserved at any of cricket's twice-a-year auctions—who secured whatever he chose to bid for was either a wealthy man or acting for one. Perhaps stocked with some

Hugh Simmonds — record payment for *Wisdens*.

of the £300,000 commission he boasted he had earned through an arms deal, he splashed out £5500 plus 10 per cent premium for the first and second editions of *Wisden Cricketers' Almanack* (1864 and 1865), and as much again on other old *Wisdens*, *Vanity Fair* caricatures, and an autograph book that contained, among numerous cricketers' signatures, that of Prime Minister Stanley Baldwin. This willingness and ability to pay grossly inflated prices tends to paralyse ordinary, sincere collectors, who are left only to hope that the raider will not return.

Although, to widespread relief, Simmonds was not spotted at subsequent sales, he did consult cricket book dealer Martin Wood, who called upon him at his office in Beaconsfield and found him wanting to sell rather than buy. Soon, however, the Law Society, having been alerted to the chain of malpractices, were on the verge of making an announcement, a move which Simmonds headed off by killing himself. He drove to woodlands near Chalfont St Giles, put a hosepipe (even this was purchased with a dud credit-card) from the car exhaust to the car's interior, switched on the engine and closed the door. He placed a book on the accelerator pedal to keep the engine running. It was not stated at the inquest whether it was a *Wisden*. His body was found on November 15, 1988. He was 40, and left a wife and two daughters, and he left over 500 people with claims against him. Divorce proceedings had also been initiated. He is surely the least mourned of all the subjects under review.

From two disparate solicitors to two doctors with much in common. They were both Oxford Blues of the 1950s, one Adelaide-born, the other from Derbyshire.

The Australian was Anthony Douglas Jose, born on February 17, 1929 and educated at St Peter's College and Adelaide University before taking up residence at Brasenose College, Oxford as a Rhodes scholar. He had already played for South Australia as a fast bowler in three matches in 1947–48, just before and after his nineteenth birthday, numbering Arthur Morris and Sid Barnes among his six victims.

Tony Jose — 'a most interesting bloke'.

The ordeal of playing at Lord's in the Varsity match must therefore have been lessened in intensity. Tony Jose played twice, in 1950 and 1951, taking 4 for 46 in the second match to help set up a Dark Blue victory. In Oxford's match against Surrey at Guildford in 1950 he bowled a bouncer which hit Geoff Whittaker on the temple and put him out of the match. It was in 1951 that Jose returned the best figures in his 29 first-class matches: 6 for 45 against Warwickshire at, of all places, Stratford-upon-Avon, on a lively pitch. The under-strength county were all out for 86 before lunch.

Jose played some county cricket himself that season and in 1952, having five matches for Kent. But his medical studies took him from the cricket field, and eventually to America, where in 1960 he was attached to the John Hopkins Hospital in Baltimore. By 1963 he was back in Australia, at Sydney's Hallstrom Institute, but in 1972, when he was nearing 43, he was working in the cardiology section of a Los Angeles hospital, and it was while there that he took his own life.

David 'Jumbo' Jowett, who played against him in 1953, when Jose turned out for Free Foresters, remembered him as 'a very genial soul', and his introversion, which might easily have been mistaken for a 'laid-back' temperament, led to his being called 'the Dozy Doctor'. A perfectionist in all things, he could not bear anything other than the best. He amused Jowett by referring to fellow player and Test veteran Gubby Allen (then aged 51) as 'the Regius Professor of Elastoplast', such were the size and variety of bandaging the former England captain was forced to put on to protect himself from strains and hernias before taking the field. Oxford captain Alan Dowding, a fellow Australian who grew up with Tony Jose, described him as 'a most interesting bloke, complicated, highly intelligent, sensitive—and a brilliant heart specialist'. He remembered him too for his all-round athleticism. He was a good Aussie Rules footballer, and his widow recalled he became a fan of American football: 'perhaps the discipline intrigued him; medical research demands discipline'.

Ian Gibson was born in Glossop, Derbyshire, on August 15, 1936 and was educated at Manchester Grammar School, where his cricket records stood for over 30 years until Michael Atherton burst on the scene. At barely 17 Gibson was a

Ian Gibson — outwardly casual, overwhelmed by responsibility.

good enough middle-order batsman and legspin-googly bowler to earn selection in Lancashire's 2nd XI. At Oxford University he entered the elite ranks of those who have played in four Varsity matches at Lord's, though he was not on a winning side in those contests between 1955 and 1958. His best moments came with the top Oxford score in the match in 1957 (63), and twice (1956 and 1957) he took Dexter's prized wicket.

In 1957 he played the first of his seven matches for Derbyshire, in a summer which brought him the satisfaction of his only first-class century, 100 not out for Oxford against Gloucestershire at The Parks, and his best bowling figures, 5 for 29 for the University against D. R. Jardine's XI at Eastbourne. It also brought him his highest score for Derbyshire, 66 not out at Ilkeston against Notts (including Dooland), an enterprising innings which secured a first-innings lead.

Like Jose, Gibson put his career in medicine ahead of his cricket, and was seen no more on a first-class cricket field after 1961, signing off with 46 and 3 as opening batsman for Derbyshire at Bournemouth, when Hampshire's victory gave them the County Championship.

Less than two years later, young Dr Gibson was dead. Contemporaries at Oxford remember him as a sociable young man, perhaps weighed down at times by fairly fierce paternal expectation. He was only 26 when he gassed himself on May 3, 1963, at Bowdon, in Cheshire—not his first attempt—and the strain induced by overwork was seen as a contributory cause, 'Jumbo' Jowett, a close friend, goes deeper however. Gibson was, he says, outwardly very relaxed and seemingly casual in his approach to life in general and sport in particular—as was Jose. He writes:

> When he played for Derbyshire the professionals were amazed at the casual manner in which he would take very difficult catches in the outfield.

Gibson completed his training at Guy's Hospital, but in the autumn of 1961 his girlfriend called on Jowett and said that Ian had suffered a nervous breakdown. He went home, up north, to convalesce, and Jowett next saw him in a Wardour Street pub in London just before Christmas 1962:

> I invited him to play in my MCC side against Abingdon the following summer. He told me then, as had his fiancée a year earlier, that the reason for his mental breakdown was that he felt so inadequate as a doctor—he had been a houseman at a London hospital as the final part of his training—as he could not cope with having to make decisions that could literally kill or cure. Perhaps his seemingly lackadaisical approach to life was a cover for his lack of confidence . . . this awful sense of responsibility got him down.

How anyone so highly-strung could ever have bowled leg-breaks and googlies so successfully remains a mystery. Jowett concludes:

> What I was very concerned at was that, having accepted my invitation to play in my MCC match, he wrote to me three weeks before he committed suicide explaining that he couldn't, after all, play as he had a recurrence of his affliction, *and I*, to my eternal regret, put his letter on one side, planning to answer it, but never actually did so. I often wonder to myself whether, if I had written a supportive but cheerful response, the situation would have turned out differently.

In the early winter of 1978—*not* the peak time for suicide as one might suspect: spring and summer bring the upturns in statistics—Tony Davis, top Berkshire batsman, shot himself through the head at his home in Reading. He was headmaster of Reading School, 47 years of age, a Royal Navy, MCC and Minor Counties player who played two first-class matches in 1967, falling to Intikhab Alam for 16 and 37 in Minor

Tony Davis — Berkshire's brooding and enigmatic captain.

Counties' exciting match against the touring Pakistan side at Swindon, having opened for MCC against Oxford University in May and made only 4 at a very damp Parks.

That same season he scored a century before lunch in Reading School's all-day match against Romany, an occasion which gave the author not only a first-hand glimpse of Davis's neat batsmanship but also an impression that he was, perhaps, rather more stern of humour than many a batsman who has been applauded from the field. Perhaps he was still immersed in deep concentration and bound by a nervous tension, but to a smiling 'You took your time!' he could muster only a suspicious glare.

Anthony Tilton Davis was captain of Berkshire throughout the 1960s, and was a Reading man through and through. He was born in the town, on August 14, 1931, and died there 47 years later. His affection for Reading School, where he taught for so many years, was deep and patent, and it was the threat of its conversion to a comprehensive school which is said to have contributed to his fatal depression—that and the failing of one of his eyes, and the recent loss of his father. E. S. Holt wrote of him in Reading School's cricket history, published in 1986: 'He was a man who would have supported any denunciation of the 1960s, and a man for whom cricket, within the school and outside it, was of enormous importance.' The reference to the 1960s pointed to the social rebellion that, probably at worst in cricket terms, meant floppy long hair stuffed into batsmen's and fielders' sunhats. At a time of meagre success by Reading School, the headmaster himself (Davis) took charge of the 1st XI, 'an innovation which received a mixed response from the players', and a dramatic revival occurred in 1971 and 1972. Up to 1977 the school's cricket prospered, under Tony Davis's 'galvanising if sometimes over-critical influence'.

The chronicler described Davis as 'an enigmatic man almost impossible to sum up briefly'. Holt recalls his presence on the boundary during school matches: 'coughing, whistling, or making comments about the game into his tape-recorder', all of which induced nervousness into the cricketing pupils. 'His captaincy was variable,' Holt wrote, 'and depended much on his volatile moods.' Davis was often heard to express his displeasure on the field. When Old Redingensians were fielding to some dreary and unimaginative Berkshire Gentlemen batsmanship he called across to the slips from his station at short leg: 'We'll have to drop this fixture next year.'

Davis captained MCC sides against his school, and once blazed a furious 141 not out, an exhibition launched with some punishing and indignant shots against a school opening bowler whose long hair offended. The lad conceded 45 runs off four overs. A couple of years later Tony Davis fumed as his MCC opener pottered around for 11 runs in an hour and a half. Unable to stand any more, he retired the batsman and strode out ready to batter the school into submission, only to lose his off stump first ball. The poor bowler paid for it later that week, when Davis smashed him for several sixes, to 'restore discipline to the boy'.

A. T. Davis was endeavouring to retain Reading School's independence in the face of the Government's plan to bring it into the comprehensive system. It all became too much for him. That terrifyingly tight temperament snapped at his home in Craven Road, Reading, on November 21, 1978. The school, 12 years later, remained the only boys' grammar school in Berkshire.

Tony Davis had been in the Royal Navy during national service. Another from the Senior Service, Reigate-born Trevor John Duncan Grant, who played one match for Sussex in 1946, was found dead in Cabin 14 of the ward-room on HMS *Ganges* at Shotley, near Felixstowe, Suffolk, on October 11, 1957. He had shot himself through the head. He was 31. Grant, a lieutenant-commander, could scarcely have enjoyed a briefer county career. The match, against Hampshire at Bournemouth in July 1946, was over in two days, Sussex being caught on a drying pitch on which first Jim Bailey with left-arm spin and then Tom Dean with leg-spin took five wickets in an innings. Grant's dismissals, both on the second day, were at the hands of Lofty Herman, whom he had caught in Hampshire's innings. Opening with Harry Parks, Grant made 0 and 6. No reason is known for his suicide 11 years later.

Nor, probably, will the reason ever emerge for the suicide of one of the most promising of post-war schoolboy cricketers, R. H. Thompson, of Harrow School. Hugh Thompson made news in the glorious, sunlit Compton-Edrich summer of 1947 by scoring a polished 71 for Harrow against Eton at Lord's with the King, the Queen, the two princesses, and Lieutenant Philip Mountbatten in attendance. It was a patient innings, studded with strong drives, and it supported the belief of masters and friends that young Thompson had it in him to rise to the very top, perhaps one day captaining Yorkshire, the county of his birth.

Then, on May 28 of the following year, on the day that Lancashire's Malcolm Hilton created a sensation by dismissing Don Bradman for the second time in the match, 17-year-old Hugh Thompson hanged himself in a bathroom at the school. At the inquest in Wealdstone, his father (a school governor) and his housemaster stated their beliefs that the boy had been 'on top of the world', and the coroner was left merely to conclude that 'a sudden mental derangement must have prevented him knowing what he was doing'. His shocked team-mate Robin Marlar, who became highly successful as an off-spinner for Cambridge and Sussex as well as a writer on the game, confirms Thompson's exceptional batting talent, and asserts that schoolboy suicide, especially by hanging, has never been exactly a rare thing. In a weird sort of way it has often been seen to have a fashionable touch to it, a romantic, cultish, heroic flavour, with a copycat influence. Unquestionably there have been instances of play-acting which went wrong. This young man can surely only have succeeded after a serious attempt if the burden of some

Hugh Thompson — hanged himself at 17, reason unknown.

adolescent problem had grown to unbearable dimensions, or a clinical depression had gone undetected and unexpressed.

Another of his contemporaries remembers Thompson's 'caustic tongue' and detected a 'superior air about him', but Hugh's sister, in Yorkshire, still cherished a photograph of him on her sideboard over 40 years later.

There is a suicide attempt somewhere in the United Kingdom every two-and-a-half minutes, with 5000 per annum proving fatal. The causes are mainly identifiable. But the victims of chemical or hormonal imbalance are among those whose secret agony is inexplicable and therefore most terrifying. There is, too, the less apparent suicide, who takes the slow alcoholic path through comforting lift after lift, each linked by depression and overlaid with the certain knowledge that extinction is being hastened. Dylan Thomas knew it, and so did Brendan Behan and masses of others, Colin Milburn probably among them, and perhaps including Alex Reid, a wicketkeeper from Dominica who had a trial—which came to nothing—before the West Indies party was chosen for the 1957 tour of England. Thirty-one years later, in May 1988, he was found dead in his home in Bradford, Yorkshire, having drunk—an inquest was told—over 10 fluid ounces of whisky. He was 58, and if he had carried through a reckless death wish, it would at least have gladdened his last moments to have known that *The Times* described him as 'the former West Indies wicketkeeper'.

A Minor County cricketer of much lesser eminence than Tony Davis apparently drowned himself in April 1990. John Rowland Dinwiddy, a keen player, a Free Forester, whose 'wrong-foot' fast-medium bowling earned him a couple of games with Suffolk in 1956 (without success), was a distinguished member of staff at Royal Holloway & Bedford New College, where he had worked for 20 years. Although some of the staff thought he had looked unduly worried, and seemed to have lost his customary keen interest in what was going on, it came as stunning news that he had disappeared, his car and clothing being found by the Thames riverbank at Runnymede on April 19. His body was found nine days later. He was 50, and left a wife and two daughters. A colleague spoke of his 'lovely' nature, and of how quiet and easy to get on with he had been. John Dinwiddy was a scholar, educated at Winchester and Oxford, an assistant master at Eton, a lecturer in Uganda, a chairman of the University Board of Studies in History, an expert on Jeremy Bentham, and a cricket-lover who forsook the game in later years, such was the pressure of work. He was due to give his inaugural lecture as Professor of Modern History the following month.

Before any attempt is made to analyse the mass of preceding material, to blame cricket or to excuse it, there is one more tale to be told, perhaps as much a classic case as Stoddart's or Gimblett's or Faulkner's.

13

'Turnip-head' Trott

There is a plot in Willesden cemetery, west London, that is forever Australia. Beneath the forlorn tumulus, marked only with a peg showing 'P613', lies the body of Albert Edwin Trott, Anglo-Australian cricketer, who hit a towering six over the Lord's pavilion, averaged 102.50 for Australia in Tests against England, and once drew from his Middlesex wicketkeeper, fellow alcoholic Gregor MacGregor, the remark: 'What a pity you haven't got a head instead of a turnip. You'd be the best bowler in the world.'

He may not have been university material, but no cricketer from Victoria and none—with the possible exception of W. G. Grace—born of the Victorian era has been at the core of so many amusing anecdotes and the subject of so many quips as Trott. His father, Adolphus, was a perky character, judging from impressions of his non-stop 'Mr Jingle' commentary while scoring for the South Melbourne club when his sons Harry and Albert were batting together. *The Bulletin* later commented: 'Great cricketers and good-hearted fellows, the Trotts deserved happier endings.'

G. H. S. (Harry) was six years older than Albert and was the third of the family of eight children. Chunkily-built and dreamy-eyed, he was a superb batsman who went on to play in 24 Tests, touring England in 1888, 1890, 1893 and (as captain) 1896, when he scored his sole Test century, a courageous 143 following a first-innings duck attributed to the awful backdrop at Lord's, where there was still no sightscreen at the pavilion end. The century only just came: he was dropped on 99. He and the diminutive Syd Gregory had a partnership of 221, then the highest in Test cricket. A tantalising, sly leg-spinner too, and no mean tactician, Harry Trott, a Melbourne postman, was a genial and popular captain, and as shrewd as any that his great contemporaries ever saw. He was to spend much time in later years in mental asylums, confounding his team-mates' impression of a man who never let the acute tensions of cricket affect him. When MCC bowled his Australian side out for 18 at Lord's, he deflected the mighty Spofforth's commiserations with the comment: 'Things could hardly be worse. But tell me, Spoff, are there any decent leg shows on at the theatres?'

Harry died in November 1917, aged 51, his only son also having lost his grip on life, supposedly through his father's constant breakdowns. The news of his own younger brother's suicide three years earlier can only have added to Harry's mental agonies.

Albert Trott, though destined to play fewer Tests than elder brother Harry, made a bigger mark on the game for a number of reasons. He not only has the biggest batting average in Ashes Tests, but he also played for his adopted England. His performances in first-class cricket were staged in New Zealand and South Africa as well as in his native Australia, and most memorably in England, where for several years his batting, and more particularly his bowling, astonished cricket-lovers around the turn of the century as they cast their eyes over the sports pages of the newspapers.

With those Oriental eyes and spreading moustache, 'Alberto' seemed certain to be a star from his teenage years. He practised with fierce determination, placing a wooden crate in front of stumps to represent the obdurate 'W. G. of

Albert Trott — Australian reject, Middlesex hero.

Australia', George Giffen, and learning to spin a fastish ball around it. His imaginative and adventurous mind directed his vast hands and strong body to deliver every ball known to man—preferably all in the course of one over. At a time when bouncers were rare, he could dig in the most uncomfortable lifter; at will, he could move the ball either way in the air, and off the pitch; his yorker was a beast of a ball, no easier for a batsman to repel even after a forcible warning from a team-mate than Trott's evilly disguised slower ball, which could make the best of them look ridiculous.

Harry Lee, who played a few games for Middlesex as a young man when Trott was nearing the end of his career, recalled how the Australian could play tricks with novices in the dressing-room, spinning a lacrosse ball all sorts of bizarre ways, making it leap up and hit the unsuspecting in the nose and working it with those powerful fingers so that it would bounce back against the direction in which it was delivered. In a match, he would lower his arm, impart bodycheck, and make the ball swerve alarmingly to slip, from almost a baseball pitcher's action, before cutting back towards the stumps. On a helpful pitch he could be as close to unplayable as any man has seen.

'I wish I were young again,' wrote Lee, 'and on my way to the wicket to score my first century for Middlesex at Lord's.' He might have been speaking for any keen cricketer who ever played the game—Trott as much as anyone. 'Albatrott' loved the game, and would have played on much longer had he not become fleshy through drink, and unsound of health. Lee, who used to sit and watch cricket from the Mound Stand at Lord's until he was 90 (he died in 1981), was among the last to survive with first-hand memories of 'old Trotty'. He used to refer to young Lee as 'Oi' or 'Boy', and by all sorts of other calls, obviously lacking Keith Miller's amazing memory for everybody's name (other, it seems, than his own sons'!). Lee recalled that when a wicket fell, Trott would often trot off for a pint of beer or a tot of whisky—for which a doting spectator would pay, naturally. He could resist no diversion. When a fellow called Bates, who played a couple of times for Middlesex in 1909, displayed a little trick of spitting pellets at umpires and unsuspecting batsmen, Albert Trott immediately had to go one better by filling his mouth, a dozen pellets at a time, and firing them in all directions.

He had made his debut for Victoria in 1892–93, and in 1894–95, the season of his elevation to the Australian Test team, he took 7 for 85 against Tasmania. He had routed all kinds of opposition in Melbourne club cricket, having entered the club game at 15. John Barrett saw his great potential at the South Melbourne club's net practice. Dr Barrett, who carried his bat through Australia's innings at Lord's in 1890, suggested the youngster settle down and bowl with a break one way or the other instead of mixing them all up, with the consequent inevitable loss of accuracy. Trott tried a leg-break, and the ball flew over the top of the net. The next was an off-break—leg-break to left-hander Barrett—and took out the leg stump. 'There was not a prouder man in Australia that day than myself,' Barrett proclaimed.

Trott was an innocent and ingenuous young man. When, in a club match, having switched from Harry's South

Trott — bowled every ball known to man.

Melbourne club to East Melbourne, he accidentally kicked the stumps over in the act of bowling, he was no-balled for his clumsiness. When asked later why he hadn't pointed out to the umpire that this minor calamity hardly constituted a no-ball offence, he replied that he thought a new law must have been brought in since the previous season. Not that it would have concerned him unduly, for he finished with 8 for 51, and sizable talent money of £3. It was not only batsmen he sometimes startled. In another Melbourne club match one of his swifter deliveries killed a swallow.

His debut for Australia came in January 1895, when Australia were two down to Stoddart's England team with three to play, and he went in at No. 10 with his side 157 for 8. Another wicket fell immediately, but he and Syd Callaway hit the tiring England attack all over Adelaide Oval to add a priceless 81 for the last wicket. Trott was soon picking

Lockwood off his slatted pads high over the leg field to land the ball in a buggy in the driveway, and driving Tom Richardson, the warhorse, into that wide expanse down the ground for five scampered runs. He was 38 not out when Richardson bowled Callaway for 41.

Trott opened the bowling, but was given only three overs, Giffen and Callaway getting five wickets each as England, distressed by the hellish heat, subsided to 124, 114 behind. Billy Bruce (80) and Frank Iredale (140) then extended Australia's lead well beyond sweating England's hopes. Trott actually found himself fielding as substitute for England when Lockwood's finger was split.

When Trott went to bat in this second innings the situation was very different. Australia were 283 for 8 (397 ahead), and the bowlers were going through the motions. Sixty-four runs were added before Iredale was caught-and-bowled by Peel, and then Callaway came in for a repeat of the first-innings last-wicket stand, worth 64 this time. Albert Trott was left unbeaten with 72; Australia's 411 left England in need of 526 for victory.

Trott, still only 21, might well have been satisfied with 110 runs in his maiden Test match without being dismissed, but the best was yet to come. MacLaren and Ward made a sound start of 52. But then Trott claimed his first Test wicket when MacLaren lofted one and was caught. Next he bowled Ward, splitting the stump from top to bottom with a murderous delivery. Giffen bowled Philipson, and as the evening shadows crept across the oval, Trott hurt Jack Brown with another.

Next morning, with the pitch still playing fairly well, Trott bowled Brown off his pads with one that kicked sharply and broke back. Brockwell hit out, and Trott pocketed a return catch. Next ball, Peel, on a 'pair', went the same way, and Trott had five wickets. He served a nasty ball to Ford, the tall left-hander, and brother Harry held the catch at his familiar position of point. Albert then bowled Briggs third ball, and enticed Lockwood to drive through the hot, thin air for Iredale to complete the catch. England nine down for 130, eight wickets to Trott, who then finished the massacre by catching Richardson off Giffen. Australia by 382 runs on the fourth day, and a new national hero had been created.

To his 110 hard-hit runs he had added bowling figures of 8 for 43 off 27 six-ball overs, earning himself a guinea a wicket from one admirer and a loaf of bread from another. The ball was presented to him, and the England captain, A. E. Stoddart, paid him the following tribute:

> I can't help congratulating our young friend Trott, and I rather credit myself for having, on the first occasion I saw him play, said he would be one of the finest cricketers Australia has ever seen. I hope Mr Trott will visit England—at least, I hope he will *not*!—but if he does come we are always pleased to welcome cricketers such as he.

Thus spoke Trott's future amateur Middlesex fellow cricketer, both to shoot themselves within eight months of each other.

Melbourne's *Argus* newspaper depicted 'Saint Albert Trott' in a stained-glass window, while a versifier saw the funny side of hero Trott's mauling of England with these clever lines from 'The Kangaroo' to Mr Stoddart:

> You didn't expect it, my sonny?
> Yet, truly, complain you must not;
> For you wanted 'a run' for your money,
> And, complying, I gave you 'A. Trott'.

As the two sides prepared for the fourth Test, another paper expressed the view that he would not be playing for Victoria much longer since Sussex had made him an offer to qualify for that county. Firstly, though, he set about enhancing his reputation further. In the Sydney Test he watched Australia's first six wickets go down for 51 on a spiteful pitch after Stoddart had put them in and let Peel, Richardson and Briggs loose in conditions that suited them perfectly. But Joe Darling, held back to No. 8, clouted Briggs into the tennis court, and as the pitch became firmer, he and Harry Graham turned the match round. They put on 68, and when Darling was out, Trott came in at No. 9 and helped Graham add 112 more.

It was not instantly a clean continuation of his cavalier batsmanship of Adelaide, for Richardson hit Trott sickeningly as soon as he went in, and it took the fieldsmen several minutes to restore the young Australian. Graham, 'the Little Dasher', raced to his century, uniquely twinning a hundred on Test debut in Australia with the one he made on debut in England in 1893, before being stumped off Briggs, and after Jarvis's quick departure, C. T. B. Turner came in to support Trott in a last-wicket stand of 45, raising the total to 284. Trott was left 85 not out, and had thus scored 195 runs to date in Test cricket without being dismissed.

The second day's play was washed out, and it rained some more on the Sunday, so that by Monday, with the sun beaming down on a mud-heap, batting conditions could hardly have been worse. England were bowled out twice, for 65 and 72, to lose by an innings, and while Giffen gave Harry Trott a few overs, in which his leg-spin accounted for three wickets, Albert was not asked to bowl at all in the match. Turner and Giffen wiped out the rest of the wickets (Lockwood was absent injured), thus conceivably denying young Albert the chance of improving his best Test figures.

At two-all, Australia and England went into the final Test at Melbourne a month later, Trott having celebrated his twenty-second birthday in the meantime. The deciding Test turned into a classic. England responded to Australia's 414 with 385 (MacLaren 120) and eventually needed 297 for victory. A third-wicket stand by J. T. Brown and Albert Ward amounted to 210 in under two-and-a-half hours, and an epic match ended in England's success by six wickets on the fifth day.

Albert Trott failed to deliver to his home crowd the sort of stirring stuff he had provided at Adelaide and Sydney. He was caught at cover for 10 in the first innings, giving himself a Test average (205) at last, and Richardson bowled him for a duck in the second, thus halving that average. From 49 overs in the match he obtained only Brown's wicket for 140 runs.

Short of falling down a mineshaft, it still seemed certain that the strapping young Victorian had a bright Test career ahead of him. But Australia didn't want him.

Brother Harry was elected captain of the 1896 Australian side to tour England . . . but not until after it was chosen (Billy Bruce was one of the selectors), and the omission of Albert Trott seems one of the craziest in all Test history. He may have been short of form at the crucial time, but his potential ought to have been abundantly obvious, and was to be borne out in the years that followed. He did journey to England, not with Sussex in mind, but Middlesex. Stoddart was almost certainly an influence in this, and possibly the wandering Australian player and umpire Jim Phillips too.

While qualifying for the county, Trott secured an engagement on MCC's ground staff at Lord's, and lost no time in showing a likeness for English conditions. He was paid 30 shillings a week plus £5 for appearing in a first-class match and £3 for a second-class. Before his English career was much advanced he found himself in the ironical position of fielding for Australia in the Test at Lord's, with W. G Grace and Stoddart batting. Harry Donnan had damaged a hand, and Harry Trott found—or called—his brother on as substitute. Many felt it was Albert's rightful place to be part of that Australian side. But it was to be no more than a passing fantasy. Years later, Patsy Hendren wrote that when the two brothers passed each other in Oxford Street, Harry called out, 'Hullo, you young beggar!' To which Albert replied 'Hullo!' And they kept on their separate ways.

Albert threw all his colonial energy and enthusiasm into English cricket, playing here, there and everywhere and looking forward to the day when he could walk out onto the field with the Middlesex professionals. Came 1898, and he was qualified at last. And almost immediately he suffered a bad hand injury—off the field—and missed a month's cricket.

Still, he finished with 102 wickets for Middlesex in that

first season, including 8 for 83 against Notts at Trent Bridge. This was his third bag of eight in an innings already, for in addition to the 8 for 43 in his first Test match, he had taken 8 for 53 at Lord's for MCC against Oxford University in 1897—as well as all 10 for 49, including a hat-trick, against Oxfordshire at Lord's at the end of that summer, and 10 for 19, with another hat-trick, against XII of Devonshire Park at Eastbourne in August.

Lord Hawke lost no time in snapping him up for his tour of South Africa that winter, 1898–99, and it was there that he added two England Test caps to his three Australian. The experience did nothing to enhance that whopping Test batting average, for his four innings brought him only 23 runs. But he took nine wickets at Johannesburg and eight at Cape Town to give him an overall Test bowling analysis for his two countries of 26 wickets at 14.96.

On that South African tour (he had played in Pretoria the winter before, hitting 215 not out in one match and taking 8 for 8 and 10 for 22 in others), Trott made the first of his eight first-class centuries. It came in an innings of 539 for 6, and among the Transvaal opposition was the ill-fated Vincent Tancred, whom Trott bowled to number among his seven first-innings victims. Trott's 101 not out was begun on his twenty-sixth birthday. In the next game, against XV of Pretoria, he bowled Tancred for a duck, and the South African returned the compliment by catching Trott for 1.

The opposition on those matting wickets was sketchy throughout, but his 168 wickets on the tour were 61 more than the next man, Schofield Haigh, and slightly behind Haigh on average at 9.67. Frank Mitchell wrote of him, after more than three months' fairly close observation, that

> . . . not everyone is gifted with the temperament and also, may I add, stomach of Albert Trott, to whom everything came alike, fair weather and foul, good food or no food, sleep or no sleep; it was all the same to him—an ideal professor for a tour.

Trott sat, resplendent in straw boater and blazer, beside Lord Hawke (whom he generously contended as having 'no side whatever') in the official team photograph, and must have started to feel that life outside the Australian Test XI was quite bearable after all. Besides, Plum Warner—in contradiction of MacGregor's 'turnip' remark—had just branded him as being 'the best bowler in the world'. And Trott had quite enjoyed speaking at the Graaf-Reinet CC dinner, and proving himself the best fisherman in the side when they were taken out deep-sea fishing.

He fell for the customary tourist's temptations too, as Warner recorded:

> One of the funniest things I have seen was Trott, Tyldesley, Haigh, Board, and Cuttell boarding the train just before we left Bulawayo, armed to the teeth, like so many stage pirates, with battle-axes, assegais, blunderbusses, and the like. These murderous-looking implements completely filled up the passage of the saloon carriage.

At three in the morning, en route to Matjesfontein, their train banged into another, and the weaponry was scattered noisily, Trott finishing with a dislocated thumb.

He dressed as a priest for the fancy-dress party on board ship back to England, an unlikely disguise. His fast bowling with its brilliant variations and his mighty hitting (often he smashed the ball clean out of the South African grounds), together with his readiness to laugh and set up practical jokes, render him an early version of Botham, but there were several feats to Trott's credit which remain unmatched.

He launched himself into the 1899 season with gusto. Darling's Australians were on tour in England, and their old team-mate, the reject from Melbourne, was on hand to greet them in their Eastbourne match against 'An England XI', which was rubbing it in a bit. He paid heavily for his three wickets and made few runs with his heavyweight (3lb) bat. Nor did he do much in the first MCC match. But by the last day of July in this first of his greatest two seasons he

Trott — A hit over the Lord's pavilion, made all the sweeter by having been off Australian bowling.

was about to make perhaps the most famous hit in history. Medium-pacer M. A. Noble bowled, and Trott, having had a few warm-up hits, now caught the ball perfectly on the up and sent it sailing heavenwards. As the ball became a speck, 'Alberto' put his hand over his eyes and peered with delight as his shot achieved its end: it bounced on the reverse slope of the Lord's pavilion roof, hitting a chimneypot, and toppled into a garden beyond. It was not the biggest hit ever seen by the pavilion-dwellers, for some hits have crashed into the upper reaches while still going upwards, but it remains the only one to clear the roof. Only that same season, Trott had launched a stronger hit, off Fred Tate, which was still rising when it cannoned into the MCC emblem on the left-hand tower.

Noble soon had him. Another attempt at a big hit spooned the ball into third man's hands, with Trott's score 41. Later in the match he bowled Trumper.

That spring Trott had been one of *Wisden*'s Five Great Players of the Season, and yet the best was still to come—even if only for two spectacular summers. In 1899 he took 239 wickets at 17.09 and scored 1175 runs at 22.03. His two centuries were 164—the highest in his first-class career—against Yorkshire at Lord's, the last 137 runs coming in 90 minutes, with two blows landing the ball on the top balcony of the pavilion and several others striking the old Tavern; and 123 against Sussex, also at Lord's, a week later. Twice that season he took eight wickets in an innings, once for Middlesex and once for C. I. Thornton's XI at Scarborough.

The following year, 1900, saw him passing the 200 wickets/1000 runs mark again, his wickets costing a little more, his batting average increasing a point or two. Centuries came for Middlesex against Gloucestershire at Lord's and for The Rest against Surrey & Sussex at Hastings, while his 8 for 47 against Gloucestershire at Clifton was not even his best analysis of the season. At Taunton he took all 10 Somerset wickets for 42, only the fourth instance of a maximum by an Australian-born player.

He was the chief attraction on the county circuit, a rough-and-ready virtuoso, aggressive, unpredictable, entertaining. He could bat with fair orthodoxy or slog with ferocious power. His bowling was demonic and threatening in its range. When, between county matches in 1900, he played for MCC against Hampstead at Lord's, it seemed he could do whatever he chose on a cricket field: innings of 57 and 171 accompanied bowling figures of 9 for 77 and 7 for 98.

Constantly he teased and outwitted and permitted himself the occasional guffaw. One opposing batsman, who had made it known he considered Albert to be overrated, was handed a folded piece of paper as he took his guard, and told not to read it until his dismissal. Trott's first ball hit him in the stomach, second ball went through a wild swing, and third removed his middle stump. On his way back to the pavilion, the batsman was at liberty to read the note, which stated: 'Trott is to receive £5 if he hits you first ball, gives you one you cannot hit, and clean bowls you in the first over. Is he a good bowler?'

All who played with and against him came away with a tale or two to tell. Wilfred Rhodes remembered how Trott would mimic his Yorkshire accent, but getting it slightly wrong: saying 'Thy knows' instead of 'Tha knows'. None who saw it could ever forget his running-out of Gill of Somerset, when he stopped a hard drive and threw the ball backwards through his legs to break the wicket at the bowler's end. Plum Warner was most amused when Trott, answering an enquiry as to which was the next stop while they travelled by train through France, looked at his ticket and said, 'Why, Prix, you fool.' He'd read the French word for 'price', and pronounced it 'pricks'. ' "Pricks" was good,' relished Warner, 'but "you fool" was even better.'

Warner, the Middlesex opener who captained the county as well as England, was transparently fond of Trott: 'Poor Albert! He was a good soul. He had a heart of gold and was as simple as a child, and he was one of those people who compel attention.'

Little is recorded of Albert Trott's private life, though it is thought that his marriage in February 1897 (the newlyweds sailed straight off to England) did not last. Of his tendency to depart from the straight and narrow after cricket hours there can be little doubt. He was interviewed by the police, though not as a suspect, after a Taunton woman was murdered early this century. Trott had called on her whenever Middlesex were in the town (that much was known), and her reputation was scarlet.

Gambling probably accounted for much of what money he made. Lord Hawke detected this weakness during the South African expedition:

> Albert Trott had quaint ways. He came to me one day and asked if he could have some money advanced to him

> to send to his brother in Australia. I complied, but that money undoubtedly went to a 'bookie' in Cape Town. At Johannesburg Alberto repeated the same tactics. I answered that I would send it myself if he gave me his brother's address. I never received it.

His successes and his mischief went on beyond those two sensational seasons of 1899 and 1900, but the decline had already begun. With each passing season the tallies of runs and wickets went down while his alcohol consumption—and his weight—went up. His one century per season between 1901 and 1903 each came at Lord's, his average sliding down by a run or two per annum. His wickets reduced in number and the cost rose, and opponents learned to fear him less, even though he was only just passing the age of 30. The last time he took eight wickets in an innings was in 1901, when he did so three times (adding a century to his 8 for 54 against Essex) all at Lord's, where his massive popularity was becoming tinged with frustration among fans who wanted him to do well forever, and marvelled at the match-winning bowling partnership he had established with the paramount medium-pacer J. T. Hearne, which did so much to help Middlesex to the County Championship in 1903.

Instead of spending winters in Australia, he had taken to coaching and playing in Hawkes Bay, New Zealand, between Middlesex seasons, though joining up with Warner's 1902–03 MCC side, and going on to Australia with them, to take 4 for 88 against his own State, Victoria, and 6 for 88 against New South Wales. Perhaps those extraordinary doubles of 1899 and 1900 had left the public expecting too much of him, but he remained a major figure of entertainment, holding most of the catches that came his way with those great bucket hands of his, usually positioned at slip, where he could quip to wicketkeeper and batsman or anyone else who might listen.

In a match for the Players against the Gentlemen (he played in 13, without great success) at The Oval in 1903 the wicketkeeper, pint-sized Herbert Strudwick, asked him how he signalled his famed faster ball. Trott told him that he didn't. How would Struddy be able to 'find' it then? 'That's all right,' growled Albatrott, 'you'll soon find it.'

Like most keepers of that time, Strudwick stood up at the stumps for all but express bowling. He wrote years later of how he discovered Trott's extra-fast ball:

> In his third over he tried to bowl a fast yorker. I did not see much of the ball, as it came in between the batsman's legs and the leg stump, and hit me *full toss* plumb on the left foot. It was awfully painful and it made me hop. Trott came up to me, laughing all over his face, and said, 'Did you find it?'

His cruel streak showed when donkey-drop bowling was served up at him, as sometimes happened in the Golden Age, when high-flighted, rolled leg-breaks, often down the leg side, were delivered as tempters and potential partnership-breakers. Trott simply swivelled and smashed them straight at the terrified wicketkeeper. Asked by one if he had ever hit a keeper this way, he answered: 'Yeah, and bloody near killed him!'

For all his astounding feats, the unprecedented doubles of 1899 and 1900, the fast-forward and very physical centuries, even the 15 wickets against Sussex at Lord's in 1901 (including Fry and Ranji in both innings, *Cricket* contriving not to mention Trott's name once in its 200-word match report): for all this, his best-known achievement remains the 1899 hit over the pavilion at Lord's.

But close behind it comes the near-farce of his benefit match, Middlesex v. Somerset, at Lord's in May 1907. Fellow Victorian Frank Tarrant, a brilliant player, stole the early honours for Middlesex, scoring 52 and then taking 6 for 47 with his left-armers. Middlesex eventually left Somerset to get 264 for victory on the third day, and Trott demolished the visitors in the most spectacular way. First he took four wickets with four consecutive balls—and almost a fifth as Fred Lee was beaten, a bail was nudged, and the ball went for four byes. The procession of four consisted of Lewis, Poyntz,

Sammy Woods (another Australian) and Robson, the first lbw and the next three all bowled. He soon caught Lee off Tarrant (having served that bowler earlier in the innings with a catch to dismiss P. R. Johnson), and with Somerset 97 for 7, Trott bundled the remaining three wickets out with a hat-trick. O. C. Mordaunt was caught by Mignon, the Reverend A. P. Wickham was bowled, and Mignon clinched the hat-trick for Trott and the match for Middlesex by catching Albert Bailey, the No. 11.

Trott's celebrated quote after the match was 'I've bowled meself into the workhouse!' But the crowds, such as they were, had come in already over the three days, with 7044 paying on the opening day of the match. His devastating 7 for 20 had merely shortened the match by a couple of hours. The true culprit was the cold, damp weather, which kept thousands away.

One report said that Trott punched himself in the head for depriving himself of a few extra pounds from latecomers on that third day. Sammy Woods tried to cheer him up by presenting him with a straw hat with seven rabbits painted on the ribbon, all running into the pavilion. Alberto wore it with pride, but it did nothing for his luck and form. *Wisden* reported that for the rest of 1907 his bowling 'became quite harmless'.

The fires subsided towards ash, and in 1910 he played his last match for Middlesex, when he was 37, and then took up umpiring. Random photos from 1911 to 1913 show him in long white coat and often in his favoured wide-brimmed sunhat or stetson, moustache drooping on the features of a man who looks considerably older.

Dropsy caused him pain and depression, and added to his bloated appearance. Doubtless had those old photographs been in colour, Trotty's nose and cheeks would have shown as alcoholically florid.

His health dragged him down to the point where he had to give up umpiring during the 1914 season. Playing had long been out of the question. His last matches had truly weighed

Trott — an umpire in 1913, unwell and depressed.

him down to rock-bottom, as Henry Grierson remembered. He played against Trott in a minor match around 1911:

> I was trying to bowl swingers with the leg side packed, and poor Albert was in dreadful trouble with them. Finally he walked towards point, leaving the sticks clear on the leg side, and was quite happy when he was bowled behind his back. Ireland commiserated with him on bagging a brace, but Trott said 'That's all right, sir, and it's the third pair I've got this season.' Rather pathetic from a man who, only a few years before, could have hit us all into the pavilion almost at will.

Near the end he was seen watching the Thespids beating the Cross Arrows at Lord's, having played for the Arrows against Cockfosters himself some 15 years earlier, hitting 44 fours in an unbeaten 207. Now, the spent figure slouched by the boundary rope offered his match summary: 'Well, the Arrows have bitten off more than they can chew today.'

For the last two-and-a-half years of his life he lodged in Denbigh Road, Willesden, in a house since demolished, run then by a Mrs Mary Crowhurst. He had entered St Mary's Hospital on July 20, 1914 under the care of Sir John Broadbent, but after eight days of tedium Trott insisted on going home. The hospital authorities paid his cab fare to his lodgings.

Depression and sleeplessness moved him to ask his landlady if she could get him a sleeping draught from the chemist, but the chemist refused, and Trott shook his head when Mrs Crowhurst broke the news. 'Oh, dear, I can never go through another night,' he groaned.

At two o'clock that afternoon, July 30, five days before the outbreak of the First World War, Mrs Crowhurst heard a shot in Albert Trott's room. She opened the door and saw him lying dead on the bed, a Browning pistol in his hand. He had shot himself through the head. He was 41.

Trott's lodgings in Willesden, since demolished.

He had scribbled a 'will' on the back of a laundry ticket, leaving his wardrobe to his landlady and some photographs to a friend in Australia. Money found in the room amounted to £4.

The coroner's jury returned a verdict of 'suicide whilst of unsound mind', and MCC sent a telegram to the inquest to the effect that the club, his employers for so long, would be responsible for the funeral—though they did not reach as far as a gravestone. His younger brother Fred, who had also been on the MCC staff before settling in Scotland and having success as a pro (he named one of his sons Albert Edwin), sent a message to say he was unable to attend the inquest.

An imposing wreath lay on the coffin as it rested in the mortuary, the note reading 'With love and deepest sympathy to dear old Trottie.' Had a memorial been erected, his cricket figures—special though they were at 10,696 runs at just under 20 and 1674 wickets at 23, with 452 catches—would not have been the most appropriate material for inscription. And yet the character, the skill and the humour of the man might almost have been on too grand a scale to be contained adequately in a slab of marble. One short sentence might have said it all: 'No-one's enemy but his own.'

He died half a world away from his birthplace, broken and alone, in the confines of his rented room. Not for him the touchingly flamboyant self-extinction of the Anglicised American, cited in Alvarez's book, who, wearing bowler hat, black jacket, pinstripe trousers and polished shoes, with rolled umbrella over his arm, wedged himself into the rocks at Land's End so as to be as near as could be to—and facing—his native land, the United States, while the overdose of sleeping pills slowly removed his consciousness.

World of Cricket led its August 8, 1914 edition with three-and-a-half pages on Trott, beginning with eight lines from English-born Australian poet, bushman and horeseman Adam Lindsay Gordon, who shot himself in 1870. Rather, some lines from another Australian, Rupert Atkinson, published in 1908, might serve more aptly to escort Trott's ghost as it stomps along the boundary at Lord's on a moonlit night:

Stale years had shrouded him. He could not bear
Each day to feel the dizzy moments fall
Moment on moment, till each hour became
Time crumbling, smothering him. He could not dare
Endurance of the future, and withal
Death-refuge caught him, gibing at his shame.

14

Cricket Innocent?

Is cricket to blame? I once thought so. But I'm no longer convinced. The game may be responsible for exposing, often with some rawness, a man's inner frailties, but these were implanted at birth or during adolescence. If not, they came with disillusionment in later life, when unfulfilled desires and ambitions, or jealousy, or fatigue, or the inability to do any longer what could once be done becomes a lethal weapon turned in upon oneself.

Cricket is only superficially a team game. Essentially it is an individual and lonely game, with multiple odds stacked against each contestant. In this, it is a fairly faithful reflection of life. At the same time, it might be argued that cricket's apparently unduly high levels of suicide and divorce (one random statistic: in 1980, six Middlesex cricketers were having their marriages dismantled) match those of Hollywood, and actually exceed the respective national norms.

But the key question must be: are the psychological strains imposed by the playing of cricket—when it is a means of livelihood, but also, not negligibly, when it is an amateur passion—are these strains more damaging than the everyday and cumulative mental stresses familiar to milkmen, mortgage brokers, or medical practitioners? More pertinently, are cricketers overcast by the drawn-out, stressful demands of the sport more than their brethren in other sports?

Cricket's virtues are renowned. Played well, it gives thrilling satisfaction to the performer; it also gives vast spectator pleasure; and—to those who need it—it offers broad scope for warm companionship and comfort. Withdraw the first and last of these, and the void created presents itself as a potential hardship at best and fatally damaging at worst.

The tyranny and terror of the first realistic if long-distance view of old age and the evils of old age itself encompass the inabilities to do things that once came easefully and naturally—not just bending the spine into bowling or flicking arthritis-free knuckles across a leg-break, or running a quick three and facing up to the next ball with lungs still well under control. These are not the only losses. Mocking shadows replace the freedoms of choice as they fade away with the accumulation of years during the unremitting inevitability of the physical wind-down.

This may have explained the deaths of some of the middle-aged cricketers in this alarmingly long cavalcade. Had Harold Gimblett stayed on the farm might he not have had a smoother and comparatively untroubled (and longer) life? If A. E. Stoddart had had children and had permitted himself more of the company of his numerous old friends, would he not have come to terms with the loss of those days of glamour and hero-worship which he navigated with as much grace and modesty as gratification, and gone on to a ripe old age, perhaps even surviving the financial jeopardy wrought by the Great War?

For some, a future without cricket was unthinkable. For them, surely, it cannot be said that it was the stresses of cricket which precipitated a spiritual decline, but rather the threatened *loss* of cricket? Yet even the prolongation of a career in itself, cheating Time for a time, may not be sufficient to allay depression, for to be trying in vain to repeat earlier youthful triumphs can be as painful physically and morally as collapsing while trying to jitterbug with folk a third one's age or sprinting for a train 35 years after leaving school and thereby courting a coronary occlusion.

Half-hearted cricketers are extremely rare. This game gets a grip on people such as only religious fanatics might comprehend. The secret of survival would seem to hang on the ability to execute a timely and gracious transition into committee room, spectator's enclosure, or umpire's coat. So many retiring cricketers talk—with what really seems slightly questionable foundation—about 'putting something back into the game', when what they need most is a continuing connection with the familiar pastime or profession which has given them so much pleasure, pride and even pain for 20 or 30 years. Time beats us all. It's merely a question of whether we're knocked out, lose on points after a gallant fight, or throw in the towel.

The nature of cricket is such that it tears at the nerves of all participants who want to take it seriously or are forced to take it seriously. But of all the subjects in this book, the great majority were beset by deteriorating health, acute financial anxiety, helpless addiction to the bottle, marriage problems, or a kind of intrinsic instability, even madness, innocently induced by chemical change in the brain or in some cases by the hideous experience of front-line warfare. The mounting depression overwhelmed them. The adversities of later life have proved too crushingly heavy. That they played cricket—many of them for a livelihood—may after all be seen as incidental. The tensions of the game fray the nerves, and in at least one case, that of Surrey and England batsman Ken Barrington, have induced premature if 'natural' death. Barrington, like Gimblett, was highly strung (though outwardly cheerful and amiable to one and all) and a helpless worrier. Cricket's vicissitudes took his anxieties by the arm and ran them to the fatal edge—in his case heart attacks of increasing severity. He would have been prey, presumably, to similar pressure had he been an airline pilot or a social worker. Like so many who have been studied in this book, Barrington had a high degree of neurotic anxiety in his natural make-up. Whether such souls are lured into cricket by its challenging uncertainty is a matter which still awaits conclusive findings. What is certain is that cricket seems to have produced an inordinately high number of suicides. And yet there seem to be external explanations for almost all of them.

Is cricket, therefore, off the hook? I believe so and I hope so, though the tentative conclusion surprises me when I recall preliminary suspicions and contentions.

Shrewsbury feared terminal illness; Hardy was shattered by trench warfare, and Gimblett by slaughter witnessed; Scotton was deranged; Bull had desperate money worries; Dr Gibson felt grievously inadequate; Burke seemed to have lost everything that mattered to him; Relf could not face threatened bereavement; Faulkner was worn out; Partridge was addicted to drink, the sinister depressant; Sarbadhikary could not cope with a downward spiral in circumstances; Trott could not stand being left with only pain and dreams; Stoddart could no longer bear the loneliness. All had their reasons. None, as far as can be told, was ever seen wandering around like the doomed comedian Tony Hancock, volume of Kant under his arm, questioning despairingly for the true meaning of life. But all—in common—took their leave of this world without significant consideration for those left behind, such were the blind depths of their despair.

And yet . . . might it still not prove that if, after all, there can be a satisfactory life after cricket, it somehow can never be more than a hollow set of ruminations and 'do you remembers', with only the very strongest of will defiantly claiming to have dismissed the past and to be looking only to the future?

Alvarez states that John Donne ('No man is an island . . .') 'finally negotiated his mid-life crisis by taking holy orders instead of his life'. He further quotes Boris Pasternak in his *An Essay in Autobiography*, an exemplary definition of the implications of suicide:

> But a man who decides to commit suicide puts a full-stop to his being, he turns his back on his past, he declares himself a bankrupt and his memories to be unreal. They can no longer help or save him, he has put himself beyond their reach. The continuity of his inner life is broken, his personality is at an end.

'Turns his back on his past' . . . 'his memories unreal' . . . these notions stab at the very heart of cricket, for it is the most backward-looking of games. Its heroes and even its 'half-heroes' are not usually forgotten, for some years after their withdrawal at least. Perhaps even being interviewed long after the battle, or being toasted at a reunion dinner, is not sufficient balm to ease the painful joints and curb the fierce and impossible wishes to be young again and active. Pasternak probably came as close as man might to defining the spiritual consequences of self-extermination. Only those who have beheld the private pergatory can know. Alvarez, a joyously triumphant failed suicide himself, goes no further than to suggest that the great Russian knew by dint of close proximity and not necessarily by experience.

From another angle, the much-loved and self-confessed manic depressive Spike Milligan touches a chord familiar to all but the most insensitive when he says: 'It is as though something has snapped and I have lost my ability to be resilient to difficulties, especially unjust things or people not responding in a decent way.' The Goon genius might excuse the follow-up: 'Like a shocking umpire's decision against me? Or being dumped by ungrateful, unfeeling, unintelligent selectors?'

Cricket's freemasonry affords the chance to all its members to help each other to get by. The chance of constant companionship is there, albeit that it remains subject to forbearance of the boring, the arrogant, the conniving, the insincere. The game is not free from malevolent forces, of course, and neither can it ever supply solutions for essentially personal problems too deep to analyse even by trained professional people, let alone to be expressed on paper. But cricket offers escape, refuge, reassuring continuity: comfort factors found also in authentic orthodox religions.

Cricket 'fanatics' sometimes have their enthusiasm deflated by the oh-so-resigned and solemn dictum: 'What do they know of cricket, who only cricket know?' So, as a final thought-link to the theme, let us draw from someone who may only just have heard of this all-consuming game. French writer Albert Camus claimed: 'Suicide is prepared within the silence of the heart, as is a great work of art.' At Test level, we may well be enduring an occasionally abstract and violent age; but cricket is an art, is it not? Who would deny that it, too, lies in the silence of the heart, expanding to enchant, torment, consume?

Bibliography

Many books, booklets and periodicals have been consulted. The main sources are as follows:

Ego 7 James Agate (Harrap 1947)
A History of Honor Oak Cricket & Lawn Tennis Club M. B. Alexander (1965)
Cricket: An Illustrated History David Rayvern Allen (Phaidon 1990)
Cricket on the Air ed. David Rayvern Allen (BBC 1985)
The Savage God: A Study of Suicide A. Alvarez (Weidenfeld 1971)
Who's Who of Cricketers ed. Philip Bailey, Philip Thorn, Peter Wynne-Thomas (Newnes 1984)
It Isn't Cricket Sid Barnes (Collins 1953)
The Observer on Cricket ed. Scyld Berry (Unwin Hyman 1987)
New Zealand Cricketers R.T. Brittenden (Reed 1961)
Hit for Six Gerald Brodribb (Heinemann 1960)
England Over Dudley Carew (Secker 1927)
The Faber Book of Cricket ed. Michael & Simon Davie (Faber 1987)
History of Indian Cricket Edward Docker (Macmillan 1976)
Suicide: A Study in Sociology Emile Durkheim (1897)
The Guardian Book of Cricket ed. Matthew Engel (Pavilion 1986)
Harold Gimblett: Tormented Genius of Cricket David Foot (Heinemann 1982)
'*My Dear Victorious Stod*' David Frith (1970)
Clean Young Englishman John Gale (Hodder 1965)
A History of Cricket Benny Green (Barrie & Jenkins 1988)
The Ramblings of a Rabbit Henry Grierson (Chapman & Hall 1924)
Notes on Some Early Arrivals in Otago No. 4 G. J. Griffiths (1971)
At the Double Richard Hadlee with Tony Francis (Stanley Paul 1985)
Rhythm and Swing Richard Hadlee (Souvenir 1989)
Recollections and Reminiscences Lord Hawke (Williams & Norgate 1924)
The Family Fortune by Alan Hill (Scan 1978)
Shadows Over the Wicket E. Hoskin (Red Cross Sports Committee 1945)

100 Years of Durham County Cricket Club Brian Hunt (Casdec 1983)
The Hughie Gallacher Story Paul Joannou (Breedon 1989)
The Elevens of Three Great Schools 1805 to 1929 ed. W. R. Lyon (Spottiswoode 1930)
Fifty Years of Sport at Oxford, Cambridge and the Great Public Schools ed. Hon. R. H. Lyttelton, Arthur Page & Evan B. Noel (Southwood 1922)
The Demon and the Lobster Anthony Meredith (Kingswood 1987)
Bat and Pad ed. Pat Mullins & Philip Derriman (Oxford 1984)
Cricket Walkabout John Mulvaney & Rex Harcourt (Macmillan 1988)
Men in White D. O. Neely, R. P. King & F. K. Payne (Moa 1986)
The Cream of Cricket William Pollock (Methuen 1934)
With Stoddart's Team in Australia Prince Ranjitsinhji (Bowden 1898)
Never a Cross Bat Tom Reddick (Nelson 1979)
Cricket Prints R. C. Robertson-Glasgow (Werner Laurie 1948)
46 Not Out R. C. Robertson-Glasgow (Hollis & Carter 1948)
More Cricket Prints R. C. Robertson-Glasgow (Werner Laurie 1948)
On Top Down Under Ray Robinson (Cassell Australia 1975)
It Never Rains . . . Peter Roebuck (Allen & Unwin 1984)
Blindfold Games Alan Ross (Collins 1986)
Cricket in Doncaster and District Philip L. Scowcroft (Doncaster Library 1985)
The Players: A Social History of the Professional Cricketer Ric Sissons (Kingswood 1988)
A Sussex Cricket Odyssey Laetitia Stapleton (Ian Harrap 1979)
Twenty-Five Years Behind the Stumps Herbert Strudwick (Hutchinson 1926)
Cricket in Many Climes P. F. Warner (Heinemann 1900)
Gentlemen v Players 1806–1949 Sir Pelham Warner (Harrap 1950)
Twelve Days of Grace G. Derek West (Darf 1989)
Century at Newlands 1864–1964 S. E. L. West & W. J. Luker (Western Province Cricket Club 1965)
'Give Me Arthur' Peter Wynne-Thomas (Barker 1985)
County Champions (various) (Heinemann 1982)
The Cricket Almanack of New Zealand
A History of Cricket at Reading School (Reading School 1986)
MCC Cricket Scores and Biographies Vol XV (Longmans 1925)
Wisden Cricketers' Almanack

Periodicals: *The Bulletin; Cricket: A Weekly Record of the Game; The Cricket Field; The Cricketer; The Cricket Statistician; The Journal of the Cricket Society; Natal Witness: Sportsworld* (Calcutta); *The Times; Wisden Cricket Monthly; The World of Cricket.*

Index